WARS OF BLOOD AND FAITH

Books by Ralph Peters

Nonfiction

New Glory
Never Quit the Fight
Beyond Baghdad
Beyond Terror
Fighting for the Future

Fiction

Traitor
The Devil's Garden
Twilight of Heroes
Flames of Heaven
The Perfect Soldier
The War in 2020
Red Army
Bravo Romeo

Writing as Owen Parry

Fiction

Rebels of Babylon
Bold Sons of Erin
Honor's Kingdom (Hammett Award)
Call Each River Jordan
Shadows of Glory
Faded Coat of Blue (Herodotus Award)
Our Simple Gifts
Strike the Harp

WARS OF BLOOD AND FAITH

The Conflicts That Will Shape the
Twenty-First Century

Ralph Peters

STACKPOLE
BOOKS

Published by
STACKPOLE BOOKS
5067 Ritter Road
Mechanicsburg, PA 17055
www.stackpolebooks.com

Printed in the United States

First edition

10 9 8 7 6 5 4 3 2

Library of Congress Cataloging-in-Publication Data

Peters, Ralph, 1952-
  Wars of blood and faith : the conflicts that will shape the twenty-first
century / Ralph Peters.
    p. cm.
  ISBN-13: 978-0-8117-0274-4 (hc)
  ISBN-10: 0-8117-0274-X (hc)
  1. Military art and science—History—21st century. 2. War—Forecasting.
3. World politics—21st century. I. Title.
U42.P48 2007
355.0201'12—dc22
                                              2007006628

To my fellow "graduates" of the 1st Battalion,
46th Infantry Regiment

"It is fatal to enter any war without the will to win it."
—General Douglas MacArthur

Contents

Introduction

Where We Are Now

Far too many academics measure "intellectual rigor" by the volume of their footnotes. Yet, the rigor of mind that matters as we face a challenging world is the power to sweep aside the layers of prejudice and preconceptions masking reality, to free ourselves of the comforting assumptions—the cultural footnotes—that impede our understanding. The most bewildering quality in our national leaders and those who advise them, Democrat or Republican, is their unwillingness to think honestly about the world around us. Prisoners of educations as close-minded as anything the Middle Ages offered, the members of our ruling elite (for want of a better word) may become wily tacticians but have not produced a serious strategist from among their number in at least a half-century.

These men and women are prisoners of our intelligentsia's illusions about humankind, of our reactionary dogma regarding international statecraft, and of our absurd insistence that "all men want peace," with its corollary fantasies of bloodless war and a lawyer's faith in the power of negotiations. Insulated by their privileges and wealth from the American people as well as from the ferocity beyond our shores, our leaders and their understudies live in a through-the-looking-glass world in which religion is anachronistic nonsense, the power and tenacity of hatred is denied, and the globe's passionate discords are reduced to statistics. In a bloody world, few of those who assume the right to lead us have ever had a bloody nose.

The goal of many of the essays and columns in this book is to provoke the complacent, to challenge the (deadly) traditional wisdom, and to encourage Americans to think for themselves. As the years pass, I have ever-greater faith in the American people, but ever-less confidence in our leaders. On black days, I cannot help feeling that, were Washington's entire governing class and its courtiers swept away, with only the Constitution and the Bill of Rights preserved, the government rebuilt from the intial confusion might better fulfill the ideals of our Founding Fathers, while confounding those who have lost the ideals of service.

We are led by vultures, not eagles.

In the middle of the last century, a grand hullabaloo followed the publication of a critique of our educational system, *Why Johnny Can't Read.* We're overdue for a companion volume, *Why Washington Can't Think.* The advertising copy for such a book might note that, despite Washington's status as the richest, most powerful capital city in history, where advanced degrees are ubiquitous, innovative thought not only doesn't exist, but has become distinctly unwelcome. Washington is incestuous and elitist, as closed to outside ideas as a paranoid religious cult. No matter their party affiliation, insiders at work in government or the media arise from mini-dynasties, attend the same schools and universities, share a disdain for military service, play musical chairs with the same government positions, rotate through the same cluster of (wildly misnamed) think tanks, attend the same usual-suspects policy briefings, read the same books and newspapers, live in the same neighborhoods—and dread the embarrassment threatening anyone who challenges Washington's dysfunctional, but comfortable, way of interpreting the world.

This unwillingness to risk appearing foolish or simply out of step destroys the possibility of innovative thought. Genuinely new ideas will *always* be mocked by the establishment—initially. A man or woman unable to see beyond his or her next job in the next administration is not going to risk diverging from the norm. What passes for debate in Washington is really a bizarre form of agreement, of witless collusion: The policies proposed may stand in superficial opposition one to the other, but are based on the same flawed premises. Hoping to doctor the world, we begin with a false diagnosis that reassures us, however unhelpful it is to the patient. I don't know who first produced the wonderful line that "Washington is Hollywood for ugly people," but it's even more stinging to note that Washington is the one arena in which the cowards finish the game with the most medals.

Washington is *afraid* to think. Because so many of the answers are terrifying.

I deplore the advertising approach that tells us that we "deserve" a Caribbean vacation, an usurious home-equity loan, or just a cheeseburger. But I believe with all my heart, mind, and soul that our country deserves better leaders. I revere the rare men of integrity on Capitol

Hill, such as Senator John McCain or Senator Joseph Lieberman, but our corrupt political parties regard them as threats to be managed, not as inspirations to be emulated. I sometimes doubt that I will live to see another man—or woman—of honor live in the White House.

Speaking to military audiences, I joke about taking a "GPS approach to strategy." The Global Positioning System tells you where you are on the globe, while the first step in designing a realistic strategy is to calculate where we are in history. If you don't know where you are, you're unlikely to devise a sound route to the future.

Where are we, then? Many of the pieces in this book attempt to fix our present location along the fast-running river of history—as a number of mighty currents shift the river's course beneath our hull. We are at the beginning of a genuinely different age, struggling to act effectively amid a torrent of changes so disorienting that the natural tendency in every civilization and subordinate culture is to turn to yesterday's verities for reassurance or to embrace simplistic answers that transfer the blame for local problems onto distant enemies. This is as true for members of Congress as it is of members of al Qa'eda.

Among the diverse currents flowing simultaneously into this wild river, the following are the most critical for our national purposes:

The Age of Ideology is over. This is discussed at length in the book, but the essential point is that we have just passed through a brief, aberrant period in history. Running roughly from 1789 to 1991, the Age of Ideology was a time of unaccountable mass delusion, when human beings convinced themselves that individuals could reason out a better architecture for human societies than human collectives could arrive at organically. From the obscure to the notorious, humanity flirted with man-made programs for utopias. Concocted nationalisms and Marxism-Leninism, Nazism, and Maoism killed hundreds of millions: As human failings frustrated those in charge, the attempts to perfect humankind led inevitably to the GULag and to Auschwitz, to the butchery of the Cultural Revolution and the killing fields of Cambodia. The wars of the Age of Ideology were defined by their inspired savagery.

Although ideologies still echo—not least, in Latin America—their maddened glamor is gone. We have returned to the historical mainstream, abandoning conflicts over artificial systems of social organization in favor of strife provoked by those ineradicable causes, religion and ethnicity. As the title of this book suggests, the bleeding over political systems is largely finished; we have returned to the historical norm of wars of blood and belief, of conflicts driven by faith and tribe—the two forms of identity that function enduringly as Darwinian survival mechanisms for human collectives. This sudden, profound change matters enormously for our statecraft and our approach to warfare, since the techniques that work against opponents inspired by ideology fall woefully short when applied to enemies aflame with divine visions or the lust to avenge old or imagined wrongs done to their kind. The lessons we thought we had learned (often incorrect, in any case) about diplomacy and military affairs over the past two centuries are now largely irrelevant—but we resist abandoning a worldview with which we're comfortably familiar, just as an Afghan villager clings to his own verities. No matter how vociferously, even sincerely, we deny it, our wars will be fought over religion and ethnic identity. Those wars will be cruel and hard.

Globalization has contradictory effects. The pop-bestseller notion that globalization (and its sorcerer's apprentice, the internet) is bringing the world together gets it more than half wrong. First, globalization isn't new, it's just gaudier. Second, far from bringing us together in one big, happy family, the internet is the greatest tool for spreading hatred since the development of the movable-type plate for the printing press. Third, and most critically, globalization may, indeed, unite the most-privileged of the world's citizens, homogenizing their choice of auto-mobiles or vacation playgrounds, but among the masses its primary effect is disintegrative, collapsing new and fragile national identities back into narrower tribal and religious affiliations. From Belgium to Burundi, identity is growing more exclusive, not inclusive.

The fundamental question humankind asks in the year of our Lord 2007 is "Who am I?" The responses are largely what they would have been three hundred years ago. This Age of Globalization and technological wonders is also the new age of superstition, primitive faith, and blood loyalty.

The post-colonial era has barely begun. This is a theme I've returned to for years—it gains no traction in Washington because it overturns the entire system of diplomacy upon which we rely (with such dismal results). The notion that the postcolonial era was a mid-twentieth-century phenomenon is utter nonsense. After European imperialism deformed the world for five hundred years, the damage could not be undone in a generation or two. We shall be lucky if the postcolonial era concludes in another two centuries (it has already lingered for two-hundred years in Latin America and apparently has a few generations more to go).

While much of the developing world suffers under the legacy of the European-model state itself, the gravest practical problem left behind by imperialism's retreat is the prevalence of arbitrary borders—designed by Europeans for the benefit of Europeans. From West Africa through the Middle East to Southeast Asia, Europeans divided the world among themselves with little regard for geography and less for local identities or the desires of their subjects. As a result, states as diverse and vital as Nigeria and Iraq, Sudan and Afghanistan, Congo and Indonesia are all Frankenstein's monsters sewn together from ill-fitting body parts. As the Soviet Union collapsed, the United States and our allies entered a series of conflicts whose common cause was arbitrary, dysfunctional borders; phony statehood; or both: Kuwait's liberation, Somalia, the wreckage of Yugoslavia, Afghanistan, Iraq. . . . In each case, the state's frontiers made no ethnic sense or ignored religious legacies. According to the wisdom of the Age of Ideology, ethnicity and religion were destined to fade away. Instead, ideology faded away, leaving ancient, indestructible identities behind: Arab or black African, Sunni or Shi'a, Christian or Muslim, Kurd or Arab, human beings remain who they were a thousand years ago. And they like it that way.

The struggles in which we now are engaged, as well as the wars that will haunt our future, are bloody manifestations of a deformed world struggling to return to its natural condition. While our diplomats cringe at the mention of changing borders—as if all existing frontiers were eternal—borders are changing as you read these lines. By attempting to preserve a perverted European design for the world, we have placed ourselves on the wrong side of history. There are many things for which we shall have to fight, not least our survival, but it's a travesty of our heritage and values to send our troops to preserve international boundaries designed by the European tyrants that our ancestors fled.

The European-scorched world has embarked upon a long and difficult process of recovery. The process threatens the theories upon which our academics and diplomats have built successful careers. In the manner of intellectuals everywhere, they will cling to those disastrously wrong theories as our soldiers bleed for the vanity of those who would not invite them to their dinner tables.

Taken together with the massive migrations underway around the world—the new *Voelkerwanderung*—this inevitable collapse of unnatural borders is the greatest practical strategic dilemma we face.

Women's freedom is the defining social issue of our time. The deepest disagreement between civilizations and cultures is over the role of women. Admittedly, the issue is barely mentioned in this book, although it has a substantial place in previous volumes of mine. It demands to be mentioned here, though, since its strategic implications are profound, yet utterly disregarded in Washington: The Islamists' horror at the prospect of equal rights for women is the most powerful underlying cause of the turmoil we face in the Muslim heartlands.

The greatest social revolution in history has been the acceptance of the equality of women with men in our civilization. It has doubled our human capital, immeasurably enriched our culture—and made life a great deal more pleasant. But the image of the female as a treacherous, insatiable she-devil incapable of controlling her animal desires haunts traditional societies. Nothing so threatens, alienates, and excites our Islamist enemies as our acceptance that women are fully human. Imprisoned within a civilization of infantile sexuality (Freud is more useful than Clausewitz here), the Islamic fear of the female would be hilarious were it not so monstrous and deadly. We do not cast our endeavors in such terms, but our current wars are about female emancipation (even as our blundering in Iraq has, tragically, reversed the trajectory of women's rights from Basra to Baqubah). The greatest cultural divide today is between those civilizations that honor women as free human beings and those obsessed with women's "honor." The civilizations that continue to oppress women are bound for comprehensive failure, leaving them a source of unending rage and violence.

There is no way to wage a bloodless war. Even after all we have endured since September 11, 2001, our governing elite refuses to accept that war cannot be waged according to the prejudices of the media or the concerns of lawyers. There are many reasons for this naiveté regarding what it takes to win a war, from the lulling promises of defense contractors to pure wishful thinking, but the basic cause of our national misperceptions about warfare is that our leaders lack experience in uniform. They did not serve, their children do not serve, and their children's children will not serve. Our ruling class and its aspirant members disdain military service as beneath them. Their election-year appearances at military bases might as well be visits to a zoo.

The ascendancy of the alchemists and astrologers of conflict—academic theorists—further divorces our governing class from warfare's reality. In yet another bizarre phenomenon, we turned for our understanding of warfare to professors and pundits who never wore a uniform, dismissing the hard-won insights of those who actually served. The pernicious sprawl of think tanks bears much of the blame, but the primary impetus for this shift from trusting the general's experience to believing the professor's generalities was simply that military men gave uncomfortable answers, while the academics provided reassurance. Rejecting the American tradition of piling on and winning, we fell in love with graduated responses, surgical strikes and precision weapons, and the belief that mortal enemies could be persuaded to give up if we just impressed them with our capabilities.

In Iraq, as I write, the situation is dire, but did not have to be so. We tried to make war on the cheap, only to make the endeavor vastly more expensive—in every respect—than it needed to be. In warfare, whether against powerful states or elusive insurgents, there is no substitute for fighting as hard as you can. As long as we are unwilling to fight—to *really* fight—our military efforts are bound to fail.

As in so many other respects, our leaders and their acolytes in government and the media live in a fantasy world without real threats or consequences. Others die for their mistakes. And when things go awry, the privileged tell the rest of us that "Victory isn't possible." But victory is always possible for the United States. We have the capabilities to win any conflict on our own terms, but our sheltered political class and the media and academic circles to which it looks for reassurance lack the strength of character and will to fight for anything beyond personal advancement. The most privileged Americans today are a grotesque realization of 1960s icon Grace Slick's snarl, "I'd rather have my country die for me."

The media can now determine a war's outcome. This relates, of course, to the preceding point. The media have been enflaming and distorting conflicts since at least the sixteenth century, but across the past four decades we've seen a decisive shift from a domestic media that could influence a war's outcome (as in Vietnam) to a global media that can overturn the result of a battle by forcing it to a premature conclusion (as in the First Battle of Fallujah). The media's sense of entitlement-without-responsibility results in an establishment that doesn't report reality but willfully shapes it. While the media's components are certainly various, the anti-American strain (Freud again) is so powerful that we must regard the media as a whole as a combatant in our conflicts—which means enforcing logical rules on its behavior. We must not permit a hostile, self-adoring media to decide who wins our wars.

There are, of course, many other factors at play in the strategic environment, but I believe that those listed above are as decisive as they are ignored. We mock the delusions of Islamist madmen, but their surreal view of humankind is no more absurd than our own slovenly jumble of self-serving beliefs. Proud of our imagined rationality, we, too, live in a strategic dream world.

Our political leadership, Republican and Democrat, is unprepared for twenty-first-century reality. And you and your children are going to pay the price.

—Presidents' Day 2007

PART I

The Twenty-First Century Military

The Shape of Wars to Come

Armchair General

March 2006

The twenty-first century will see an unprecedented expansion in the varieties of organized violence. The argument over whether the future will bring back big wars or extend the current pattern of asymmetrical conflicts misses the point. The United States military will continue to wage "small wars" but must be prepared for the possibility of greater conflicts. There is no choice involved. And the fiercest challenges may come neither from conventional nor irregular forces as we know them, but from governments and organizations willing to wage war in spheres now forbidden or still unimagined. The nature of warfare never changes, but its surface manifestations will mutate savagely in the coming decades.

Beyond the question of *how* men, gangs, tribes, nations, and faiths will fight, *what* they will fight about appears grimmer still. This will be a century of contradictions: The age of supertechnologies is also the new age of superstition, of great religions reduced to cults that worship bloodthirsty bogeymen. Seek to deny it though we may, we face decades of religious wars—between faiths, but also within faiths. The defining struggle of our time—the source of conflicts great and small—will be between those who believe in a merciful god and those who worship a divine disciplinarian. This philosophical divide will kill many millions.

Desperate, failing civilizations will confront triumphant ones. While racial hatreds tragically persist, wars *within* racial groups will

3

kill more human beings than conflicts between races. Humans may hate a distant enemy in theory but prefer to kill their neighbors in practice. Tribes—a term forbidden twenty years ago—are back, even in Europe, where godlessness is simply another faith, if one devoid of comfort. Men will fight about all of the traditional sources of conflict, from global economics to access to wells and parcels of grazing land, but the most frequent wars and lesser conflicts will be between those who disagree over the interpretation of a single faith, as well as between different tribes within the same racial group. Often, both differences will manifest themselves in the same conflict—with atrocity the result of compounded hatreds.

The genocidal impulse isn't an anomaly. Humans are hard-wired for it. Only civilization and the rule of law occasionally allow cultures to control the enduring longing to exterminate those perceived as enemies.

Here in the West, we have our own superstitions that complicate warmaking. The insistence on the part of leftists and unthinking academics that all humans want peace; that all conflicts can be negotiated to a gentle ending; that all cultures and civilizations are morally equal; and that all foreign barbarities are somehow our fault is reminiscent of the papacy's insistence that the evidence had to be rejected, that Copernicus and Galileo were wrong. Our internal "culture wars" are waged between those who have created a pretty, but utterly unfounded, fantasy of a peaceful nature for humankind and the new Newtonians who recognize that the data this planet generates every day suggests otherwise. The new inquisitors insist that we can pretend war away. In consequence, the greatest impediment to effective warfighting by the U.S. military is the double-barreled nonsense that war is never necessary and that, when we do find ourselves at war, we must fight with exaggerated restraint. Even after 9/11 and the blood-cult terrorism encountered in Iraq, the American intellectual class refuses to think honestly about war.

Of course, it's natural for Americans or Westerners in general to look at conflict through the lens of our own recent experiences, but our wars and interventions are merely the best publicized—and far from the grimmest. For most of humanity, the American-led interventions in Afghanistan and Iraq, with their broad adherence to restrictive rules, would be an incomprehensible experience.

More instructive examples of what the future holds would be the 1980s war between then-Sunni-dominated Iraq and Shi'a Persia, in which over a million soldiers and civilians died, with millions more wounded; the twin civil wars in Sierra Leone and Liberia, in which children served as shock troops and societies collapsed into anarchy; the drug lord insurgency in northern Mexico that subverts state authority; or the decade of interrelated wars in Rwanda, Burundi, and eastern Congo (formerly Zaire) which took at least two million lives—mostly civilians—most killed at close quarters and many butchered with knives.

We Americans—liberal or conservative—share a deluding belief that all problems have answers, if only they can be found, and that all conflicts can be brought to a resolution, if only we hit on the right formula. But this is an age of insoluble conflicts—of confrontations that can only be "solved" by ethnic cleansing and other barbarities, of conflicts likely to ebb and flow throughout our lifetimes. After a few hundred years of pretending that warfare might be limited by laws, savagery is back in fashion.

Except in North America and northwestern Europe, the great religious wars of the last two millennia never really ended—they were only taking naps, due to the exhaustion of one party or both. The Sunni–Shi'a contest is thirteen centuries old—as old as, but deeper than, Islam's struggle with the West. The struggle between Islam and Hinduism threatens to go into nuclear overdrive. And the racial and religious jihad of Arabs against black Africans may be on the verge of exciting a startling reaction. All of these are endless wars, punctuated by stretches of phony peace and falsely divided by historians into separate struggles.

The world wars of the last century, then the Cold War—the last great struggle within the West—clouded our understanding of the longer, greater tides of history. Now, with bewildering speed, history has come back, insisting on its durability and casting the last hundred years as an aberration. We have reentered the long river of struggles over elemental issues: God and blood. We have to reset our calendars and recalibrate our mentalities.

In this century, the Battle of Manzikert is more relevant than the Battle of Midway, and the overarching struggle will be about interpreting God's will.

TERROR AND ITS MYTHS

The nature of historical records misleads us: Terrorism may be an older form of violence than warfare. Certainly, its recorded pedigree is lengthy enough, from the Assassins through John Brown to al Qa'eda. Yet, for all of the studies of terrorism in print, we fail to make the essential distinction between the two basic types of terrorists: Those who have political goals, however far-fetched, and those who believe they are on a divine mission. Grasping the difference is crucial to fighting them effectively.

Elsewhere, I've termed these two archetypes "practical" (or political) terrorists and "apocalyptic" terrorists. Both sorts can be deadly, but the danger from the latter is a magnitude greater. Political terrorists—the kind with which we grew familiar over the past two centuries—have earthly goals. They seek to change systems of government or to assert group rights, not to jump-start Armageddon. Political terrorists are often willing to die for their cause, but they would rather live to govern. Sometimes their grievances are legitimate. The most hardened must be killed or imprisoned, but others end up in parliaments. Except for the truly deranged—such as Timothy McVeigh—they rarely seek to create mass casualties among civilians.

Apocalyptic terrorists, fired by their stern vision of religion, regard death as a promotion—making them far more dangerous opponents. These ultrazealots have little regard for the suffering even of their coreligionists. They excuse atrocities great and small as serving the self-evident will of their god. Among the worst, the impulse is simply to destroy—Israel, America, less devout Muslims, or a world they find unsatisfactory and immoral. While apocalyptic terrorists may announce political goals, no concessions would satisfy them. It is impossible to negotiate with a man who believes that his god is whispering into his ear and telling him to kill you. Religion-fueled terrorists, by their nature, cannot accept compromise. This is the ultimate zero-sum game, with a demanding god as judge and referee. Historically, the only way to deal with apocalyptic terrorists has been to wipe them out. Instead, we worry about their legal rights when we capture them.

Faced with the most implacable—if not yet the most dangerous—enemies we ever have faced, we try to tame the threat they pose by employing the terms of political science and sociology. But these are madmen spawned of devilish myths. Recasting them in our own image only deludes us as to their nature and intent. And fanaticism does not preclude genius. Horrific though it was, 9/11 was a brilliant act of strategic judo, exploiting our own civilization's laws, technologies, and openness against us. Although the terrorists woefully misjudged the American reaction, the strikes themselves were an artful aerial choreography of death that riveted the world. The true "wonder weapon" of our time isn't one of the hyper-expensive high-tech weapons we designed for our dream wars, but the suicide bomber—dirt cheap, deadly, and even more precise than a satellite-guided bomb.

The only good news in our struggle with terror is, first, that the brutality of our enemies eventually will force us to take them seriously, and, second, that terrorist movements ultimately fail unless they can bind themselves to a popular insurgency *and* face a weak-willed state whose power is already decaying. Despite the toxic media coverage, these conditions do not exist in Iraq. But we need to worry about them converging elsewhere in the Middle East.

We can win the global struggle with Islamist terror. *If* we take the fight seriously.

INSURGENCIES

Unless terrorists gain control of a full arsenal of weapons of mass destruction, they will not be able to do as much damage to states and societies as full-blown insurgencies. In Iraq, for example, terrorism cannot force the disintegration of the state, but any number of possible insurgencies could. The dividing line between a terrorist group and an insurgency lies between the inability of the former to attract mass support and the ability of an insurgent movement to mobilize the population whose cause they claim to represent.

For all of the drama of terrorist attacks, insurgencies and the civil wars they spawn kill vastly more human beings. Those insurgencies range from Latin-American narcotics syndicates that challenge governments (the term "narco-terrorist" is wrong—these rich, powerful groups wage postmodern insurgencies) to classic ethnic or religious resistance struggles, such as those that recently plagued Sudan, Ivory Coast, Ethiopia, much of central Africa, Sri Lanka, Nepal, Turkey, the Russian Federation, and dozens of other states.

Insurgencies are harder to fight than terrorist movements, at least in the sense that more killing is required. Fighting terrorists may take longer, but insurgencies command more active support—and they're increasingly well armed. Nor do all insurgencies originate outside of a government—the butchery in Rwanda had its origins within the state apparatus. The Hutu Interahamwe militias targeted an ethnic group, not the government. Subsequently, the new Tutsi-dominated regime in Rwanda sponsored a bloody military operation in Zaire (now *Congo* again) that amounted to insurgency-as-invasion. Overall, the forms of insurgency and its motivations are expanding, exacerbated by a world of faulty borders and revived competition over religious and ethnic issues.

In trying to understand twenty-first-century conflict, it's helpful to view human societies as mass organisms, as ecosystems of flesh and blood. The bewildering violence we see in the developing world reveals attempts by complex human systems to regain their equilibrium after being forced out of their natural balance by European colonialism and its legacy of ill-drawn borders. Societies around the world are trying to put themselves right—and the default impulse is to do it through violence. Of one thing we may be certain: Until the international community takes the improbable (but essential) step of devising a system for peacefully correcting bad borders, we will see no end of insurgencies and civil wars.

Had we wished to design a world where conflict was inevitable, we could not have done better than yesteryear's Europeans, who drew borders in dazzling ignorance or cynicism, forcing together people who hated one another, or separating those who felt a historical affinity. Add in the revival of religion-as-blood-cult, and counterinsurgency warfare looks like the primary mode of fighting that civilized states will face in this century. The violence in the developing world over the past six decades was just a rehearsal.

CONVENTIONAL WAR

At present, it appears that the only possible conventional-warfare challenge to the United States would have to come from China. It's a war that neither party desires, but states often tumble clumsily into war. Thus, it's instructive to consider what a future war with China might look like, if only because its scale would be greater than any other unexpected, conventional clash.

First, it must be stressed again that a general war with China is unlikely to occur. Defense contractors have done their best to exaggerate China's military capabilities, but Beijing's forces remain two full generations behind our own technologically, and China's military has yet to display the culture of flexibility and internal communication essential to twenty-first-century warfighting. The Chinese have impressive military thinkers, but their executors lag far behind. Often accused of seeking to compete globally with the United States, most of China's far-flung endeavors are desperate attempts to secure the fuels and raw materials critical to the country's continued expansion. Beijing must maintain high growth rates to keep a restive population under control—China's leaders are far more worried about internal strife than about "American aggression." China may have interests from Sudan to Panama, but its armed forces would have difficulty reaching Taiwan in a war with the United States.

That said, we would be foolish not to accept the possibility of war with China—as long as we do not allow our analysis to become a self-fulfilling prophecy. And an honest model of a conflict with China raises a number of potential surprises for which our own armed forces and government are not adequately prepared. Our recent conventional operations have been ground-force heavy, with swift armored advances followed by gritty infantry combat in cities. We've seen that our Army and Marine Corps are too small for their global responsibilities. Yet, a war with China would be overwhelmingly a naval and airpower conflict—at least in its initial phases. Unless China came apart in the course of the conflict, we would be unlikely to invest ground forces in an effort to control Chinese territory. Instead, we would attempt to devastate China's military and essential infrastructure from a distance. The most probable land encounter would be a fight to the south, in Myanmar, for control of the old Burma Road, a trade lifeline for southern China (although we would first seek to control the route through a naval blockade—which would require Indian support).

In the broader struggle, we would be apt to get some unpleasant surprises. First, a war with China would be long, not short, and could well spread to other parts of east or southeast Asia as Beijing tried to alter the terms of the struggle. Our initial strikes from the air and sea would rapidly demonstrate the limitations of precision weaponry to inflict decisive—or even convincing—destruction on a powerful enemy with great strategic depth. China's larger number of aircraft would begin to tell as our ordnance and even our pilots grew exhausted, leading to a standoff in the air.

At sea, the initial exchange would be similar, but grimmer. Instead of repeating the great fleet actions of World War II on a strategic scale, our naval encounter with China would look uncannily like Jutland, Part Two: The Pacific Version. After inflicting more damage on our fleet than we anticipated in our war games, the Chinese would grasp that the price of sustaining their effort was too high. Withdrawing to the protection of their air-defense umbrella, Beijing's navy would become as immobilized as the German Imperial Fleet in the Great War—while our Navy would dominate the crucial sea-lanes, without being able to close in for the kill.

This would still be a naval war—but our Navy's decisive role would come in a postmodern form of commerce-raiding, closing off all trade with China (for years, not weeks or months), while standoff strikes interdicted future pipeline routes across Central Asia. The crucial theater of war would be the Indian Ocean, the waters that carry the vital trade that allows China to function as a modern, industrial state. Virtually all of the grandiose studies on high-tech wars brought to swift conclusions would prove worthless, while the old naval theorists who recognized the criticality of controlling seaborne trade would be vindicated: The strategic truth we ignore is that globalization has made control of the world's sea-lanes more important than ever before. Instead of great fleet-on-fleet battles, our Navy's essential contribution will be stopping, seizing, and occasionally sinking merchant vessels on the high seas. Our future Navy will combine the traditions of the Union Navy's blockade of the Confederacy with a twenty-first-century version of the South's bold commerce raiders. A conventional war with China would also have daunting unconventional aspects, but those are discussed below.

NUCLEAR WAR IN THE TWENTY-FIRST CENTURY

As ever more states come to possess nuclear weapons, the likelihood of their use increases exponentially. But the identity of the parties to the next nuclear exchange might surprise us. Without question, we should worry about all forms of weapons of mass destruction in the hands of terrorists—although nuclear weapons are difficult for nonstate actors to acquire, deploy, and use. Terrorists might stun us with the detonation of a small nuclear device (destructive enough, certainly), but the grand nuclear duels of the future are apt to be between states or multistate alliances led by newly emerging nuclear powers.

A war between China and the United States would be unlikely to turn nuclear, although Beijing might threaten nuclear use as a last, desperate gambit. The long-feared nuclear exchange between Pakistan and India remains a possibility—a probability, should religious fanatics seize power in Islamabad. Israel must always worry about nuclear weapons in Islamic hands, but Tel Aviv's retaliatory capacity remains a deterrent against all but the maddest regimes.

Instead, the smart money would bet on a nuclear exchange between Iran's Persian Shi'as and Sunni Arabs in neighboring states. We worry, rightfully, about Tehran's quest for nuclear weapons, but we fail to understand the context of the mullahs' adamant refusal to interrupt Iran's nuclear program. We see ourselves as the potential target, but to the degree that the Iranians consider us, they view nuclear weapons as an essential deterrent, not as first-strike tools. We take third place, at most, on Tehran's targeting list, while Israel and Sunni Arabs tie for first place—and, if recent history is any precedent, Sunni Arabs may occupy the top spot.

Although Pakistanis are not Arabs, Islamabad's bomb is a Sunni bomb—paid for by Saudi coreligionists. Tehran wants a Shi'a bomb as a counterweight. The opening section of this article noted that the bloodiest conventional war since 1945 was fought between Saddam's Iraq and Khomeini's Iran. The Iranians, who suffered a disproportionate share of the casualties, have not forgotten—disabled veterans in the streets are a constant reminder. This grudge match is just pausing between rounds.

One of the many reasons to hope for the success of our efforts to help Iraqis build a unified, rule-of-law government is that, should Iraq fail, the chances for a regional conflagration would skyrocket. Arabs, Persians, and Turks all might join in a bloody squabble over Iraq's dismembered parts—should Tehran possess nuclear weapons by that time, it would not scruple about using them to prevent a defeat by Persia's and Shi'a Islam's age-old enemies. The single factor that might prevent nuclear use under such circumstances would be the weakness of Arab armies in the post-Saddam era. Iran's military could win a conventional fight—unless Saudi Arabia called in enough chips to persuade Pakistan to open a second front.

All of this remains speculation, but the other variable is that Iran will not be the last state to pursue nuclear arms. Nuclear use during the Cold War was prevented primarily by a sense of rational self-interest and by fear. A future, fanatic, nuclear-armed regime may be neither rational nor afraid.

BEYOND NUKES

With rare exceptions, recent discussions about "asymmetrical warfare" have focused on nonstate actors employing terrorism or guerrilla techniques against Western militaries. Yet, across the coming decades, any state with which we found ourselves at war would pursue unconventional means and strategies in an attempt to offset our conventional advantages.

For example, a general war with China, as described above, might settle into an atmosphere of "phony war," of wary armed confrontation after an initial bloodletting. Our own asymmetrical effort would be to starve China of resources, trade and financial instruments. For its part, China would attempt to expand the range of warmaking activities, attacking our communications and electronic infrastructure at home, manipulating the global media in a struggle to command world opinion, and seeking to convince the American people that the cost of continuing the war was prohibitive. To that end, Beijing might even attempt to wage biological warfare based upon genetic engineering, betting that its larger population could more easily absorb significant losses than could ours.

China would attempt to strike at our domestic weaknesses, just as we would assault China's—with both sides resorting to nontraditional means. For us, the overcentralization of our food supplies and the interwoven character of our electrical grid would be enormous vulnerabilities (especially if compounded by a devastating epidemic). A national supply system that relies on massive warehouse complexes and interstate trucking worsens the centralized food-production problem for us. Our economies of scale and sophisticated just-in-time delivery techniques could prove appallingly fragile—a

Chinese village is better equipped to feed itself than most American small towns today (to say nothing of our cities), and the general goods, the availability of which we take for granted, would quickly become scarce under pandemic conditions.

We would try to divide China's population into a regime camp and a new-nationalist peace movement. While Chinese chauvinism is powerful, discontent grows daily beyond the success-story cities (which have their own vast, combustible slums). An operational goal would be to incite a governmental overreaction to unrest— crudely put, to set Chinese to killing Chinese. Simultaneously, Beijing would attempt to divide Americans politically.

China is far more aware of its internal weaknesses than we are—as we continue to search desperately for a mighty enemy to replace the Soviet Union. The most instructive action taken by the Beijing government in the past twenty years wasn't the Tiananmen Square crackdown, but the ferocious response to the spread of the Falun Gong cult. Cognizant of their national history, China's rulers feared the rapid spread of a charismatic religion. For centuries, the great upheavals in China, from peasant revolts through the Taipings and the later Fists of Righteousness (or "Boxers"), down to the secular cult of Mao, have had a messianic, millenarian character. China's present rulers dread the rise of a new, seductive religion within the country far more than they do any external threat. And given the resurgence of religion-as-an-excuse-for-violence in our time, Beijing's fears may be accurately placed.

And we must be careful what we wish for: Were China's government overthrown by the rise of a new religion, we might find the new China more aggressive and dangerous than the wary state we face today. The most asymmetrical aspect of a war with China might be its outcome—unleashing forces we have not yet imagined.

NO "END OF HISTORY"

All of this brings us back to rekindled religious passion as the motive force for conflict in this new century. Far from seeing an "end of history," we're experiencing history's return with a vengeance. From the sorry close of the last century at Srebrenica to the beginning of the new one on 9/11, we've found ourselves in a great age of transitions: From the Europe-spawned "Age of Reason" that perished at Auschwitz, to the new age of faith gathering global impetus; from the Western cult of technology to the resurgence of superstition; from an age that sought to impose the rule of law, to the age of hyperlawlessness; from the age of a world ordered by Europe, to a world violently disordered by Europe's colonial legacy.

Rarely has the end of a century and of a millennium coincided so neatly with a sudden break in values, beliefs, social organization—and the modalities of war. We long for recent verities, now collapsed, and find it almost as difficult to face the ferocity and unreason of this new age as our enemies find it to cope with our dominance. We live at a time when men refuse to believe what they see before them, preferring to believe in things they cannot see. Our enemies are the prisoners of a cruel vision of their god, while we are captives of our myths of a benign world.

The conflicts of the coming years will force a sense of reality upon all of us.

Living, and Dying, with Suicide Bombers

USA Today

January 4, 2006

After spending trillions of dollars on high-tech armaments, the United States finds itself confounded by a dirt-cheap weapon of genius: The suicide bomber. The ultimate precision weapon and genuine "smart bomb," the suicide bomber is hard to deter and exasperatingly difficult to defeat. This is the "poor man's nuke." For a few hundred dollars (or less) and a human life, a suicide bomber can achieve strategic effects the U.S. Air Force can only envy.

For all of the claims that technology would dominate the twenty-first century—and not only in the realm of warfare—we find that impassioned faith still trumps microchips. Armed with a fervent belief in his god's appetite for blood, the suicide bomber can dominate headlines around the world with a few pounds of explosives. A paradox of the Information Age is that it's simultaneously the new age of superstition. As calcified social orders collapse under the pressures of global change, those who feel most threatened flee into debased, occult religion. Increasingly, fanaticism finds outlet in shedding the blood not only of unbelievers, but also of coreligionists whose beliefs are seen as imperfect.

The suicide bomber views himself (more rarely, herself) as fulfilling a divine mission whose execution will be rewarded in paradise. How do we discourage an enemy who regards death as a promotion? How do we identify the religious madman among the masses in time to stop him from killing? On a practical level, defeating the increasing numbers of suicide bombers is our most difficult security mission.

HOMELAND VULNERABLE

Except for 9/11, suicide bombers have conducted their missions abroad. That's going to change, but it's a credit to the patriotism and decency of American Muslims that none of our fellow citizens has strapped on a bomb and walked into a Wal-Mart. Nonetheless, our enemies will find a way to bring their deadly campaign back to our doorsteps.

The suicide bomber is so powerful a weapon that not even the terrorists have realized its full potential. Today, we see intermittent, localized attacks. The suicide bomber is at the same stage of development as the tank was in World War I: Used in small numbers, armored vehicles did not achieve and sustain critical mass. We need to prepare for the suicide-bomber blitzkrieg, when murderous zealots come at us in waves.

The obvious forerunners of today's Islamist fanatics were the Assassins, the notorious cult that operated from Persia through Syria in the eleventh and twelfth centuries. Armed only with sacramental knives and patience, the Assassins terrorized governments by killing sultans and grand viziers. It took the invading Mongols—the all-time masters of counter-insurgency warfare—to destroy the Assassins in their mountain strongholds.

But assassination became commonplace in the Muslim world thereafter. The Assassins came from an off-shoot sect of Shi'a Islam. Today's suicide bombers are overwhelmingly Sunnis, but the pattern of waging an asymmetrical conflict through carefully planned murders is a tradition, not an aberration.

To be fair to the Assassins, they attacked only the mighty, not the masses. And, as Bernard Lewis, the giant of Middle Eastern studies at Princeton, pointed out, Islam's prohibition against suicide meant that yesteryear's murderers allowed themselves to be caught and suffer torture rather than kill themselves. But the new age of faith is also an era of the perversion of religion, from the primitive blood-cult evident in ritual beheadings to the rationalization of a suicide bomber's death—not as self-murder but the consequence of a brave attack in the conduct of holy war. Nor should it be as difficult as we assume for Westerners to grasp the psychology at work in the suicide bomber. Our own history is full of martyrs and religious warriors who went boldly and knowingly to their deaths. In every culture, the really good haters die well.

WHO ARE THEY?

Deplore his act though we rightly do, the suicide bomber, who imagines himself a defender of his threatened faith and humiliated people, is the extremist equivalent of the soldier we revere for throwing himself on a grenade to save his comrades' lives. Our rules for self-sacrifice are different, but the psychology is uncomfortably familiar. The results may differ terribly, but the motivation has filial roots.

We see only the indiscriminate carnage, the apparent madness. Until we recognize his crazed valor, we cannot understand the suicide bomber. And it's much harder to defeat an enemy you don't understand.

Suicide bombers are recruited from the ranks of troubled souls, from those who find mundane reality overwhelming and terrifying. The suicide bomber longs for release from the insecurities of his daily experience. He is fleeing from life every bit as much as he's rushing toward paradise. He dreads women, sin, and doubt.

Hypnotized by faith and excited to ecstasy, he can walk into a children's clinic and press a detonator. No heart-rending child's face will stop him. His god will forgive the innocent. Nothing matters but the divine will as interpreted by the masters of terror—the most brilliant psychologists of our time.

We have faced enemies more dangerous, but none so implacable.

The world's great strategic struggle of this century is between those who believe in a generous, loving god—in any religion—and those who serve a punitive, merciless deity. The suicide bomber has chosen his side.

Shattering Warfare's Rules

USA Today

January 4, 2006

The U.S. military faced suicide bombers in the past: In the closing months of World War II, Japanese kamikaze pilots flew bomb-laden planes into U.S. Navy ships. The kamikazes generated casualties but could not change the outcome of the war. Strapped into their aircraft, those who volunteered to die for the "divine emperor" were the closest thing we ever faced to today's Islamist fanatics. But there were key differences: The kamikaze pilots were disciplined military men attacking military targets. Their goal wasn't to slaughter civilians but to stave off defeat. They were fighting for an imperial idea, not for a global religious crusade.

We fought Muslim fanatics before, too. In the wake of the Spanish-American War, the Moro insurrection in the southern Philippines pitted impassioned jihadis against the U.S. Army. It took years, but the Moros were defeated by superior organization, a battlefield ruthlessness impossible in today's media environment—and Gatling guns. The combat was so brutal, we developed the famous M-1911 .45 caliber semi-automatic pistol to stop attackers who were frenzied by religious visions and drugs. Yet, even the Moros weren't intent on suicide. Willing to die to drive out the unbelievers, they didn't seek death.

We fought other faith-inspired enemies, from the Boxers in China to the Ghost Dancers on our Indian frontier—opponents whose trust in mystical spells or totems to ward off bullets failed to armor their flesh against modern rifles. Still, every such enemy fought to win, however hopeless the odds. None intended to die for the sake of dying.

Driven by a nihilistic desire to achieve salvation through slaughter, today's suicide bombers are a genuinely new phenomenon. With their twin goals of self-annihilation and creating mass carnage, they've fundamentally shifted the battlefield's rules—and its location. We've heard a great deal about our high-tech "revolution in military affairs."

Welcome to the counterrevolution.

Heroes with Bulldozers

New York Post

January 20, 2006

America's soldiers are always good for a surprise: The enthusiasm the Army's combat engineers show for our mission in Iraq would dumbfound even our military's most fervent supporters.

Privileged to speak with officers and NCOs from the Army's Maneuver Support Center in Missouri last week, I came away proud to have worn the same uniform as those men and women. Every one of them had served in Iraq or Afghanistan. Now they were briefly back home, working hard to incorporate combat lessons learned into doctrine and training the young soldiers they'll lead during their next Mideast tours. All that nonsense about a "broken Army"? What I heard was the conviction that we're not only doing the right thing in Iraq, but doing it far better than the media tell the American people.

Along with those combat engineers, the audience consisted of infantry, military police, and chemical corps leaders—veterans all. Not one was discouraged by the political tempests blowing in Washington (where the hot air is a prime cause of global warming). The best word for what our soldiers displayed is *zeal*.

I only wish my fellow citizens were given an honest view of our troops—their morale and their accomplishments—along with a fuller sense of our military's complexity. Yes, the infantry leads the way, along with the other combat arms. But who hears about the combat engineers? Even though they often lead the infantry? Well, here's to the heroes who clear the minefields, defuse the improvised explosive devices (IEDs), blow open the doors, dig the trenches, build the defensive barriers, renovate the schools and clinics, plunge into the tangle of wires that passes for an electrical grid—and fight as infantrymen when the need arises.

When you see those dramatic photographs of infantry teams taking down an urban target, the soldiers up front are often combat engineers, opening a path for the grunts to go in.

Every branch of our Army makes its own unsung contributions, but a glimpse at the combat engineers offers a sense of how complex the Iraq mission really is—and how bravely those in uniform have faced up to the challenges. So here are a few anecdotes from the officers and NCOs I met last week:

- All a soldier has to do to make headlines is to whine to a reporter. But we don't hear about the NCO lying in a stateside hospital ward who, after losing an eye defusing an IED, begged his visiting commander to help him get back to his unit in Iraq.

- In the past, active-duty leaders often dismissed the National Guard as "weekend warriors." Not anymore. The highest praise I heard was for a "dump-truck" outfit, the 1457th Engineer Battalion from the Utah National Guard, that served in Baghdad and central Iraq. A colonel described them as remarkably brave and resourceful. Operating at as low as 65 percent of their authorized strength, those mountain lions from the Rockies never ducked a high-risk mission—whether they'd been trained for it or not.

- When the highly paid contractors failed to show up with the bullets flying, combat engineers often were thrown in to get the electricity working out in the boonies. And they did. But all we heard about were the problems in Baghdad—where the contractors were responsible.

- Having just returned from Iraq, one officer said, "I'd give up my promotion to go back." Even allowing for the moment's enthusiasm, that family man believed that his sacrifices made a vital difference. Why don't men like him make the evening news?

- Even during an occupation, the Army has to train for its full range of missions. At a division commander's request, our engineers built a tank-gunnery range with sixty-four miles of protective berms to keep the main-gun rounds from going astray. One example among many—all in a day's work for the bulldozer boys.

- That day's work includes some of the most dangerous missions in Iraq—defusing IEDs. The equipment and techniques have gotten better, but it remains a nerve-wracking challenge. Combat engineers volunteer to do it.

- As in the Army's better-known units, our combat engineers see impressive reenlistment rates. Soldiers sign up knowing they'll be sent back to Iraq. Tough as it is, they love what they do. As one command sergeant major put it, "This is what they signed up for. This is what it's all about."

Of course, no list of this sort can begin to capture the courage of these soldiers. They have families they love and the prospect of long lives in the greatest country on earth. Yet, they continue to risk death or mutilation because they will not quit on America—or Iraq—in the middle of a war. At a time when we're bombarded with so much doom-and-gloom nonsense from those who'd like to abandon the world to terrorists, it's a shame we don't hear more about the men and women who stay in uniform, who do our nation's toughest work and receive so little credit from the know-it-alls safe at home.

Harvard and Yale? Keep 'em. The finest Americans are those who have gone through the School of the Soldier. A "broken military"? Nope. Anyway, if it was broken, the combat engineers would fix it. Under Fire.

Bloodless Theories,
Bloody Wars

Armed Forces Journal

April 2006

During the Second World War, American and British air-campaign planners attempted to force the Nazi war machine into collapse by attacking crucial links in Germany's national infrastructure. According to the theory, hitting well-selected individual targets would paralyze entire systems. So, at an enormous cost in lives and aircraft, we went after German rail junctions and ball-bearing plants, engine factories and Romanian oil fields. We were, in short, executing Effects-Based Operations, or EBO, the current darling among "revolutionary" concepts.

Of course, the Wehrmacht had to be defeated on the ground. The Allied bombing campaign certainly aided in that defeat, but it was not decisive in itself. No matter how many railroad marshalling yards we struck, the Reichsbahn found work-arounds. As for bombing the industrial infrastructure, at the end of the war more than 90 percent of Germany's production capabilities remained intact (contrary to popular belief), giving the defeated country a launching pad for its postwar "economic miracle." In early 1945, German combat aircraft production was increasing. Those expensive attacks on "vital" nodes helped the war effort but could not have won the war alone had they lasted for a generation. Germany's lack of home-country petroleum reserves severely hampered the Nazis—but the advance of the Red Army did vastly more to interrupt fuel supplies from the east than did the EBO efforts of the 1940s.

The primary problem we face in preparing for future wars is an intellectually corrupt budgeting and procurement process, a system that forces the services—especially the Navy and Air Force—to make extravagant, impossible-to-fulfill claims for the weapons they wish to buy. It isn't possible to argue that a system will be "useful." To appear competitive, each system has to be "revolutionary."

Compounding the damage, each of the services (except the Marine Corps) has fallen into the trap of designing its strategy to fit the systems it wants, rather than devising an honest long-term strategy and then pursuing the weapons best fitted to support that strategy. We have gotten the process exactly wrong. No sensible person would argue against the potential benefits of new military technologies—but those technologies must be relevant to genuine wartime needs, not merely sexy platforms for air shows. The services become so mesmerized by their in-progress procurement programs that any challenge to a system's utility is treated as an attack on the service itself.

The truth is that we lie. Precision-guided weapons are marvelous additions to our arsenal. They save lives, spare resources, and accomplish crucial missions. The fallacy is to believe they can win wars by themselves. The abysmally failed "shock and awe" campaign that was supposed to persuade Saddam Hussein to surrender by demonstrating our techno-prowess should be a lesson to us all: Take the enemy's psychology into account, don't engage in wishful thinking, and worst-case what it takes to defeat your opponent.

Nonetheless, at the Joint Forces Command and in the Air Force, proponents of Effects-Based Operations now suggest that, by striking just the right pressure points, we might bring China to its knees. Well, China's already on its knees—a position that gives China greater inherent stability than our own top-heavy military and hyperdeveloped national infrastructure possess. The crucial question in any war is, "What will it really take to force our enemy to surrender?" We know what it took in Nazi Germany. And in Imperial Japan. To defeat China, we'd have to inflict at least a comparable level of destruction. EBO isn't a strategy. It's a sales pitch.

Yet, EBO also reflects a recurring American delusion—the notion that, if only we can discover it, there must be a formula for winning wars on the cheap. EBO and other schemes for sterilized techno-wars have surprisingly deep roots in our military culture—

the American vines were grafted onto diseased European root stocks.

Far from being a brand-new, breakthrough concept, EBO is rooted in the nineteenth-century cult of Gen. George B. McClellan's favorite military theorist, Baron Antoine Henri Jomini—the Swiss-born, French-speaking military charlatan who seduced the engineers produced by West Point with his geometrical "the calculus is all" approach to warfare. Presenting himself as the heir to Napoleonic thought, Jomini got the emperor dead wrong (only his Ulm campaign makes any sense in Jominian terms), reflecting, instead, the mannered approach to warfare that was generally prevalent between the Peace of Westphalia in 1648 and the cannonade at Valmy in 1792.

Although there were many exceptions to the "mannerly war" school of that long eighteenth century—such as Marshal Turenne's scorched-earth campaigns in the Rhineland and the life-or-death battlefield ferocity of Frederick the Great—many of the period's conflicts within Europe were "cabinet wars" about slight alterations to frontiers. (Wars against the Turks were always fought with greater savagery, as were conflicts in the Polish empire, Ukraine, and Russia.) Elegant campaigns sought to capture a single fortress, the loss of which might make a series of other fortresses untenable. Reverting to the maneuver dances of Renaissance condotierri, who had no wish to waste the lives of their expensively equipped and trained Landsknechte, post–1648 generalship often consisted in giving greater priority to preserving the king's regiments than to defeating the king's enemies. While the brilliant combination of the Duke of Marlborough and Prince Eugene led to one decisive victory at Blenheim, the former's campaigns in Flanders, although waged brilliantly on the terms of the age, were limited in scope. Most Western European wars fought between the destruction of the Spanish tercios at Rocroi and the rise of Napoleon simply aimed at moving a dynasty's football a bit to either side of the fifty-yard line.

Napoleon revolutionized European warfare with his strategic vision, his ruthlessness, and his disregard for the accepted rules. The odd thing is that only Clausewitz, who fought against him, "got" Napoleon. An aide-de-camp to the emperor, Jomini interpreted Napoleon's campaigns through the long-dead eyes of the marshals of Louis XIV.

This arcane history matters because the U.S. Army never signed up for Clausewitz (not even in the 1980s, when he was quoted more often than he was read). Ours was instinctively a Jominian military when it came to theories of warfare. We did—and do—want checklists, formulae, easy how-to instruction kits. Clausewitz, a soldier of incomparable integrity, provided insights, not answers. Jomini, the hustler in uniform, laid out warfare as a board game, as an engineering problem, ever calculable for those who got the math right. Clausewitz is difficult and unsparing. Jomini is as superficial as a television commercial. Our choice was predetermined.

Clausewitz long remained unknown to American officers, but Jomini had become a must-read for our most-ambitious officers by the end of the 1840s. (Until he was translated, they read him in French; how much they understood is another issue entirely.) Compounding the problem, our military ancestors assumed that the French military was the world's best model to emulate, missing the fact that Napoleon had been a grand anomaly. Thus, officers such as McClellan not only took Jomini to bed with them, but also tailored their uniforms and trimmed their mustaches to appear as French as possible. (Those well-known Civil War caps of ours were based on French kepis, and the surest measure of a Civil War officer's vanity, whether he wore blue or gray, was the number of photographs taken of him with a hand burrowed into his tunic à la Napoleon). Even the Prussian triumph in 1870–71 hardly convinced us that the French military might not be the be-all and end-all, and we were still studying French tactics well into the bloodbath of the Great War.

Our Civil War was won by the officers who didn't read Jomini—or who read and dismissed him. By contrast, the Union's debacles were often shaped by Jominian thinking. Most notoriously, McClellan thought in terms of campaign geometries and strategic coups de main—EBO, in fact. McClellan fought as an eighteenth-century French marshal, worried more about the embarrassment of losing than the advantages of victory, building a lovely army—then fearing to risk it—and, above all, imagining that the right combination of maneuvers might force a determined Confederacy to surrender.

McClellan's inept Peninsula Campaign—the worst example in our history of an entire army failing because of a single man's incompetence—was supposed to present the Confederates with check, then checkmate, by fatally threatening Richmond. Of course, he didn't reckon on Robert E. Lee or Stonewall Jackson, soldiers who were more inclined to fight than to theorize. McClellan's attempts to "leverage strategic nodes" were all about his own genius, with no regard for a living, thinking, fire-breathing enemy.

Most of the Army of the Potomac's early campaigns tried to play Jominian chess with the Army of Northern Virginia—which kept knocking over the board. But even the Confederates were not entirely immune to Jomini's influence. Both sides angled against the other's capital city, imagining that its possession would inevitably mean victory. Lee's two invasions of the North—the latter of which forever crippled his army—were Jominian, aimed at out-flanking Washington by invading Pennsylvania and making the Army of the Potomac's position militarily and politically untenable. The Gettysburg Campaign was EBO without smart bombs.

Tactically brilliant and strategically myopic, Lee seems always to have been torn, influenced by his studies and his background as an engineer, yet sensing that the war had to be won by attrition—a strategy he could not afford. Early in the war, when John Singleton Mosby commenced partisan cavalry operations in the Union rear area, Lee worried that the effort would rob him of mounted troops badly needed for reconnaissance and on the battlefield. With some difficulty, Lee was persuaded to allow Mosby to operate with great autonomy, and the Gray Ghost did, indeed, tie down a lopsided number of Union troops with EBO-style raids on crucial nodes, such as rail junctions or supply trains. In the end, though, Lee's instincts proved right. Mosby was a glorious annoyance but could not deliver winning blows against the enemy. The Confederacy was quantitatively incompetent—and Mosby's valiant efforts only diluted Lee's battlefield punch. The Civil War had to be won by generals who grasped that victory would not come with fallen capital cities, interdicted rail lines, or clever maneuvers but only with hard, bloody, relentless fighting. There was no cheap way to win.

Thereafter, the Army read Jomini intermittently but fought Indians, as well as the Boxers, the Moros, and then Pancho Villa. Then the Great War exploded every fashionable theory, from those of Jomini's French heirs (such as the tragic Ardant du Picq) to the fatal Prussian oversimplification of Clausewitz. Attempts at bold Jominian strokes, such as Winston Churchill's Gallipoli Campaign, ended in disaster (Liddell-Hart's "indirect approach" is pure Jomini). For the soldiers involved, it was one of the grimmest wars in history (ending with a devastating influenza epidemic). Military theory dissolved in a bloodbath.

Jomini went into eclipse thereafter, but his spirit had been embedded in the U.S. military. His formulaic approach to making war was a perfect fit for the psychology of the world's leading industrial power, the country that made progress by making things. Giulio Douhet, Italy's false prophet of airpower, was a peculiar bastard descendent of Jomini, convinced that airpower alone would decide the next war. (Sound familiar?) Likewise, the American general Billy Mitchell—in some respects a courageous figure—exaggerated the capabilities of airpower as surely as do today's Air Force theorists.

Mitchell got it partly right—a particularly dangerous situation. As a result, the Army Air Corps got it partly wrong, although it fought heroically. The Allied bombing campaign over Germany in the Second World War was a marriage of American industrial power and eighteenth-century military thought, by way of Jomini: Just press the right node hard enough and Jack will spring out of the box, waving a white flag. In the end, the raw destruction of German and Japanese cities was far more useful in inculcating a useful postsurrender sense of defeat in our enemies than were our costly attacks on strategic nodes. But nothing was as useful as old-fashioned battlefield victories.

Inevitably, the Cold War saw renewed efforts to discover the alchemical formula for easy victory. Far from the great age of American military strategy, this was its nadir. From Mutually Assured Destruction to the Pentomic Army (which appears to be coming back), phony intellectualism obscured a poverty of minds and practical confusion. The most strategically incisive document of the era remains the film *Dr. Strangelove or: How I Learned to Stop Worrying and Love the Bomb*.

The neo-Jominians of the 1950s and early 1960s produced calculations far beyond their ancestor's scope, certain that they knew precisely how the next war must be waged.

Instead, we got Vietnam.

One could rehash this endless tug of war between our military theorists, who never fail to come up with new clothes for their emperor, insisting that this time they really do know how to win wars cheaply (in terms of blood and bother, if not financially), and the fighting generals and colonels who have to step into the mess the theorists have made and clean it up while the bullets are flying. Contemporary generals such as Mattis and Wallace are the heirs of Sherman and Sheridan—not afraid to fight and ever ready to ride to the sound of the guns. On the other side, you have the theorists, who have them outnumbered, if not outgunned. No matter the empirical evidence, theorists will always insist that they know a better, easier way to wage war than the men who must actually fight it. Compounded by the power of the defense industry and the political momentum of legacy weapons systems, the theorists win. In peacetime.

When the first early man discovered that he could bind a sharp stone to a stick with a leather thong, you can be certain that he turned immediately to his pals across the campfire and shouted, "I've just achieved the ultimate revolution in military affairs!"

There's no end of such revolutions. Only the End of Days will see an end to military innovation. And we're told, again and again, that the nature of warfare has changed. But the nature of warfare never changes—only its superficial manifestations. On the battlefield, Cain still squares off with Abel. The technologies evolve, but it's still about killing the enemy until the survivors raise their hands—and mean it.

Even as our soldiers and Marines fight primitive (but intelligent) enemies in Iraq, Afghanistan, and elsewhere, we're told that the evidence before our eyes doesn't really mean anything, that the next war is going to be different, that technology really will do the trick this time. If the United States still exists a hundred years from now, I have no doubt that your great-great-grandchildren will also be assured that, while the theorists were wrong for the past century (or two, or three), they really have it figured out now and that technology really is going to be decisive this time.

Appropriate technologies are essential. But flesh and blood wins wars. The only Effects-Based Operations that mean anything are those that destroy the enemy's military, the opposing leadership, and the population's collective will. Bombing well-selected targets helps. But only killing wins wars.

Oh, and a last note on Effects-Based Operations: Any combat doctrine that cannot be explained clearly and concisely will fail.

Hawks for Dissent

The Washington Monthly

May 2006

Pop quiz: Who was our secretary of war—the closest figure we had to a secretary of defense—in 1942? Too hard? Then who was FDR's trusted adviser on how to wage the Second World War?

The secretary of war was Henry L. Stimson. But it is General George C. Marshall whom we remember, the man who shaped a war-winning strategy and then went on to win the peace with the Marshall Plan. Secretary Stimson's performance was competent and constructive, but he did not interfere with military operations. By contrast, everyone remembers that Robert S. McNamara was the secretary of defense as the Vietnam War went awry, but few could name the nation's most senior military officers in any given year of that conflict.

Unpalatable as it may be to those raised on Oliver Stone's rein-vention of history, the truth is that our nation's most successful wartime partnerships have been between presidents and generals: Lincoln and Grant, Wilson and Pershing, FDR and Marshall. Such professional, non-political relationships brought us a remarkable century of victories, from Mexico City to Tokyo Bay.

Thereafter, the miserable road to Saigon—and Baghdad—was paved with the best intentions. Six decades ago, the National Secu-rity Act of 1947 inserted buffers between presidents and their top military men, leading immediately to a series of military debacles or, at best, stalemates. Instead of Marshall speaking—respectfully but frankly—to FDR, we got McNamara huddling with LBJ and, now, Donald Rumsfeld, who never saw combat, interpreting warfare to a president who never saw combat. Instead of making battlefield decisions based upon military necessity, the rise of powerful secretaries of defense resulted in combat decisions based upon political expediency.

Defense secretaries, not dissident retired generals, have politicized our national security. As for the recently invented "requirement" for retired officers to remain silent and apolitical, would we really like to strike George Washington and Dwight D. Eisenhower from our history books? After all, it was Eisenhower, the former soldier, who warned us so presciently of the military-industrial complex, while secretaries of defense—one after another—merely shoveled money into its maw.

The Goldwater-Nichols Act, an echo of Vietnam, was supposed to guarantee unfiltered military advice to the president. It didn't work. The elaborate superstructure of the contemporary presidency, with its many gatekeepers, excludes the nation's senior military leaders from the frequent, intimate, and unconstrained contact with the president that served us so well in the past. Too much has been delegated: While the president has the indisputable right to dismiss military leaders (as Lincoln certainly had to do), he also has the duty to study the professional advice of those who will lead our troops into battle before overruling it. With the approval of Congress (and increasingly without it), the president makes our strategic decisions, but it is his obligation to the American people to make informed decisions.

Today, however, our presidents do not hear unvarnished, depoliticized military advice, and the situation has never been graver than under the current administration. Presidential interviews with generals are essentially pre-scripted, with vetted talking points—political courtiers control access to the president and determine what the president will hear. Only the president himself could change the situation by demanding to hear a range of military views (without commissars at the shoulders of the generals). President George W. Bush, who has chosen war as a policy tool, may be the American president most isolated from sound military advice.

BRASS ATTACKS

At least six retired combat commanders have now gone public with the sort of technical—not political—criticism I've heard for years in private conversations with our generals. None of the critics has anything to gain personally. Indeed, each has much to lose by speaking out against any aspect of the most vindictive presidential administration since the Nixon era. Dissenters are automatically blackballed from the lucrative defense industry jobs that corrode the ethics of retired senior officers, and they'll never be offered plum posts in any future administration, Republican or Democrat. In addition, they've had to undergo savage and dishonest personal attacks in the media from support-the-administration-at-all-costs conservative columnists, from retired officers who draw their paychecks from a defense industry that has plentiful reasons to be grateful to Donald Rumsfeld, and from serving officers promoted by the secretary of defense—not least the chairman of the joint chiefs, Gen. Peter Pace—who are not supposed to take public political positions, but who have, nonetheless, been slavish in their praise of Rumsfeld.

Remarkably, our gotcha media have given Rumsfeld's high-ranking uniformed supporters a pass while falling for the red-herring issue of civilian control of our military. Nor have our media investigated the defense industry and Bush administration ties of the retired officers who appear as television talking heads or write op-eds condemning the critical retirees. Were reporters or broadcast producers to do the slightest legwork (or keyboard work), they would uncover blatant conflicts of interest—it's as if a talk-show host interviewed an oil-industry executive on the rising price of gasoline without revealing his corporate allegiance.

The crucial issue, though, is the bogus charge of insubordination threatening the good order of civil-military relations. It's a spurious claim that has nonetheless been embraced uncritically by the orthodox on both the left and right. Instead of being alarmed that former soldiers—with no political ties or agendas—searched their consciences and then went public with their criticism of a notoriously imperious defense secretary, we should celebrate the fact. Each of these men played by the rules, retiring before speaking out. None prejudiced good order. Not one stands to profit from his courage (quite the contrary).

If former officers cannot speak out on complex military issues, to whom can we turn for expert advice? To politicians who never deigned to serve in uniform themselves? To pundits equally lacking in military experience? To defense industry publicists? Surely, lifelong expertise should hold some value in our specialized society.

As someone who supported the destruction of the Saddam Hussein regime, who continues to support our efforts in Iraq, and who recently returned from Baghdad humbled by the commitment and courage of our soldiers and Marines, I am outraged by the disinformation campaign this administration has conducted against honorable and patriotic critics. Those on the pious right never fail to invoke the First Amendment when it suits their purposes, but now that six retired generals, without coordination or organizational support, have criticized one of the least popular figures in the Bush administration, freedom of speech is suddenly un-American; criticism is a threat to the republic; and, according to one newspaper aligned with the administration, military retirees who dare to question the performance of the Office of the Secretary of Defense should be prosecuted.

We celebrate whistle blowers in corrupt corporations such as Enron, in the worlds of finance and health care, and even in the FBI. Yet, what national endeavor deserves greater scrutiny than the conduct of our wars? Do we truly want even retired military figures to remain silent if the blood of our fellow citizens, our national prestige, and our wealth is squandered through incompetence? Do we desire a Prussian military that excuses every action by claiming it was only following orders?

In twenty-two years of uniformed service, I never encountered subversive speech among my peers. Every officer I've known has taken seriously his or her oath to uphold and defend our constitution. Their ethos was loyal—and silent—service. For a retired officer to raise a voice in dissent is a grave act of individual conscience, so earnest a decision that I suspect few civilians can grasp its emotional intensity.

Of course, the administration's no-holds-barred defense of Secretary Rumsfeld is really a defense of itself. From disseminating talking points against the critics to thousands of retired flag officers, to instigating op-eds (not a few of which have been bluntly dishonest), the administration's response to criticism has been character assassination combined with a skillful effort to shift the terms of the debate. We have been told that the critical retirees are simply gripers, disappointed in their military careers. What we're not told is that Major General John Batiste, the decorated former combat commander of the 1st Infantry Division in Iraq, turned down a third star rather than continue to serve under Secretary Rumsfeld, or that Major General Charles Swannack, another critic, led the Army's elite division, the 82nd Airborne, in combat in the Sunni Triangle. Every officer who's spoken out has had a successful career and is respected by those still in uniform. Yet voices closely tied to the Office of the Secretary of Defense, some belonging to former officers who took off their uniforms well over a decade ago and who have never walked an infantry patrol in Iraq, insist that Rumsfeld's critics somehow don't have the "big picture."

This is just a lie. Who better to understand and explain the unnecessary challenges our troops have faced and continue to face than the combat leaders who signed the letters of condolence to bereaved families (not using an autograph machine, as the Secretary of Defense did)? Should we put our trust instead in biased pundits, administration surrogates, and a battery of yesteryear's military retirees who've fed heartily at the defense-industry trough and rely on continued access to the Pentagon?

CAPTURING THE PRESIDENT'S EAR

There is a cost to our nation from celebrity defense secretaries such as Robert S. McNamara, who shrugged as 50,000 American troops died; the tragic Les Aspin who, for political reasons, would not provide our troops in Somalia with a single company of tanks; and now Donald Rumsfeld, who seeks to take credit for the successes of others, while shunning blame for the casualties his obstinacy caused. The common denominator of these defense secretaries is that they politicized our military and its decision-making processes. It hasn't been the generals or admirals who have done so.

From the era of Winfield Scott through that of George Marshall, there was a logical, practical distribution of labor between the executive branch, Congress, and senior military leaders. Our presidents and legislators decided if, when, and with whom we would go to war (this process, too, has broken down under a series of imperial presidencies). Presidents, while keeping Congress informed, determined the broad outlines of our grand strategy. But our elected and appointed leaders allowed military professionals to determine the details of how our military would organize for war and how wars would be fought on the ground. It was an imperfect system, but it delivered a history of victories.

While the generals and admirals should never be given a blank check, we must return to our lost tradition of listening with an open mind to their professional advice about how to defeat an enemy we have determined to take on (or who has determined to take us on). The president will always be the ultimate "decider." But his or her decisions must be made after hearing unfiltered military advice, not the spin of a fellow political insider. If war is too important to be left to the generals, the battlefield is too deadly to be left to the politicians.

Yet, unwilling to address the what-happened-in-Iraq issues raised by his critics, Secretary Rumsfeld has attempted to play a shell game, blaming a hidebound Army reluctant to reform itself for all of his problems. At the same time, the Army reforms that paid off handsomely on the road to Baghdad and thereafter—for which the Secretary of Defense has tried to seize credit—were inaugurated in the late 1990s and then developed aggressively by General Eric Shinseki, the Army chief of staff sidelined by Rumsfeld for suggesting that an effective occupation of Iraq might take hundreds of thousands of troops.

To identify an organization truly unwilling to change, we need look no further than Rumsfeld's beloved Air Force. Far from driving "transformation" as he claims, the Defense Secretary has continued to buy hyperexpensive, virtually useless aircraft that were conceived in the 1980s to combat the Soviet air force. Rumsfeld's transformation program boils down to reducing our ground forces—the soldiers and Marines who rescued him from a fiasco in Iraq, where progress has been made despite his incompetence—in order to send massive welfare checks to the defense industry. One of the key worries within the military is that the administration is ignoring the serious lessons of our recent wars while continuing to purchase unaffordable and useless weapons systems that will lock our armed forces into twentieth-century warfighting models for decades to come. The defense secretary's major procurement programs are reactionary, not revolutionary.

Even if we did have a "hidebound" military reluctant to move, would we want it any other way? Contrary to left-wing myths, our generals and admirals tend to be reluctant to go to war, insisting on laying out the potential costs for decision-makers (Colin Powell might serve as the archetype of the ideal military professional). Would we prefer a military anxious to invade others? Would we prefer generals and admirals who abet the madcap visions of ideologues, right or left, rather than offering sober assessments of the risks of war? The institutional conservatism of our military occasionally has impeded the progress of new ideas (to my personal frustration during my own years in uniform), but it has generally served our nation well. Better a military that changes cautiously and eyes foreign adventures suspiciously than one that embraces every passing fad and cries for war at every provocation.

The administration will win this time around. It is able to bring to bear so much power that a half-dozen men of conscience haven't a chance. The word on the military-retiree street is that anyone else who speaks out against the Secretary of Defense will lose his defense-industry job or contracts. All the favors have been called in and scraps of access have won the allegiance of partisan columnists and talking-head generals alike. The six critics stand against the coercive powers of the Office of the Secretary of Defense, the administration behind it, the Republican Party and its loyalists—and all the wealth of our unscrupulous defense industry.

Doesn't it tell us something about the administration's awareness of the depth and breadth of its failures that it feels compelled to mobilize so many of its resources against six retired veterans exercising their First Amendment rights?

Americans who care about our country should be very skeptical of the administration's line that no military dissent—not even from retirees—is ever permissible. As a nation, we need to ask ourselves some very uncomfortable questions about the rise of hyperpolitical defense secretaries, the politicization of military affairs by both Republicans and Democrats, the isolation of the president from frank military advice, and civilian interference in the smallest details of combat operations.

When a presidential administration will not tolerate honorable, legal criticism from those who dedicated their lives to uniformed service, we should be far more worried about ideologues in power than about a few retired infantrymen on pensions.

Why Clausewitz Had It Backward

Armed Forces Journal

July 2006

Even those who have never read a line written by Carl von Clause-witz, the Prussian military philosopher, accept as truth his dictum that "War is simply a continuation of policy with other means." Yet, that statement was only superficially true for the European world in which Clausewitz lived, fought, and wrote, and it never applied to the American people, for whom war signified a failure of policy.

To characterize the conduct of other civilizations and states—from the bygone Hittite and Assyrian empires to today's Islamic heartlands, China or Russia—Clausewitz's nouns would have to be reversed: "Policy is simply a continuation of war with other means."

Conflict, not peace, is the natural state of human collectives. We need not celebrate the fact but must recognize it. If peace were the default condition of humankind, wouldn't history look pro-foundly different? Thousands of years of relentless slaughter cannot be written off as the fault of a few delinquents. Human beings aggregated by affinities of blood, belief, or culture are inherently competitive, not cooperative, and the competition is viscerally—and easily—perceived as a matter of life and death. Pious declarations to the contrary do not change the reality.

Our blindness to this fundamental and enduring principle—that all of a state's nonmilitary actions seek to achieve the ends of warfare through alternative means—leaves us strategically crippled, needlessly vulnerable, and wastefully ineffective. Only our wealth, size, and raw power redeem our strategic incompetence sufficiently to allow us to bumble forward. We continue to regard warfare as something profoundly different from all other official endeavors, as an international breakdown and a last resort (occasional military adventurism notwithstanding), but similar attitudes exist only in a core of other English-speaking countries. Elsewhere, the competition between governments, cultures, civilizations, and religions is viewed as comprehensive and unceasing, and it is waged—instinctively or consciously—with all the available elements of power.

We, not our antagonists, are the odd player out.

Regarding peace as the natural state of man, Americans not only defy history but also donate free victories to competitors and enemies. Although capable of fighting ferociously when aroused, we deny that such conduct comes naturally to us, insisting that Sergeant York merely rose to the occasion. Heritage lasts, and ours was shaped initially by visions of a "peaceable kingdom," a "New Jerusalem," a "shining city on a hill." Our earliest immigrant ancestors fled Europe's wars and strife, determined to change not only their real-estate holdings, but also human nature. This continent was to become a new Eden, and each eruption of organized violence, from King Phillip's War to Operation Iraqi Freedom, has been regarded by us as an anomaly.

Pressed hard enough, we make war brilliantly, but we never cease insisting that we are, by nature, peacemakers. This dualistic character has been addressed by a succession of scholars, but, to my knowledge, not one of them has suggested that warfare might be the human baseline: We do not rise to the occasion of war, but occasionally rise above war—remarkably often, in the exceptional American case.

Yet, it may be our predilection for prolonging even the most wretched peace that ultimately makes our wars so bloody. After a century of Euro-American conflicts, it requires little effort to make the case that the quickest way to inspire a shooting war may be to cling to the dream of peace in our time. Denying human bloodlust only permits it free rein while the "virtuous" look away. Idealistic American communists abetted Stalin's crimes, while conservatives insisted that Hitler wasn't our problem. Our domestic leftists insisted that cutting off all support for South Vietnam was the moral and humane thing to do—then, without so much as muttering "Oops!" they looked away from the massacres, tortures, and mass incarcerations that swept Vietnam, Laos, and Cambodia after 1975. The massacre at Srebrenica can't be blamed on Serb militias alone—Europe's pacifists were the enablers. Darfur screams, while we stop up our ears.

The war college motto "In peace, prepare for war" takes us farther along the common-sense highway than platitudes to the effect that "War doesn't change anything" (perhaps the least defensible claim ever made by a human being). But the truly crucial step is to realize that warfare never ceases but only shifts from one medium to others, playing now on the battlefield, later in the economic sphere, then in the cultural arena, and, always, in the pulpit. It isn't Gandhi or Bonhoeffer who looks prophetic, but Trotsky. Every economy is a war economy. And every successful businessman understands this intuitively, even if he has never thought or expressed it clearly. In this new age of wars of faith, the ecumenical obsession of the West is the religious equivalent of Neville Chamberlain's appeasement—just as Islamist crusaders are the equivalent of the prime minister's German interlocutors.

Along with our nibbling at Clausewitz, we also snack on a few crumbs from Sun Tzu, repeating, without any real comprehension, that "to win without fighting is the highest form of victory." Our assumption is that the maxim has a pacific, if not pacifist, sense: victory without bloodshed! Hurrah, hurrah! Such an interpretation is profoundly wrong. Sun Tzu's primary emphasis in that passage isn't on avoiding battle—that's secondary—but on winning by alternative means. The distinction is critical. Sun Tzu would have found Western peacekeeping operations incomprehensible: avoiding battle and losing.

Let's put the wisdom of the amalgam of authors we now know only as "Sun Tzu" in a more accurate perspective: If you can spare your own army by destroying your enemy through hunger, thirst, plague, exhaustion, poverty, mutiny, assassination, subterfuge, lies, or terror, let the enemy suffer and die while you profit from his agony, preserving your forces for battle against the next enemy, who might not be such a patsy. Sun Tzu would have regarded weapons of mass destruction as marvelous, practical tools—as long as only his side possessed them. Sun Tzu is Machiavelli without the conscience.

Even in our religious practice, we gloss over the merciless wars of the Old Testament, although Yahweh waged total war against Pharaoh's Egypt with a succession of plagues (including germ warfare, balancing out the proto-nuclear effects achieved against Sodom and Gomorrah).

The message we refuse to learn is that aggression is necessary and ineradicable. The only hope of minimizing military aggression is to channel the impulse into other, less destructive channels. If we routinely fight with other elements of national power, accepting that we are endlessly at war with our competitors, we are apt to face far fewer military contests.

The conundrum is that our military strength makes our policy-makers lazy. Neglectful of other instruments and means of national power, they inevitably find themselves forced to resort to military solutions.

The Chinese understand perfectly that policy is an extension of war beyond the crudities of the battlefield, and they act upon the insight skillfully. The Russians grasp it, too, if less coherently. Muddling Lenin, Trotsky, bitter resentment, and inherited paranoia, the Kremlin acts upon the perception clumsily (as with the depth-of-winter gas shut-offs to Ukraine and then Georgia). The French have acted as if engaged in comprehensive warfare with all other parties for four centuries, failing only because their means were never commensurate with their exaggerated ambitions.

Now our Islamist opponents, with their model of robust jihad, have made operational the idea of multidimensional struggle. They will do anything, in any sphere, to wound us as deeply as they can. In response, we debate the legality of tapping their phones.

This inversion of Clausewitz isn't merely a matter of wordplay but highlights the need for a fundamental shift in our national outlook. We need not announce to the world that we believe we're engaged in an endless war of all against all, but we must learn to act more resolutely in our own interests, to view our foreign endeavors in all policy-related spheres as aspects of an overarching strategy. The world may not be a zero-sum game (although our antagonists view it as such), but when the winnings are tallied, we want to leave the table with full pockets.

This doesn't mean that we should pursue a statist, minutely planned approach to international activities. But we do need a sense that we have a national purpose that transcends the inherited boundaries of statecraft and that our purpose is to remain dominant. At present, our formal national strategy is as narrow and unimaginative as it is insincere. It is, literally, nothing but words. Instead of working together for the common good, the various branches of our government (to say nothing of our business community) continue to undercut one another's efforts. Citing improved cooperation between departments isn't enough, given how abysmal it has been in the past. Our government needs to function as a team—something it has not done since the Second World War.

We do not need a comprehensive plan, only a comprehensive sense of mission.

We do, however, need to face the coldly cutthroat nature of the world in which we live, in which our ancestors lived, and in which our descendants will continue to live. While awaiting the New Jerusalem, we need to recognize that the old one was blood soaked (and the present one isn't much better). There is nothing human collectives do more effectively than making war. If we want to prevent or limit wars, this means we must obtain the results of a successful war through other means.

To repeat a worn-but-wise phrase (this one attributed to Trotsky), "You may not be interested in war, but war is interested in you."

One of the most pathetic manifestations of our willed naiveté is our insistence on describing foreign states as our "friends." Nations (and entire civilizations) do not have friends. They have allies, and those allies can change over time—just as yesterday's enemies can become today's allies. The British fought us twice (and not gently), after which we spent a century wondering whether we would have to fight again. Now, Britain is our closest military ally. During the Civil War, our most important diplomatic ally was imperial Russia; we later fought alongside Russia in its Soviet incarnation during World War II; and, in the wonk-Woodstock atmosphere of the early 1990s, American policy makers insisted that the United States and the new, "democratic" Russia would be best pals forever. In the intervals between and after these brief periods of alliance and fellow feeling, we feared the global spread of Bolshevism, then dreaded a Soviet-launched nuclear holocaust, and now must contend with Moscow's breathtaking lack of scruples, its revived paranoia, its appetite for blackmail, its affection for despotic regimes, its distaste for political freedom, its disregard of human rights—and its dangerous clumsiness in the international china shop (no pun intended). Is Russia now, or has it ever been, our "friend"?

Whatever one thinks of the decision to depose Saddam Hussein, the venomous pro-Ba'athist actions and anti-American rhetoric from long-standing European allies whose minor commercial interests were threatened should have brought us to our senses. While some allies are more dependable than others (because of common interests and shared values) and allies of varied worth can be desirable if the quid pro quos are not forbiddingly painful, we nonetheless must view the world as constantly in competition with us in every form of endeavor related to national power, wealth, and influence. After all, the purpose of any alliance is to take advantage of the ally—if possible, to get the ally to sacrifice and suffer in your place.

This does not mean that we should endeavor to bankrupt or weaken every country on earth, but that we must recognize when it is in our interest to undercut the capabilities and confidence of a rival—even if that rival is a nominal ally.

The Beijing government understands this with such clarity that one can only admire the intellectual integrity of Chinese strategic thinking. Confronted with integrated, well-designed challenges from China in the economic, financial, diplomatic, and—least important for now—military spheres, our response, to the extent that we may claim one, has been piecemeal, intermittent, inept, and weak. Brilliantly, the Chinese have managed to harness the greed of influential elements within our own business community to prevent the implementation of policies by Washington that might reduce China's artificial trade advantages and limit our own self-inflicted vulnerabilities. By allowing a relative handful of American corporations to grow rich, the Chinese have paralyzed our government's ability to defend our workers, our industries, and our economy. We have reached the point where lobbying veers into treason. The Chinese view our relationship as a war conducted through nonmilitary means. Under such advantageous economic conditions, they are perfectly happy to refrain from shooting.

Defense contractors, as well as desperate generals and admirals, warn of a military confrontation with China. But why on earth would China want one when Beijing is gaining all it needs through far less painful means? Certainly, countries have a way of blundering into war—but China would much prefer to avoid a violent conflict with the U.S. Why fight us, when we make a gift of all that Beijing seeks through our tolerance for rigged exchange rates, our acceptance of the dumping of manufactured products, our refusal to live up to our rhetoric about human rights, our rejection of serious policies to protect our intellectual property and copyrights—and our outright gifts of technology?

This is the Sun Tzu that we cite so glibly yet fail to understand.

The Islamist threat is even fiercer—far fiercer—than China when it comes to exploiting policy as a continuation of war with other means. Saudi Arabia, for example, has engaged in a merciless religious war against the West for more than three decades, yet it has not only done so while convincing our national leaders, Republican and Democrat, that we're "friends," but has managed to gain the protection of America's military on the cheap, even as it refuses meaningful cooperation with our forces. To preserve the profits of a handful of multinational oil companies, we protect a repellent, throwback regime that willfully created Osama bin Laden and his ilk. In country after country, I personally witnessed how Saudi money is used to spread anti-Western hatred (and to divide local societies), while America's taxpayers fund a military prostituted to the defense of the degenerate House of Saud.

We're not even mercenaries: Mercenaries at least get paid.

As for the Islamist terrorists, they've adopted a nonstate variant of the "total war" concept developed by Chinese military theorists. No front or sphere is off-limits. We are to be attacked wherever and however it is possible to do so. Indeed, a key lesson we should fear that the terrorists took away from 9/11 isn't that Americans can be killed by the thousands, but that killing Americans by the thousands costs our economy trillions.

We debate the legitimacy of propaganda broadcasts (by other names, of course), while our terrorist enemies run rampant on the internet; govern the content of our own television, radio, and print news through their calculated actions; preach apocalyptic hatred around the world (even in our own country); and exploit our own laws to paralyze us. In response, we send a female political-campaign worker from Texas on a brief tour of the Middle East to "turn the situation around." We not only lack a strategy—we lack a sense of reality.

Wishful thinking can't win wars, and it won't preserve peace. If only we could overcome our bias against honest thinking, we might find that accepting the thousands of years of evidence that government policies are a continuation of war with other means would result in the more effective use of those "other means" and, consequently, a less frequent requirement to go to war.

In one sense, the old American conviction that the advent of war confirms the failure of policy is true: We have to send our military to solve problems because we didn't use the other tools of policy boldly or adeptly. Our antagonists, from Beijing to Baqubah, recognize that victory will require the uncompromising use of every available resource. We default to guns. Certainly, terrorists do not shrink from violence, but they view violence as a means, not a solution. The target of the suicide bomb isn't really flesh and blood—it's the video camera, that powerful, postmodern "other means" of securing a military advantage without possessing a military.

By refusing to instill a warlike spirit in other fields of our national policy, we only make "real war" inevitable.

The Hearts-and-Minds Myth

Armed Forces Journal

September 2006

Mastering the languages, cultural nuances, beliefs, and taboos that prevail in a theater of war, area of operations, or tactical environment is vital to military success. It's much easier to kill people you understand.

Beyond that, cultural insights ease routine operations and negotiations, the training of local forces, and the development of intelligence. Environmental mastery helps us avoid making unnecessary enemies. But that is where the advantages end in conflicts of blood and faith: No amount of cultural sensitivity inculcated in U.S. troops will persuade fanatic believers to discard their religion, nor can any amount of American empathy change a foreign thug's ethnic identity.

Frustrated with the difficulties facing us in Iraq after being denied both adequate troop strength and the authority to impose the rule of law in the initial days of our occupation, U.S. military commanders responded with a variety of improvisations, from skillful "kinetic ops" to patient dialogue. Nothing achieved enduring results—because we never had the resources or the fortitude to follow any effort through to the end, and our enemies had no incentive to quit, surrender, or cooperate. We pacified cities with force but lacked the forces to keep them pacified. We rebuilt schools, but our enemies taught us how easy it was to kill teachers. Accepting that it was politically impossible on the home front, we never conducted the essential first step in fighting terrorists and insurgents: We failed to forge a long-term plan based on a long-term commitment. Instead, we sought to dissuade fanatics and undo ancient rivalries with stopgap measures, intermittent drizzles of money, and rules of engagement tailored to suit the media, not military necessity.

It is astonishing that our efforts have gone as well as they have.

Yet no honest soldier or Marine would argue that we could not have done better—and should have done better. Setting aside, for now, the inept leadership from the Rumsfeld Pentagon and the fateful, if not fatal, lack of adequate troop strength, we're left with one crippling deficiency on the part of our leadership: The unwillingness to recognize the nature of the various conflicts underway simultaneously in Iraq.

With an obtuseness worthy of the left's caricatures of military officers, we drew the wrong lessons from the wrong historical examples and then did exactly the wrong things. Enmeshed in bitter conflicts over religion and ethnicity resurgent after decades of suppression, senior officers ignored myriad relevant historical examples and focused instead on the counterinsurgency campaigns with which they were comfortable—and that were as instructive as dismantling a toaster to learn how to fix a computer.

REALITY'S DELETE KEY

Officers looked to operations in Malaya, Vietnam, Northern Ireland, and occasionally, Algeria for positive and negative examples. Yet not one of those political struggles is relevant to the situation in Iraq (or Afghanistan). As for the pertinent examples of insurgencies rooted in religious or ethnic fanaticism, such as the Moro Insurrection, Bloody Kansas, the Sepoy Mutiny, the Mahdist Wars, the various European Anabaptist risings, the Thirty Years' War, the Armenian Genocide, Nagorno–Karabagh, the destruction of Yugoslavia, Rwanda, Kashmir, the Pueblo Revolt, the Ghost-Dance Rebellion, 1,300 years of uninterrupted warfare between the Islamic and Judeo–Christian civilizations, and several thousand other examples dating back to the savagery chronicled in the Old Testament; well, the lessons they suggest are, to say the least, politically incorrect. So we hit the delete key on reality.

Our civilian and uniformed leaders have engaged in comforting fantasies about the multilayered conflicts we're in, while speaking in numbing platitudes. Now we're back to "winning hearts and minds."

We can't do it. Not in the Islamic world. Arabs—Sunni or Shiite, in Iraq and elsewhere—are so battered psychologically that many need to blame the West, Israel, unbelievers, Shiites, Sunnis, Kurds, and the ice-cream man for their failures. Any chance we had of winning the minds, if not the hearts, of the biddable minority in Iraq was thrown away when we failed to enforce the rule of law the moment Baghdad fell. Proclamations of American generosity fall short when you cannot walk your neighborhood streets without fear.

Even with the limited forces we had on hand three and a half years ago, we could have done more. But the Bush administration and our military leaders had fallen into the politically correct trap that spares the murderer at the expense of his victims. We weren't ready to kill enough of the right people. As a result, our enemies have been able to spend more than three years killing the people we meant to liberate. Our reluctance to kill evil men proved murderous to innocent men, women, and children, and our unwillingness to do what needed to be done leaves us at least partly responsible for the thousands of Iraqis killed and maimed by acts of terrorism—as well as for our own unnecessary losses.

The law of war is immutable: Those unwilling to pay the butcher's bill up front will pay it with compound interest in the end.

MUSH, NOT RIGOR

The new counterinsurgency doctrine the Army and Marines are developing gets the language right initially, noting that no two insurgencies are identical and that each must be understood on its own terms. Then it veers into nonsense, typified by the insupportable claim that a defection is always better than a surrender, a surrender is always better than a capture, and a capture is always better than a kill. That's intellectual mush. And it's just plain wrong.

It's Malaya again, with doughty Brits hacking through the jungle to pip-pip-wot-ho those wily communists. It's Kit Carson Scouts in Vietnam and faithful Montagnards. It's the PX at Tan Son Nhut air base (oops, almost wrote "Balad"). It's the nonveteran John

Wayne starring in *The Green Berets* and proving beyond any doubt that all good Vietnamese instinctively loved Americans and dreamed of drinking Cokes in suburban freedom. It's Mel Gibson reprising Pickett's Charge in the Ia Drang valley—and winning this time!

The well-intentioned drafters of our counterinsurgency doctrine are mining what they've recently read without serious analysis. Do they really believe that a Sunni Arab insurgent in Kirkuk is going to see the light and declare that, from now on, he's a Kurd? Or that a Shiite militiaman in the Mahdi Army is going to wake up and decide, "Twelfth Imam, Shmim-mam! I'm going to become a Sunni and move to Ramadi!"? Does anyone outside the nuthouse political left really believe that friendly persuasion will disarm al Qa'eda in Iraq? Isn't a crucial lesson of Guantanamo that irredeemable prisoners are a strategic liability? Our doctrine writers are in danger of producing a tome on procreation that doesn't mention sex.

We are in the middle of a multilayered, multisided struggle for supremacy between intolerant religious factions and age-old ethnic rivals. And we pretend that it's just another political struggle amenable to a political solution—because it's more pleasant to think so, because we believe we know what to do in such circumstances, because facing reality would force us to drastically change the way we behave in combat, and because acknowledging the truth about the situation in Iraq would demand that we question every goofball cliché about the human preference for peace that we've bought into for the past half-century.

Yet, unless we accept the truth about the kind of wars we're in—and inevitably will face in the future—we're going to continue to make a botch of things.

BLOOD TIES, BLOODY GODS

The political insurgencies of the last century were easy problems compared to this century's renewed struggles of blood and belief. In political insurgencies, some of the actors can, indeed, be converted. A capture may be better than a kill. Compromise may be possible. Dialogue is sometimes a useful tool, although even political insurgencies are best resolved from a position of indisputable military strength. Men who believe, often hazily, in an ideology occasionally can be converted—or bought. The political beliefs of the masses are fickle. Defeats discourage those with mundane goals. And a political struggle within a population otherwise united by its history can end in reconciliation even after horrible bloodshed—as in the American Civil War, the Risorgimento, the gruesome Mexican revolutions of 1910–20, and the civil wars in Vietnam, Greece, and many another gore-drenched, relatively homogeneous states.

Violence arising from differences of religious confession, race, or ethnicity is profoundly different—and far more difficult to quell. Generally, such struggles are brought to an end only through a great deal of killing. One side—or all—must be bled out. Whether cast as divinely sanctioned liberation struggles or simply about one bloodline getting its own back from another, these conflicts over God's will and ancestral wrongs are never amenable to reason. Self-righteous journalists love to claim that the first casualty of war is truth, but that's a self-serving lie; the first casualty of any form of violence is reason, that weakest and most disappointing of learned human skills.

Our exclusive focus on recent political insurgencies misleads us, because wars over tribe and God are humankind's oldest legacy, while the conflicts we choose to study all fall within a brief historical interval that stands as an aberration—the twilight decades of the Age of Ideology, which ran from 1789 to 1991, a blink in historical terms. Now we have reverted to the human norm of killing one another over interpretations of the divine will and ancient blood ties. We don't have to like it—and we won't—but we must recognize the reality confronting us. We have returned to the historical mainstream. The tribes want tribute. The gods want blood. And the killers are ready to help.

The road to Srebrenica was paved with pious platitudes, the path to 9/11 with wishful thinking. Presidents and generals may declare endlessly that we're not engaged in a religious war or that ethnic factions can be reconciled, but the first claim is a lie and the second relies for its fulfillment on intrusive military power and a strength of will greater than that of the factions in question. We are, indeed, engaged in religious wars—because our enemies have determined that these are religious wars. Our own refusal to understand them as such is just one more debilitating asymmetry. As for ethnic reconciliation, call me when Kosovo's Muslims and Serb Christians reintegrate their communities, form joint neighborhood-watch committees, and vote for each other's political candidates (and check the ingredients of the casserole that Ivo's wife brought to the potluck, nonetheless).

BLOOD AND BUDGET DEFICITS

If we want achievements commensurate with the risks we undergo and the costs we pay in blood and budget deficits, we must over-come our revulsion at the truth. Saying nice things about war to please the media or to placate noisome academics is useless, any-way, because they'll always oppose what the U.S. government does—even when, as with a dictator's overthrow and a war of libera-tion, our government implements the left's long-standing agenda. We must stop belching out chipper slogans and fleeing to simplistic models for answers. We have to start thinking beyond our moral comfort zones. When generals lack intellectual integrity, privates die for nothing.

Above all, we must regain our perspective on what truly mat-ters. We must get over our impossible dream of being loved as a nation, of winning hearts and minds in Iraq or elsewhere. If we can make ourselves liked through our successes, that's well and good. But the essential requirements for the security of the U.S. are that our nation is respected and our military is feared. Our lack of resolve and mental rigor has brought us close to sacrificing both of these advantages. And a nation that is not respected encourages for-eign chicanery, while a military that is not feared invites attack.

The Marine Corps entered Iraq with a motto that captured the essence of what our efforts should have involved: "No better friend, no worse enemy." That restatement of the carrot-and-stick approach to military operations expressed in simple terms how to fight just about any kind of enemy—including insurgents and terrorists. The problem is that no American leader, in uniform or in a $3,000 suit, lived up to the maxim consistently. Instead, we applied it in fits and starts as we tried to make friends with our enemies. In the clinch, we defaulted to the carrot.

Consider how many potential turning points we missed: We failed to enforce the rule of law while all Iraq was terrified of us and anxious for clear orders. We failed to occupy the predictable trouble spots early on and in force. We failed to display sufficient imagination and courage to break up the artificial country we inherited from Saddam Hussein and a pack of Europeans at Versailles. With our typical dread of short-term costs, we passed up repeated and justified chances to kill Muqtada al Sadr, inflating his image in the process—and paying a far higher price in the long term than we would have paid had we acted resolutely and promptly. We needed Henry V and got Hamlet. Our leaders fled from victory in the First Battle of Fallujah. Now an administration with a flagging will is determined to withdraw our troops prematurely—Mission Accomplished, Act II. And all the while our soldiers and Marines have paid the price—while reenlisting to pay it again and again.

Our men and women in uniform deserve better. They're dying not only of roadside bombs but of phony morality imposed by those who face no risks themselves. Spare a terrorist, kill a soldier. Spare a terrorist leader, kill our soldiers by the hundreds. We want to treat a country torn by rival visions of a punitive god and drenched in ethnic bloodshed as if it needs only a bit of political tinkering. We're not looking for exit strategies, just exit excuses.

The longer we wait to study and learn from the relevant conflicts of the past, the more American blood we'll squander. We have to be tough on ourselves, forcing each other to think beyond the deadly platitudes of the campus, the campaign trail, and the press briefing. Begin by listing the number of religion-fueled uprisings throughout history that were quenched by reason and compromise—call me collect if you find a single one. Then list the ethnic civil wars that were solved by sensible treaties without significant bloodshed. Next, start asking the really ugly questions, such as: Hasn't ethnic cleansing led to more durable conditions of peace than any more humane approach to settling power relations between bloodlines? Monstrous as it appears, might not the current neighborhood-by-neighborhood ethnic and confessional cleansing in Iraq make that country more, rather than less, likely to survive as a confederation? Shouldn't we be glad when fanatics kill fanatics? Are all successes in the war on terrorism merely provisional? Is this a struggle that unquestionably must be fought by us but that began long before our country existed and will continue for centuries to come? Is there a historical precedent for coping with violent religious fanatics that does not include bloodshed to the point of extermination?

Even beyond these military and strategic issues, deeper questions about humanity—the individual and the mass—await serious minds. The one useful result of the coming generations of fanaticism will be to rid our own cultural bloodstream of the poison of political correctness, white lies that lead to black results. Why does humankind love war? And yes, the word is "love." Does religious competition have biological roots? Is the assertion of ethnic supremacy as natural as the changing of the seasons? Is genocide in our genes? We do not have to celebrate unpleasant answers, but, if humanity is ever to make the least progress in reducing mass violence, we need to face those answers honestly.

The American military knew how to deal with conflicts of blood and faith. But we do not study our own history when the lessons make us uneasy. During the Moro Insurrection, the U.S. Army lived up to the Marine Corps' motto for Operation Iraqi Freedom. For the peaceful inhabitants of the southern Philippines, our soldiers and administrators were benefactors. For the Moro warriors, they were the worst enemies those fanatics had ever faced. Of course, we didn't have CNN filming our Gatling guns at work, but, then, we may need to banish the media from future battlefields, anyway. Our brutal response to the brutality of Muslim fanatics kept the peace until the Japanese invasion four decades later. And no peace lasts forever—four decades qualifies as a big, big win.

The religious movement that fired the Boxer Rebellion could only be put down through massacre. The same need to rip the heart out of violent millenarian movements, enabling societies to regain their balance, applied from 1520s Germany and 1840s China through the nineteenth century Yucatan and the Sudan, down to the Islamist counterrevolution today. Only massive killing brought peace. Only extensive killing will bring peace.

We need to grasp the basic truth that the path to winning the hearts and minds of the masses leads over the corpses of the violent minority. As for humanitarianism, the most humane thing we can do is to win our long struggle against fanaticism and terrorism. That means killing terrorists and fanatics.

The Myth of Immaculate Warfare

USA Today

September 6, 2006

Under the right battlefield conditions, sophisticated military technologies give Western powers remarkable advantages. Under the wrong conditions and employed with unreasonable expectations, high-tech weapons inflict more damage on our own political leaders and national purpose than they do on the enemy.

Precision-targeting systems and other superweapons are dangerously seductive to civilian leaders looking for military wins on the cheap. Exaggerated promises about capabilities—made by contractors, lobbyists, and bedazzled generals—delude presidents and prime ministers into believing that war can be swift and immaculate, with minimal friendly or even enemy casualties.

It's a lethal myth. The siren song of techno-wars fought at standoff range makes military solutions more attractive to political leaders than would be the case were they warned about war's costs at the outset. Inevitably, the "easy" wars don't work out as planned. Requiring boots on the ground after all, they prove exorbitant in blood, treasure, time, and moral capital.

A LESSON IN ISRAEL

In recent weeks, Israel lost a campaign for the first time after a government and its senior generals convinced themselves that a new form of terrorist army—Hezbollah—could be destroyed with airpower alone. The Israelis had become so confident in their

54

technological advantage that they neglected the readiness of their ground forces. Technology failed to accomplish the mission—as it always will in the Cain-and-Abel conflicts of our time. The army had to go in on the ground. But Israel's army, too, relied heavily on technology. Most units lacked the range of infantry skills necessary to defeat a well-prepared enemy—as I saw for myself on the Lebanese border.

Israel had ignored the lessons of America's recent military experiences. In the prelude to the campaign to topple Saddam Hussein, Secretary of Defense Donald Rumsfeld and his senior advisers deluded themselves that an air effort employing precision weapons—"shock and awe"—would convince the Iraqi regime to surrender. Ignoring the enemy's psychology, the techno-war zealots failed. We were more fortunate than the Israelis were, though. The United States had a professional Army and Marine Corps capable of redeeming the mistakes of the Pentagon leadership. But in violence-torn Iraq today, we continue to pay for the prewar fantasy that technology would solve human problems.

A paradox of this era of dazzling technologies is that the conflicts we face are born of ethnic bigotry and faith gone haywire—atavistic challenges that cannot be resolved with guided bombs or satellite imagery. Employed incisively, technologies certainly help our troops, but they aren't a substitute for troops. And they won't be. Yet, the false promises will continue.

We've been through this before. In the 1950s, large ground forces were supposed to be obsolete, superseded by missiles. Then came Vietnam, followed by a succession of brutally human conflicts, from Lebanon through Somalia to the Balkans. For the seventy-eight days of the Kosovo campaign, NATO aircraft attempted to force Serbia—a weak, miniature state—to agree to treaty terms. In the end, it took the threat of ground troops to achieve the international community's goals. After the firing stopped, we found that our expensive, sophisticated technologies had been fooled by cheap Serb mock-ups of military vehicles.

Why are defense contractors and partisan generals nonetheless able to convince Congress and one presidential administration after another that technology has all the answers? Because Congress and the White House want to believe machines will get them off the hook when it comes to sending our forces into battle. And there are huge practical incentives to buy big-ticket weapons systems from politically supportive defense contractors.

The defense industry silences military leaders who know better by employing them on generous terms after their retirement from service. The system is legal, but it's morally corrupt and ethically repulsive.

Meanwhile, the impressive-in-theory capabilities of the latest weapons cloud the vision of military planners, leading them to focus on what the systems can do instead of concentrating on what needs to be done. Rather than buying the weapons we really need, we twist the conflicts we face to conform to the weapons we want to buy. The results are flawed war plans based on unrealistic expectations—in short, Iraq.

ADAPTING TO REAL-WORLD MISSIONS

None of this means that we shouldn't pursue advanced military technologies. But they must be relevant to real-world missions. We should continue to develop unmanned aerial vehicles, which are effective, versatile, and affordable, as well as a new generation of tools for urban warfare, now the dominant form of combat.

Yet we continue to buy breathtakingly expensive systems designed to fight a Soviet Union that no longer exists, such as the $360-million-each F-22 fighter. We're buying Ferraris when we need pickups.

We have to break the habit. We must stop pretending that technology will be decisive in the flesh-and-blood conflicts our troops will continue to face. There will be no "bloodless wars" in our lifetimes. In the words of Nathan Bedford Forrest, a brilliant Civil War soldier and wicked man, "War means fighting, and fighting means killing." In an age of fanaticism and terror, confronted by enemies who see death as a promotion, we will not be able to find easy, sterile solutions to our security problems.

The promises made for advanced military technologies are all too seductive to political leaders with no experience in uniform. Hype kills. Until we abandon the myth of immaculate wars, our conflicts will continue to prove far more costly than the technology advocates promise.

Studying War

New York Post

September 24, 2006

When politicians get big things wrong, they still get reelected. When academics get big things wrong, they get tenure. When Special Forces officers get even the smallest thing wrong, people die. That gives SF leaders a seriousness you rarely encounter elsewhere—unless it's among others in uniform.

Once a year, I have the privilege of speaking to the SF and other special operations students at the U.S. Army's Command and General Staff College at Ft. Leavenworth, Kansas. The questions from those officers are by far the toughest—the most intelligent and earnest—I hear anywhere.

Why? The rest of us just read. Those officers do the things we read about.

Fresh from combat tours in Iraq, Afghanistan, or in one of the world's dark crevices, they don't argue for any party line or popular prejudice in the classroom. Their fighting's deadly, not a game of political one-upmanship. With candor and moral courage, they struggle to understand the world in which they work.

According to the media, that world's black and white. But special operators deal with reality, not cant or spin. Their world has countless shades of gray. It isn't a universe of perishable headlines, but one in which you struggle to read between an infinite number of lines.

The rest of us simplify things to get a grip on them. For these men (and women, too, in Psychological Operations and other special-ops fields), every minor complexity has to be faced. They serve and fight in environments where each gesture has nuance, where life can depend upon tone of voice, and where physical stamina is ultimately less important than strength of will.

Many will never receive public credit for the risks they've taken and the victories they've achieved to keep the rest of us safe and free. You won't always know precisely what their awards for valor represent. Their personnel files have gaps that measure operations so secret that senior officers can't access the reports. Often, their families know only that their soldier's gone, with no idea where he is and when—or if—he'll return.

Think about that. In this internet age of instant communications, when troops in Iraq jump online at the end of a mission to assure the folks back home that they're OK, special operators disappear into a black hole for months. On a military post, the other spouses might talk to their distant warrior regularly. The family of the special operator waits. And waits. Even the wives and kids have it tougher in special ops.

Each year, my feeling grows stronger that I should be listening to these soldiers, not lecturing to them. No matter how much experience we think we have of the world, it doesn't begin to rival that of special operators—or of regular soldiers and Marines, for that matter. They haven't just been to a war. They've been to wars. And each one knows he or she is going back.

The only thing you can do with officers like that is to try to help them gain a greater perspective on the ordeals they've recently left behind, to assemble their individual experiences into a coherent grasp of deeper issues, and to get at the purpose of their sacrifices in a way that goes beyond pabulum generalities.

Last week, in a classroom in a wretched building slated for demolition, we talked about Islam and its relation to other religions, about the power of culture, the reassertion of local identities, and unorthodox strategies. We discussed the tactical lessons of recent wars and the lifespans of civilizations.

One major spoke cogently of the lessons he drew from interacting with Arab officers. Another stressed the criticality of education for women in breaking the chain of societal failure (and this guy was an aviator, a category of officer better known for fly-by targeting of the human female—tell Ms. Steinem we're making progress). A Navy SEAL raised the lessons medieval Europe offers for analyzing the Middle East today.

Not exactly the *New Yorker's* snitty view of military officers. There was no bluster or swagger, no trace of close-mindedness. No matter how controversial the discussion became, no one raised his or her voice. The quality of their questions and observations was signally higher than those on any campus I've ever visited. It's the same story every year at Ft. Leavenworth. If the readers of this paper only could meet these magnificent Americans, you'd be immeasurably proud of them.

They have their concerns, of course. In off-line discussions, there was never a diminished sense of duty, but their optimism was more subdued than in previous years. Repeatedly, I encountered a sense that Defense Secretary Donald Rumsfeld's policies failed our military badly, undercutting our efforts in Iraq and Afghanistan. The officers didn't complain. They just offered sober observations on what they'd been through, what they'd seen, and what we could do better. Each one was mentally prepared to go back into the fight.

And they will go back. Their time in Kansas is a brief respite, a chance to hold their families close for a few months, to study and think. They'll soon go out again to routinely do the impossible, to track down terrorists and train potential allies, to right at least a small portion of the world's wrongs and to redeem the damage done by unscrupulous foreign leaders, hate-mongering demagogues, and, yes, irresponsible politicians here at home.

The bottom line? Some of the men and women I spoke to last week are going to die. For you.

Politically Correct War

New York Post

October 18, 2006

Have we lost the will to win wars? Not just in Iraq, but anywhere?

Do we really believe that being nice is more important than victory?

It's hard enough to bear the timidity of our civilian leaders—anxious to start wars but without the guts to finish them—but now military leaders have fallen prey to political correctness. Unwilling to accept that war is, by its nature, a savage act and that defeat is immoral, influential officers are arguing for a kinder, gentler approach to our enemies. They're going to lead us into failure, sacrificing our soldiers and Marines for nothing: Political correctness kills.

Obsessed with low-level "tactical" morality—war's inevitable mistakes—the officers in question have lost sight of the strategic morality of winning. Our Army and Marine Corps are about to suffer the imposition of a new counterinsurgency doctrine designed for fairytale conflicts and utterly inappropriate for the religion-fueled, ethnicity-driven hyperviolence of our time.

We're back to struggling to win hearts and minds that can't be won.

The good news is that the Army and Marine Corps worked together on the new counterinsurgency doctrine laid out in Field Manual 3-24 (the Army version).

The bad news is that the doctrine writers and their superiors came up with fatally wrong prescriptions for combating today's insurgencies. Astonishingly, the doctrine ignores faith-inspired terrorism and skirts ethnic issues in favor of analyzing yesteryear's political insurgencies. It would be a terrific manual if we returned to Vietnam circa 1963, but its recommendations are profoundly misguided when it comes to fighting terrorists intoxicated with religious visions and the smell of blood.

Why did the officers in question avoid the decisive question of religion? Because the answers would have been ugly.

Wars of faith and tribe are immeasurably crueler and tougher to resolve than ideological revolts. A Maoist in Malaya could be converted. But Islamist terrorists who regard death as a promotion are not going to reject their faith any more than an ethnic warrior can—or would wish to—change his blood identity.

So the doctrine writers ignored today's reality.

Al Qa'eda and other terror organizations have stated explicitly and repeatedly that they're waging a global jihad to reestablish the caliphate. Yet the new manual ignores religious belief as a motivation.

The politically correct atmosphere in Washington deems any discussion of religion as a strategic factor indelicate: Let our troops die, just don't hurt anyone's feelings.

So the doctrine writers faked it, treating all insurgencies as political. As a result, they prescribed an excellent head-cold treatment—for a cancer patient. The text is a mush of pop-zen mantras such as "Sometimes doing nothing is the best reaction," "The best weapons do not shoot," or "The more force used, the less effective it is." That's just nutty. Should we have done nothing in the wake of 9/11? Would everything have been okay if we'd just been nicer? What nonlethal "best weapons" might have snagged Osama bin Laden at Tora Bora, where the problem was too little military force, not too much violence?

Should we have sent fewer troops to Iraq, where inadequate numbers crippled everything we attempted? Will polite chats with tribal chiefs stop the sectarian violence drenching Iraq in blood?

On the surface, the doctrine appears sober and serious.

But it's morally frivolous and intellectually inert, a pathetic rehashing of yesteryear's discredited "wisdom" on counterinsurgencies and, worst of all, driven by a stalker-quality infatuation with T. E.

Lawrence, "Lawrence of Arabia," who not only was a huckster of the first order, but whose "revolt in the desert" was a near-meaningless sideshow of a sideshow. Lawrence is quoted repeatedly, with reverence. We might as well cite the British generals of the Great War who sent men over the top in waves to face German machine guns.

You can trust two kinds of officers: Those who read a great deal and those who don't read at all. But beware the officer who reads just a little and falls in love with one book. A little education really is a dangerous thing.

The new manual is thick—length is supposed to substitute for insight. It should be 75 percent shorter and 100 percent more honest. If issued to our troops in its present form, it will lead to expensive failures. Various generals have already tried its prescriptions in Iraq—with discouraging results, to put it mildly.

We've reached a fateful point when senior officers seek to evade war's brute reality. Our leaders, in and out of uniform, must regain their moral courage. We can't fight wars of any kind if the entire chain of command runs for cover every time an ambitious journalist cries, "War crime!" And sorry: Soccer balls are no substitute for bullets when you face fanatics willing to kill every child on the playing field.

In war, you don't get points for good manners. It's about winning. Victory forgives.

The new counterinsurgency doctrine recommends forbearance, patience, understanding, nonviolent solutions, and even outright passivity. Unfortunately, our enemies won't sign up for a replay of the Summer of Love in San Francisco. We can't treat hardcore terrorists like Halloween pranksters on midterm break from prep school.

Where is the spirit of FDR and George C. Marshall, who recognized that the one unbearable possibility was for the free world to lose? We discount the value of ferocity—as a practical tool and as a deterrent. But war's immutable law—proven yet again in Iraq—is that those unwilling to pay the butcher's bill up front will pay it with compound interest in the end.

The new counterinsurgency doctrine is dishonest and cowardly. We don't face half-hearted Marxists tired of living in the jungle, but religious zealots who behead prisoners to please their god and who torture captives by probing their skulls with electric drills. We're confronted by hatreds born of blood and belief and madmen whose appetite for blood is insatiable.

And we're afraid to fight.

The Man Who Wouldn't Listen

New York Post

November 11, 2006

At the climax of *Barton Fink*—the best film ever made about a writer— the protagonist's world literally goes up in flames. Bewildered, the self-absorbed playwright asks a homicidal killer why disaster had to fall on him.

"Because," the murderer tells him, "you don't listen."

In Washington, Defense Secretary Donald Rumsfeld was the man who wouldn't listen. Facing war, he dismissed the advice of those who had dedicated their lives to uniformed service, favoring civilian advisers who (to quote one observer's description of the attitude) had been "too important to waste their time in the military." Confronted by grave threats from religious fanatics, he ignored the counsel of intelligence personnel who had met them face to face. Tasked to create a democracy in the Middle East, he brushed off both the complexity of the region and the challenges of democracy.

Rumsfeld always knew better.

When the professional views of senior officers, such as the Army's General Eric Shinseki, conflicted with his predetermined agenda, Rumsfeld sidelined them. When the blood-stained evidence suggested the need for more troops in Iraq and in our ground forces overall, he denied the facts. And when his refusal to let the military plan for an occupation of Iraq proved disastrous, he pretended that everything was going according to the plan that didn't exist.

Ignoring the rule that loyalty is a two-way street, Rumsfeld broke Pentagon morale early on. He disdained the Army as hidebound, then sought to take credit for the reforms the Army had initiated before he took office. He believed that the Marines were an anachronism, that technology would win the wars of the future, and that everything that didn't shoot could be outsourced. (In Iraq, he even approved outsourcing security—and rogue mercenaries did more damage to our efforts to win the population's allegiance than any military misstep.)

Intending to cut the Army by at least two divisions and to trim the Marine Corps to free up more money for "transformation"—a code word for funneling money to favored contractors—he insisted on a war plan for the invasion of Iraq that was supposed to prove that ground forces were no longer vital to winning the nation's wars.

Yet, after his vaunted "shock and awe" air campaign collapsed and the Army and Marines had to fight their way—magnificently— to Baghdad the old-fashioned way, Rumsfeld still refused to increase the size of our ground forces, arguing that it would take two to three years to "stand up" new units.

Well, here we are, three years later—still painfully short of the boots needed on the ground. The Army and Marines, ever dutiful, are stretched thin and fight on with battered equipment.

When his nonplan for the reconstruction of Iraq failed—when the Iraqis refused to behave as he and his deputies insisted they would—Rumsfeld froze like a deer in the headlights. He never learned from our setbacks, and, three and a half years into this struggle, the Pentagon still doesn't have a strategy to win in Iraq.

Rumsfeld tried to improvise cheap solutions to the challenges posed by the most implacable enemies our country has ever faced. Religious fanatics though they be, the terrorists displayed a better grip on strategic reality than Rumsfeld ever did. Proclaiming he'd gotten an obstreperous military "under control," he was in the position of a hospital administrator who, as patient deaths soar, proudly insists he's put those worthless doctors and nurses in their place.

A talented, experienced man, Rumsfeld should have been a first-rate Secretary of Defense. Instead, he was failing in the job by the late summer of 2001. 9/11 saved him. Thereafter, our country and our military paid the price as his arrogance astonished even longtime Washington residents (and D.C. is not a city of the meek and humble).

When the military succeeded, he rushed for the microphones to preen. When things went awry, he let military officers handle the questions. He never admitted he was wrong. And he was wrong with remarkable consistency.

One man's vanity undercut Iraq's chances, squandered American lives, broke faith with our troops, and badly damaged our military. He was anxious to go to war, but unwilling to fight. Instead of leading, he interfered with those capable of leading. He micromanaged our troops, disrupting small-unit deployments, and overruling officers during combat but couldn't manage our enemies. Those in uniform felt that he disdained them.

Ultimately, Donald Rumsfeld did the impossible: He made Vietnam-era Defense Secretary Robert McNamara look good.

Killing with Kindness

Armed Forces Journal

December 2006

The Army video touting its Future Combat Systems has superb production values. Set in an unidentified country that resembles Indonesia, it opens with a get-her-phone-number enlisted medic rushing around a rural clinic to save a feverish child. Vital signs are transmitted to expert physicians in the U.S. via the FCS's satellite link, an instant diagnosis is given, and an injection of antibiotics saves the little girl.

Of course, saving sick children isn't all that the video claims the FCS can do. Rapid-fire edits cut to the detection of a suspicious character entering a tactical unit's area of operations. With the help of a handsome, Red Bull-drinking CIA type with a two-day growth of beard, a comprehensive array of sensors delivers an instantaneous facial-recognition ID from a classified database. The FCS tracks the suspected terrorist to a nearby hideout, where four more thugs wait to wreak havoc upon the innocent.

FCS to the rescue! With effortless precision, our troops close in, sending jackrabbit terrorists scampering into the cane fields. Shots are exchanged—briefly—and one terrorist crumples (no blood, however—it looks more like indigestion). The rest of the bad guys are swiftly corralled by minirobots and taken down by Officer G.I. Joe. One expects to hear those vile insurgents—who surely would rob that child of her medicine—declare, "Ya got me this time, detective, I gotta give ya credit."

The minifilm ends with a grateful mother thanking our medic—who maintains impressive grooming standards throughout—in halting English that's supposed to bring a tear to the viewer's eye. The scene called to mind Oscar Wilde's remark that anyone who doesn't laugh out loud over the death of Little Nell has no heart.

Caught up in the pace of the video, it may take the viewer a few moments to realize the triviality of the events portrayed in the film: FCS saves a child from a virus and captures five clownish terrorists.

That's what we get for more than $100 billion over two decades? A healthy kid and five hooligans in handcuffs?

What struck me most profoundly at a preview of the video was that nobody really gets hurt (our cute-as-a-hot-button medic nurtures the all-thumbs terrorist who was briefly inconvenienced by a bullet). There's no blood. The entire scenario is as antiseptic as the syringe the pinup medic uses on the sick kid. I'm told that a second video illustrates what the FCS could bring to an urban fight. I haven't seen it, but I'll bet there's no blood, torn limbs, spilled guts, splashed brains, furious curses, or screams of agony in it. Hope I'm wrong, but I suspect that FCS will be shown directing traffic.

(Since this critique was drafted, I've seen the urban warfare video. Its sterile depiction of combat—with yet another rescue of a wounded terrorist, thank you—would make an Iraq veteran howl with derision; there are a few tiny drops of ketchup in this one, but our enemies are depicted as brainless bowling pins, set up to be knocked down at no cost to the bowler, and one is left asking what the FCS can do that a 500-pound bomb can't.)

The problem here isn't the FCS, which shows great potential—as long as the Army doesn't fall into the Air Force practice of promising more than any system ever could deliver. The troubling aspect is the instinctive political correctness of the goofball counterinsurgency video (which undoubtedly cost the taxpayer as much as a good indie film, whether funded directly by the Army or by a contractor who wrote it off as a business expense). What's the fundamental purpose of FCS? One would assume it's intended to kill our enemies and destroy their ability to carry on the fight while shattering their will. That would justify the cost. But a single Special Forces A-Team could do everything in that counterinsurgency video more dependably, with a much smaller footprint and $100 billion cheaper.

Has the Army forgotten what war is? (The No. 1 complaint I now hear from officers in Iraq is about "green-zone generals" who have no idea what the streets outside their bubble are like—our military leaders are beginning to sound uncomfortably like World War I's "chateaux generals.") Is the always-dutiful, ever-unimaginative Army signing up for the Air Force's claim that technology can win the wars of the future without disturbing our enemy's beauty sleep? Do the Army's senior leaders now believe in the myth of bloodless war? Hasn't Iraq taught them anything?

Where are the Army generals honestly and honorably telling the president and the American public that "war means fighting, and fighting means killing"? It's getting harder and harder to find them. The extent to which the Army's leadership has signed up for peace, love, and understanding is appalling—and it's happened by stealth as officers whose worldviews were shaped during the Clinton era acquiesced in the Bush administration's insistence that wars could be won without annoying the enemy. When former Army Chief of Staff Gen. Eric Shinseki—a model officer—tried to tell the truth and got sent to the permanent dugout, other senior officers sympathized. But they didn't rush to defend him or argue for more troops themselves.

It's now fashionable for journalists to praise Army generals and colonels who used a light touch in Iraq. While drinking tea with the local sheik is pleasant for the fly-by commander and visiting journalist alike, the problem is that the light touch has given us the disastrous situation we face today. The big-carrot-little-stick approach hasn't worked enduringly anywhere in Iraq's Arab provinces. Meanwhile, division commanders who were actually willing to fight were condemned by their peers. War was no longer a contest of wills but a contest to see who could deliver the most gifts (bribes, really) to hostile local populations. And, of course, insurgents, militias and corrupt chieftains will always be glad to escape adult supervision as they build up their numbers, arm, train, and steal everything Uncle Sam meant to give them. In the Middle East, theft is honorable, but accepting a conqueror's largesse is bad form.

With our light-touch operations, we bought transient "successes" at the cost of nurturing the killers who are now destroying Iraq. No city where we've touted our success could withstand the terrorists, insurgents, and militias, were we to leave.

If we've forgotten the utility of killing, our enemies haven't.

The Army's knee-jerk, politically correct reaction to any suggestion that evil men need to be killed so that the innocent might prosper is the disingenuous statement that "you can't just kill everybody," as if the only alternative to uniformed pacifism is genocide. Anyway, our enemies are perfectly willing to try to "kill everybody" until they reach their goals.

In material terms, we remain by far the most powerful military on earth. In terms of strength of will or intellectual integrity, our enemies put us to shame. The terrorists are honest about their goals. We mumble platitudes and send our soldiers off to face more improvised explosive devices.

Originally, this column was going to dissect the deplorable September 21 draft of FM 3-24, "Counterinsurgency" (MCWP 3-33.5 for the Marine Corps), which appeared to have been written by Bono, two Woodstock survivors, and one disgruntled Vietnam vet. A guide to failure and the waste of American lives, the draft troubled me more than anything produced by the Army since I joined as a private in 1976. It broadly ignored our real enemies—religious zealots and ethnic supremacists—in favor of PC analysis that interprets all insurgencies as Maoist in nature. Not only is that absurd—the brief age of ideology is over and we're now back in the historical mainstream of rebellions of blood and belief—but it's willfully absurd. In the face of overwhelming evidence to the contrary, the drafters insisted on the enduring validity of models with which they were comfortable, such as Malaya or the early years of Vietnam. They want to study head colds while the Black Death is raging.

With a skin-them-alive-and-gut-them critique already written, I was assured that corrective action is being taken to produce a more sensible final document. To give the garrison Army a chance to prove it can deliver doctrine that might actually help our soldiers in the field, I'm holding my fire. But when that finalized manual appears, let's hope there's at least a single mention of suicide bombers and a few words about religious zealots and ethnic supremacists (neither of whom were included in the draft's categorization of insurgent types).

That September 21 draft's keystone chapter offers twelve lengthy paragraphs that deal with Maoist insurgencies and two—count 'em yourself—brief references to either Osama bin Laden or

al Qa'eda and other faith-fueled terrorist movements. The Bolshe-
vik Revolution got equal treatment with two paragraphs ("Back to
Vladivostok, Wolfhounds!"). Baghdad was mentioned only once,
ranking our experience there as equal in importance to the example of Che Guevara (whom we probably will not be fighting in the
near future).

The document's misdiagnosis of the threat, faulty prescriptions,
and general incoherence appeared to result from drafters defending their doctoral theses, others who were prisoners of narrow educations and poor reading habits (T. E. Lawrence, an English
neurotic who liked to dress up in flowing gowns and play spin the
bottle with Bedouins, gets three citations in the keystone chapter
and haunts the entire manual), and the pervasive atmosphere of
political correctness that has conquered so much of our military
and civilian leadership.

We've come a long, long way—downhill—since then-Maj. Gen.
Leonard Wood wrote, almost a century ago, that "The purpose of
an army is to fight." According to that goofball here's-why-we-need-
FCS video and the draft of the counterinsurgency manual, the purpose of an army is to put Band-Aids on boo-boos.

Let's all hope that the promised revisions to the manual will
inject some intellectual integrity and sobriety—but, frankly, some is
all we can hope for. Although the draft manual mentions the
importance of understanding foreign cultures, it carefully avoids
religion, which is the fundamental determinant of any culture: Men
and women are what they believe.

Consider the difference in receptivity on the part of any population (except, for now, the most secular societies in Europe) to ideological and religious insurgent movements. A villager in country X
may be convinced that Marxism or some other ideology offers him
advantages, but his commitment isn't preprogrammed and doesn't
go deep. A mere ideology can be undermined—a guiding principle
of twentieth-century counterinsurgency. But those who argue that
Afghanistan has the characteristics of a Maoist insurgency are focus-
ing on superficial techniques rather than on cultural predispositions:
In an Islamic society, the villager or urban youth is already convinced
that Islam is supremely good. The key issue is motivation, not tactics.

The apostle of an Islamo–Fascist insurgency needs only to acti-
vate a disposition that already exists in a potential recruit, to portray

the faith as under threat or betrayed and call the faithful to arms. And then you've got trouble in Kabul River City. Religious believers aren't blank slates but potential sleeper-agents, every one. It's virtually impossible to convince a man or woman anywhere that his or her religion is wrong. And, in the end, it comes down to what men are willing to die for: Faith tops the list, followed by blood ties as a close second. Ideology is way down the list and dropping.

You might convert a weary guerrilla in Latin America from Marxism to democracy and capitalism (or, at least, to narco-trafficking), but you can't persuade an Arab to become Persian or a Kurd to become Arab. Religious and ethnic insurgencies—which often overlap—are fundamentally different from and far tougher to defeat than ideological movements. Ideology is kid's stuff. Blood and belief are the real things.

So why don't we discuss religion—the most powerful motivational factor in human affairs—as an integral element of the security challenges we face? After all, our enemies insist that religion is dearer to them than all else—do we think they're just making it up to put one over on us? Where are the Western atheist suicide bombers, by the way? In the draft counterterrorism manual, I found no mention of Islamist terrorism (of course, the document is so hopelessly long and poorly written that I didn't read every word of every annex—length is the staff officer's instinctive substitute for clarity and quality).

The reason religion has been ignored as a crucial strategic factor—not only by the Army but by intelligence agencies, as well—is that political correctness rules. The dread of discussing religion as a cause of merciless violence, then getting called on the carpet for insensitivity, is so great that one editor of an official military journal told me several months ago that he had been forbidden by his superior to publish any article that mentioned religion—at a time when we're fighting Islamist terrorists and insurgents. Let's be honest: The bottom line here is that an officer's promotion has become more important than defeating our enemies.

How can we pretend to understand our opponents—or hope to defeat them—when we insist on ignoring the core of their being? Does anyone really believe that Osama bin Laden's a Maoist?

Oh, and by the way, Mao didn't invent his twelve-step program for insurgencies. The drafters of that wrong-headed counterinsurgency manual appear to believe that history started in St. Peters-burg (the cold one) in 1917. It didn't. Mao drew his lessons from centuries of millenarian, agrarian rebellions in China and, directly, from the national-chiliastic uprisings of the Taipings and the Fists of Righteousness (the "Boxers") in the nineteenth century. Maoist strategies weren't invented on the spot but exploited the millenar-ian strain that haunted Chinese history. Those who want to tell our soldiers and Marines how to subdue our nation's enemies should at least do their homework.

We'll see how the final version of "Counterinsurgency" looks. I wish the drafters well. But they must break free of the prevailing atmosphere of political correctness and deal with the world as it is, not as the Give-Peace-a-Chance Generation—now politically and culturally dominant—wants it to be. The toughest challenge, of course, is that those who have internalized a PC view of the world often don't even realize it. Instead of Chesty Puller or George Pat-ton, we have generals who rely on lawyers. And they're convinced they're warriors.

As for the Army's misguided campaign to sell Future Combat System with sleek videos so sterile they could be featured on the Car-toon Network, I walked away from that screening worried that our haste to get rid of artillery brigades—a decision that elevates supposed efficiency over guaranteed effectiveness—simply reflected our reluctance to inflict damage on our enemies. As a wary sup-porter of FCS, I want to know if, in a real war, it could flatten a city—destruction matters. In an all-or-nothing war, the capability to inflict massive devastation trumps precision. It's not that we don't need precision weapons—we need both smart bombs and the ability to render great swaths of a landscape unrecognizable—but graphic, tangible destruction is what ultimately breaks an enemy's will.

When is the last time you heard a senior Army general talk about the need to destroy an enemy? Even those whom I admire speak in petticoat euphemisms. Are officers now afraid to speak plainly—or do they really believe in the myth of bloodless war? Is that the lesson of Iraq? That friendly persuasion brings peace and, as that draft manual would have it, less force is always more? Tell that to a soldier or Marine in a firefight.

How is it that officers who are lions on the battlefield turn to jelly inside the Beltway?

Our manuals should tell us how to defeat our enemies, not how to serve them hot milk at bedtime. Videos and other tools to promote FCS should illustrate how the system will devastate our opponents, not how we can spend tens of billions to save a wounded terrorist. Senior officials and generals must speak honestly about war and stop pretending that we can win today's—and tomorrow's—conflicts without fighting.

Politically correct leadership has killed 3,000 American troops in Iraq and wounded another 20,000. Now Iraq is nearly hopeless, thanks to military theorists who think that culling sound bites from *Seven Pillars of Wisdom* serves us better than clear thinking, common sense, and fighting spirit.

It didn't have to be that way. Our troops didn't fail. Our national leadership did. And so did the generals.

Peace, sir.

Letter to the New Secretary

Armed Forces Journal

December 2006

Dear Secretary Gates,

Welcome to the second-hardest job in the world. Your immediate mission will be to shape the military component of a strategy to reach a bearable outcome in Iraq. You'll get plenty of advice on that one, so here are a few of your other won't-wait tasks:

Rebuild morale and trust within the Pentagon. Relations between the Office of the Secretary of Defense and senior officers are the worst they've been in more than a generation. We can't afford such animosity in wartime. Encourage the generals and admirals to give you their frank advice. Those in uniform don't expect you to rubber-stamp their positions—they seek only a fair hearing as professionals. Even if you reject their recommendations, they'll digest your decisions more easily if they feel they got a fair hearing.

Initiate a comprehensive reevaluation of the threats we'll face in the coming decades. There are plenty of threat assessments floating around Washington, but are any untainted by institutional or political bias? The Pentagon needs an objective threat survey that hasn't been tweaked to justify procurement programs and that hasn't been neutered in the interests of political correctness. With your intelligence background, you're the perfect man to guide this effort. You'll encounter bitter resistance from vested interests inside and outside of the Pentagon, but without an honest threat picture, service parochialism and lobbying power will continue to stymie rational force development.

And you need to rely on intelligence professionals to identify future threats, not on another "blue-ribbon panel" of political insiders and Pentagon retirees on the payroll of defense contractors.

Require each service to rejustify its procurement plans in terms of your new threat estimate. The primary reason we need an unbiased threat estimate is that there's a growing divergence between the systems the services want to buy and the enemies we face now and will face tomorrow. It isn't just a matter of affordability in the upcoming period of tighter budgets but of shaping tomorrow's force to face genuine threats, rather than fantasy projections that pander to service interests. No programs, not even those currently in the production phase, should be off-limits to termination. (Of course, Congress will make the final decisions—but you need to fight the good fight on this issue.) The positions you take on procurement will shape our military for decades to come—and may prove more important for our long-term security than your actions on Iraq.

Question transformation. While many of the disparate initiatives the services anxiously labeled (or relabeled) as "transformational" have real merit, others look dubious and destructively expensive. An objective analysis of military transformation has to consider not only theoretical potential but practical utility. A superb system is a bad buy if it has little or no applicability against real enemies. Push analysts to think boldly and objectively about tomorrow's conflicts.

Here's just one example of the many issues we must face with intellectual integrity: Nuclear battlefields may be a hallmark of the future, not just a past danger we escaped. How well would hyper-complex, communications-dependent systems perform in a nuclear landscape? The great vulnerability of twentieth-century militaries was their fuel supply; the corresponding military addiction in our twenty-first-century military is to information. Could the combat systems we're building earn their keep in an environment of ravaged communications? What if satellite links are destroyed or effectively interrupted? Are next-generation systems sufficiently robust to function effectively in a manual-and-mechanical environment? Could our enemies innovate cheap counters to our expensive, interreliant systems? These questions barely scratch the surface.

Seek a functional balance between personnel strength and acquisition programs. There's no perfect answer to the stuff-versus-people dilemma in the Era of Not Enough Money. The procurement side will argue that technologies reduce the number of troops we need in uniform, but our recent conflicts—which threaten to remain typical for decades—make it clear that there's a point at which less certainly isn't more. Technology is an enormous American advantage—yet there is still no substitute for adequate numbers of trained troops. It's not an either-or proposition but a matter of getting the combination as right as we can. And we can't afford a window of risk.

Refit the ground forces. With so much of their equipment worn out or destroyed in Iraq, the Army and Marines need immediate recapitalization. The situation in the National Guard is worse than in the active components. This is one more reasonable demand on the budget at a time when even the most reasonable demands can't all be met. These forces have to be ready, yet the money won't be there for both the next generation of land warfare systems and the full replacement of combat losses and systems stressed to a premature end of their service lives. We face a unique situation in which we now have incomparable veteran ground forces without the full complement of equipment they require to fight.

Depoliticize flag officer selection. The best single thing you can do for the officer corps in every service is to restore integrity to the promotion process—to promote fighting generals, not just those who "play well with others" inside the Beltway. Promote men capable of respectfully challenging your views, not just agreeing with them.

Mr. Secretary, you may serve only two years in this office, but you're not just a caretaker. You will have to undo various levels of damage done by the previous SecDef even as you prepare our military establishment to defend our nation in the uncertain—but certainly violent—years ahead. Since its establishment, your office arguably has never faced so many complex challenges at once. Nonetheless, you have one powerful advantage: You assume your office with great good will toward you. Use it boldly.

Quantitative Incompetence

Armchair General

January 2007

Numbers matter in war. The quality of leaders, troops, training, equipment, doctrine, intelligence, logistics, diplomacy, and strategy all matter, of course. But even the highest quality military force requires sufficient numbers of people and systems to sustain its efforts on the battlefield. And the United States Armed Forces are on a path to *quantitative incompetence,* a situation in which the numbers of troops and weapons drop so low that their quality becomes irrelevant.

The guiding principle of weapons development and acquisition in the U.S. military long has been that technological advances enable a smaller force to do more with less. To an extent, that's true. But past a point of diminishing returns, less is no longer more—it's just plain *less.* Our ground forces may already be past that point, while the air and sea services are hurtling toward numerical insufficiency.

It doesn't help to provide the world's finest weapons systems to our troops if we can't provide enough of them. High-tech's great, but numbers prevail. Ask the Wehrmacht.

We need to break ourselves of the lie that we always must buy the most expensive model of everything. A classic example is the F/A-22 Raptor, which is unquestionably the most capable air-to-air fighter in the world, but which has no present or pending enemies, and which, with total costs tallied, approaches $350 million per airframe.

We need more than techno-dazzle. We need to buy relevant and affordable systems in sufficient numbers. This requires a profound change in our thinking—in the defense industry and Congress even more than in the military. Industry likes to vend big-ticket items, since far more profits can be submerged in one nuclear submarine than in a million sidearms. And Congress does what the lobbyists from the defense industry want.

Our military needs to take a stand for common sense, to insist that numbers matter. Our ground forces are already stretched thin in Iraq and Afghanistan, yet future weapons buys may be funded by reducing the Army by at least two (of ten) divisions, with simultaneous cuts of up to 20,000 Marines. That is a risk we cannot take in an age of asymmetrical, Cain-and-Abel warfare. At some point, we will run out of grunts to pull guard duty.

Equally alarming, the long-term trend in the Air Force and Navy has been for whistles and bells to trump strategic utility. Our Air Force is already lean with 4,500 fighter aircraft. The expense of buying the F/A-22 Raptor and then the Joint Strike Fighter/ Lightning II will reduce the total number to 3,000—and that's an *optimistic* projection. Worse, these next-generation aircraft have exponentially higher maintenance requirements, resulting in fewer sorties available in an extended fight. Compounding that vulnerability, the reduced fleet will mean fewer pilots get trained. It's a downward spiral headed for a crash.

Our Air Force needs *more* airframes—UAVs (unmanned aerial vehicles), new bombers, more transports, and refueling aircraft. We're buying Maseratis and Ferraris when we need a fleet of pickup trucks and minivans.

In the worst-case scenario, a war with China, we wouldn't face the short, sharp fight that technology-*über-alles* advocates imagine. Beijing wouldn't succumb to "shock and awe" Part II. Instead, we'd face a new "Trojan War," a decade-long struggle that would drain our national resources. It wouldn't matter if an F/A-22 could knock a dozen bandits out of the sky if the Chinese could put thirteen in the air.

We need forces sufficiently large to take serious hits and keep on coming back.

Our Navy has increasing, not diminishing, global strategic requirements that necessitate more hulls on the water. Fewer ships, no matter their quality, just won't cut it. The times demand presence. We never reached the dream of a 600-ship Navy, and we won't. But we do need a 400-vessel force on the world's waters. That means buying affordable ships and accepting judicious trade-offs.

In an ideal world, we could buy the best of everything in abundance. But we don't live in an ideal world. Budgets will get tighter, not more generous. And the Army and Marines already face a price tag of tens of billions to rebuild, refurbish, and replace systems destroyed or worn out in Iraq.

We have to stop pretending we can have it all.

We need balance: A calculated mix of superhigh-tech and mid-tech weapons that gives us niche qualitative superiority *and* robust numbers. In the personnel sphere, we have to fund people even when that means foregoing some advanced weapons. In twenty-first-century conflicts, we can't just draft Johnny Nextdoor and hand him a Springfield rifle.

Watch where the money goes. If the Office of the Secretary of Defense and Congress continue to fund hyperexpensive systems of marginal relevance at the expense of the men and women who fight and practical weapons that work, we're in trouble.

The United States has the finest, most experienced military in the world. But numbers matter. History offers inspiring examples of small forces defeating far larger ones in individual battles—but in great wars and lengthy conflicts, numbers tell.

Rebels and Religion

Armed Forces Journal

January 2007

"How long will you sleep? How long until you wake up to Allah's will? Rise up and fight Allah's fight! The time is now! The evil-doers must pay . . . even if there are but three of you, if you surrender to Allah and seek your honor only in Him, you need not fear a hundred thousand enemies. But strike, strike, strike! The time is now! The wicked are nothing but dogs . . . strike, strike, strike! Show them no pity . . . do not consider the suffering of the godless . . . show them no pity! Do not let your sword grow cold . . . throw down their towers . . . strike, strike, strike while the day is yours! Allah goes before you! Follow Him! Follow Him!"

The words of Osama bin Laden? Of Ayman al Zawahiri? Or of Muqtada al Sadr? Maybe Hassan Nasrallah? The late Ayotallah Khomeini? President Ahmedinejad of Iran?

No. Every line is taken from a letter written by the Reformation-era Protestant extremist Thomas Muentzer to the citizens of Allstedt near the climax of the "Peasants' War"—the chaotic series of popular uprisings that swept much of Germany, parts of Austria, and northern Switzerland in 1525. The only "cheating" I did was to translate *Gott* as "Allah," rather than as "God."

For the record, longer excerpts from the lengthy letter can be found in *Der Deutsche Bauernkrieg* by Guenther Franz, first published in 1933, before the German Democratic Republic's entertaining attempt to claim Muentzer, the religious fanatic, as a communist forerunner.

Muentzer held an apocalyptic worldview and believed that the Second Coming was close at hand; his interpretation of events and his rhetoric bear an uncanny resemblance to those of President Ahmedinejad, who is anxiously awaiting the Twelfth Imam. Muentzer didn't generate his blood-soaked portion of the Peasants' War out of a vacuum, but exploited existing secular discontents— much as Osama bin Laden and other terrorist leaders have done. And he soared to his brief term of power by publicly defying the powerful—as Muqtada al Sadr has done.

Muentzer and the gruesome rebellions of his age, when politically frustrated men fervently embraced extremist religion, have more to tell us about the challenges we face from Islamist extremism today than do more recent waves of revolutionary struggle, when secular ideologies briefly eclipsed the appeal of faith. By studying only political terrorism of the sort we faced in the late twentieth century, we miss our enemy's inspiration, conviction, and passion and underestimate the alacrity with which he rejects "civilized" rules: His god's will trumps our mortal conventions.

Politics may inspire action, but religion inspires sacrifice. Our obsession with finding "logical" reasons for suicide bombings and terrorist massacres deludes us: Only by acknowledging the integrity and intensity of our enemy's faith can we begin to understand him—and to combat him effectively.

The Peasants' War (a misnomer, since it also drew in urban dwellers, out-of-work soldiers-for-hire, and even some disgruntled noblemen) exploded in early 1525. By the end of the year, the wild-fire local revolts, which were never effectively coordinated with one another, all had been put down. The brutality with which they were crushed ensured that there would be no early repetition of the challenge to the existing order. But for all its apparent suddenness, the Bauernkrieg had deep historical roots. What makes it especially relevant as a case study for our own troubles is that the pattern of radicalization offers a template that applies to many, if not all, outbreaks of millenarian passion, of the belief that the End of Days is nearing and that God wants help in speeding up the process through retributive violence.

The Bauernkrieg isn't just a historical footnote, but a perfect-storm model of how religious extremism masters a receptive population and rapidly excites it to violence in a god's name. From the suicidal revolt of the Zealots in Palestine almost two millennia ago, through countless chiliastic uprisings around the globe, to the evolution of Middle Eastern terror over the past four decades, the pattern of how practical dissatisfaction and political frustration open the door for impassioned religious movements seeking holy vengeance has been remarkably consistent since the Old Testament era.

We should've seen this coming.

A RETURN TO TRADITIONAL LAW

Unrest in the German-speaking lands simmered for at least a century before it boiled over in the Peasants' War. Working before World War II destroyed many of Germany's archives, scholars discovered numerous examples of local disturbances that ranged from brief riots to extensive plots for revolution throughout the fifteenth century. (The uprisings often employed the Bundschuh, a peasant's lace-up footwear, as their rallying symbol.) The troubles consistently arose from the efforts of regional princes or the Habsburg emperor to centralize authority and enforce a uniform "Roman" legal code intended to rationalize rights and obligations throughout a broader domain. (Much the same role was played by the artificially created states of the modern Middle East as they sought to consolidate power.) For the peasants, as well as for many burghers in the towns, this often meant the loss of traditional privileges and the imposition of new, onerous taxes and obligations. The first, raw uprisings demanded a return to traditional "German" law, often only oral codes handed down over the centuries—just as Middle Easterners defend their local traditions and inherited social structures today.

Most of the pre-Bauernkrieg uprisings in the German-speaking world were readily—often savagely—put down (when not discovered in the planning phases and interdicted). Rights continued to erode, and a sense of injustice prevailed. Local populations felt disoriented by rapid change originating from distant sources (echoed, again, in the Middle East today). Increasingly, calls for the preservation of traditional rights and the old Germanic folk law were supplanted by an insistence that "God's law" should prevail, a social order based upon biblical texts (Sharia, anyone?). The worse the frustration and stasis created by the authoritarian regimes of the day, the more frequent the invocations of a divine order became.

That's exactly what has happened over the past sixty years in the greater Middle East.

The explosion of 1525 involved a crisis of governmental order; an eruption of fundamentalist faith in the wake of Martin Luther's confrontation with the papacy; a split between establishment and dissident clerics; Luther's translation of the Bible into German (the effects rapidly exceeded Luther's vision of orderly reform); the destabilizing influence of the movable-type printing press (the internet of the day); the availability of out-of-work soldiers who had learned their skills in recent foreign wars that exposed the weakness of the period's superpowers (an obvious corollary with the Islamist veterans of the Afghan-Soviet struggle); a popular sense that conditions were unjust and that religion offered a viable alternative power structure; divine reassurance in a period of disorienting change; and above all, the appearance of charismatic radical fundamentalists with a gift for rhetoric and no scruples whatsoever about turning to violence.

That is the pattern of the Middle East today. The first, nationalist revolutions were secular and aimed against foreign rule or alien systems. But even where the revolutions succeeded, their results disappointed. Strongmen kept the people down (sometimes backed by Moscow, but supported all too often by Washington, whose diplomats, like the Habsburgs, placed stability above all other mundane considerations in international affairs). The popular sense of grievance endured and grew with the belief that legitimate rights were being denied and economic progress was stymied by external forces. Paranoia deepened (another similarity to the Bauernkrieg). The clergy split between an approved establishment and radical renegades bent on a stern reformation. Retributive violence came to seem not only a means but an end.

The exemplary case of the Palestinians demonstrates the transition from faith in political solutions (negotiations between states), through the initial attempts to use terror to accelerate the political process (Black September and Fatah), to disaffection with secular leaders and a new ardor for fundamentalist religion of a sort that until recently seemed foreign to Palestinian society (Hamas). When men failed to deliver, the people turned to a vengeful god whose prophets promised empowerment and triumph.

Iran offers another example: The shah's repression inhibited organic political development just as the nascent globalization of awareness held up foreign examples that simultaneously enticed and terrified the population. Left with no legal recourse, the masses turned increasingly to a fundamentalist variant of their religion that promised to uplift them, absolve them, and avenge them. Fitting perfectly with the historical pattern, a charismatic, uncompromising figure—the Ayatollah Khomeini—arose from the clergy. A frustrated population discovered that actions recently considered crimes were now pleasing to their god. The new theocracy quickly outdid Savak, the shah's notorious secret police organization, in barbarity. Yet the masses were intoxicated—sufficiently so to embrace the enormous sacrifices of the Iran-Iraq War and to remain entranced in large numbers more than a quarter-century after the Revolution of the Mullahs.

PLAGUE OF FANATICISM

The lessons of all these transitions from unaddressed discontents to religious fanaticism hold true for violent outbreaks down the centuries on virtually every continent and in all major faiths. When regimes insist that time must hold still and deny traditional or perceived rights, fundamentalist religion is always lurking nearby. At the beginning of *The Plague,* Albert Camus speaks of how a bacillus can lurk, dormant and undetected, only to reappear unexpectedly when conditions are right. Extremist religion has its own bacillus, and it has proven impossible to exterminate: There are no proven antibiotics for the plague of fanaticism. When political sanitation goes wanting, it strikes.

Yet that does not mean religious extremism can be addressed strictly through political measures (or through diplomacy, that great Western superstition). The only chance to minimize the violence is to intervene early on to create political and social breathing space for restive populations. Once religious extremism has taken hold, the pattern cannot be reversed. This is an absolutely vital point for American leaders to grasp. If the banner of jihad (or a crusade) has been raised successfully, the peaceable kingdom is finished. Only shedding blood ruthlessly can eliminate or at least reduce the problem—the enemy enraptured by faith must become more terrified of you than he is of his god. Usually you must kill him.

This matters vitally today as the United States, disappointed by its experience in Iraq, threatens to return to its disastrous "Habsburg" policy of the latter half of the twentieth century, in which the greatest democracy in history and the beacon of humankind supported a long parade of vile dictators and authoritarian regimes in the interests of stability.

The great strategic problem today isn't instability. The current instability confronting us is the result of our insistence that outwardly stable Middle Eastern states were the highest geopolitical good in the region. The great enabler of Islamist terrorism has been the artificial stability imposed on the Middle East by local despots backed by foreign powers. Increasingly, populations saw no hope of meaningful change. Right on schedule historically, charismatic religious bigots stepped in to offer not only hope, but a divine dispensation. It cannot be repeated too often or too forcefully: When human beings see no hope of remediation on this earth, they become susceptible to the prophets of religious violence, to the argument that their God wants them to punish their oppressors. And their conversion is a one-way street.

The paradox is that suicide bombers who "martyr" themselves to force a return to a traditionalist society are the product of societies in which secular progress came to a halt. Whatever his social class, the man who sees no palatable future is easily seduced by the myth of a better past. Whether late-medieval peasants convinced that German tribal laws had let their ancestors live closer to Eden or today's Islamists struggling to "restore" the caliphate—whose days of glory were over a thousand years ago—those who find the here and now intolerable are easy prey to self-appointed prophets promising a return to a lost golden age through the time machine of millenarian violence.

LIVING WITH INSTABILITY

President Bush has stated again and again that we are not at war with Islam. And although some elements within the Islamic world are certainly at war with us, let's hope that Washington does not excite even more Muslims to align with our enemies by reverting to our failed policies of the Cold War era, when any dictator would do as long as he was "ours."

We must learn to live with higher levels of foreign instability and not seek the false peace of the secret policeman if we are ever to see an end to the tumult by which we find ourselves troubled today. The temptation will always be there to support a strongman abroad when our will weakens at home, to align ourselves with those who seem powerful in mundane terms, while we miss the eternal power of the religious impulse and fail to grasp the all-or-nothing nature of the pursuit of the Kingdom of God. This problem is especially acute as we face 2007. In December, the Iraq Study Group issued a report whose implicit message was that there is no greater geopolitical value than stability. Bewildered by the demons our attempt to conjure democracy unleashed in Iraq, we long for the "good old days" in our own way, just as Islamists long for their own version of a better yesteryear. Both visions share a fundamental dishonesty, since the good old days are always a fantasy. Any American leader who imagines that the dark decades of the Cold War, when global nuclear annihilation loomed, were better than the current instability has lost his or her grip on historical reality. Even with the looming advent of a nuclear-armed Iran, we are far better off in 2007 than we were in 1957.

At the same time, we are paying now for geopolitical debts run up in the Cold War decades. After the long oppression of the colonial era, newly independent populations expected miracles—and got the shah, or Saddam Hussein, or at best Gamal Abdul Nasser. We are now at the painful beginning of a new era in which a world whose borders and structures of government were horribly deformed during the European imperial period and then by the ideological strictures of the Cold War is attempting to sort itself out through Darwinian collective action. Where we see daily acts of violence and alarming unrest, a longer view reveals human cultures and societies that were forced out of their organic equilibrium trying to right themselves. Historically, that has never been accomplished without bloodshed.

But the struggle of human collectives to find a new, functional balance is an issue beyond the scope of this essay. Of immediate relevance to us is the burden of our own new myths and the manner in which our chosen illusions prevent us from achieving success against extremist religious movements. Our fantasies run from the insupportable nonsense that the Middle East is amenable to diplomatic solutions, through the absurd notion that wars can be waged gently, to our insistence that religious differences can be reasoned away. We engage in wishful thinking every bit as irrational as Islamist claims that the American people will be converted to Islam.

Once the plague of religious passion has broken out into the population, the only solutions are the age-old remedies for the Black Death: Burn it out ruthlessly or let it burn itself out. The first course is unpalatable, the second catastrophic. Confronted with religious fanaticism, we cannot simply hope the epidemic will peter out before it does too much damage. Once we have become the target of violent religious movements, we have no practical choice but to respond with the unwavering use of force. Of course, we shall not do that. Not yet. And so we will pay, and fail, and wonder what happened as we stare at the ruins.

The legitimate authorities of his day confronted Thomas Muentzer's thousands of armed followers promptly, before his particularly destructive brand of rebellion could spread to other provinces where the revolts had been less fanatical. On May 15, 1525, Muentzer's ragtag army awaited battle on a hill north of Frankenhausen, confident that God would deflect the cannonballs of their enemies. The nobles opposing them had united various military contingents through forced marches to be certain of an overwhelming superiority. In the end, it was hardly necessary. When their faith did not divert the first cannonballs from the massed target, the rebels broke and ran, with only a few small bands of fanatics putting up any resistance during their disastrous rout. Their campaign of burning abbeys and castles, of plunder and the execution of "God's enemies" was over, and the ruling powers made certain there would be no recurrence by slaughtering more than 5,000 of Muentzer's followers in the fields and ditches. The bloodshed was horrific—yet it was far less gore than would have been spilled had the rebellion been given time to spread more widely. The battle on that hill near Frankenhausen was the Tora Bora of the day—but the authorities had no illusions about the nature of their enemy or what it would take to defeat him. Their Osama bin Laden wasn't allowed to escape to continue to preach his crusade.

Muentzer had been a defiant lion in his days of power, sentencing opponents to death for offending God and justifying apocalyptic excesses. But when his ad hoc army of peasants and townsmen fell apart, he fled—only to be apprehended disguised as a sick man in bed. His belief that the Kingdom of God was at hand had shaped his every action; defeat shattered his faith. He broke under torture, recanted his beliefs publicly, and went to the scaffold discredited. His treatment was brutal. And it worked. The world could see that Muentzer's god had failed him.

A few leaders of the Peasants' War were able to flee to Switzerland, the Pakistan of the day, but the resolute nature of the response by the authorities to the series of uprisings that inflamed Germany proved thoroughly effective—the only brief successes gained by the insurgents came where local officials dithered. Faced with insurrections of any kind, but especially with faith-fueled rebellions overheated by millenarian rhetoric, the response must be prompt and fierce. Early ferocity saves countless lives—a paradox that the liberal Western soul cannot yet bring itself to accept. Mercy can follow victory but cannot precede it.

For us, there are two pressing challenges: combating the enemies already standing against us and preventing the needless creation of more enemies. The first issue demands a new sense of reality about the nature of warfare and the motivations of our opponents. The second requires that we avoid the seductive lure of the strongman who promises us the illusion of peace and thus plays into the hands of religious fanatics.

The imposition of another term of artificial stability in the Middle East isn't a solution. It's a trap.

Progress and Peril

Armed Forces Journal

February 2007

The final version of Army FM 3-24, "Counterinsurgency," (MCWP 3-33.5 for the Marine Corps) deserves applause for coming a long way fast. The September 21 draft was a jumble of platitudes and a prescription for continued failure. After key leaders in the Marines and Army realized how badly the doctrine had gone off track, earnest debate and long days spent rewriting and editing the document resulted in a useful manual that begins to come to grips with the actual challenges facing us, instead of simply repeating the failed recommendations of the last century's counterinsurgency (COIN) "experts."

The manual now admits the existence of religious zealots and ethnic demagogues— salient insurgent types the previous draft ignored—and accepts that some enemies are irreconcilable and must be killed. It states bluntly that "old, strongly held beliefs define the identities of the most dangerous combatants in these new internal wars." The draft field manual's most foolish claims, exemplified by its "paradoxes of counterinsurgency," have been qualified, and the text now stresses the importance in many COIN operations of a "high ratio of security forces to the protected population." If only more of our military leaders had stressed that point to their civilian superiors four years ago.

Yet FM 3-24 still doesn't swing open the door to the future of COIN warfare; at best it's a hinge between the failed dogmas of the twentieth century—myths embraced by soldiers and civilians alike—and a growing sense that the reality on the ground in Iraq and elsewhere contradicts the theories we were fed. This document isn't meant as definitive doctrine but as a stopgap. Responsible leaders in the Marines and Army recognize the need for an ongoing process to continually improve our COIN doctrine. The manual will help officers think more incisively about the problems facing them, but many of the solutions it offers, nonetheless, are outdated and dubious—when not foolhardy.

It isn't just our armed forces that are in a period of transition, but also our entire civilization, including both the vanguard English-speaking nations and reluctant Europe. The half-century between the resurrection of Germany as a federal republic and September 11, 2001, might well be labeled "The Age of Frivolity" by future historians. Despite the dangers of the Cold War era, the breathtaking expansion of American wealth and power led our population into a sense of detachment from the travails and dangers that never stopped afflicting much of the globe. Despite intermittent recessions and a series of distant wars, the party never ended: Life just kept getting better for Americans.

For Europeans, the internal discipline as well as the external protection provided by America's presence and power permitted not only an unprecedented spread of wealth across social class lines, but also nurtured a blithe attitude toward both distant troubles and the suffering of neighbors behind the Iron Curtain. Europe became a continent of Marie Antoinettes.

Then came September 11. Americans sensed at once that a profound break had occurred between a confident, easy past and a painful reimmersion in the world. Marx, not God, is dead, and old enemies have been reinherited. Europe lags in grasping that the Age of Frivolity is over (and will resist facing the grave new world as long as possible), but reality will carve its initials in Europe's flesh soon enough.

The legacy of that Age of Frivolity persists, however, in our own military circles. Despite repeated failures and graphic casualties, military alchemy refuses to yield to science, and comfortable prejudices continue to stave off the acceptance of chilling facts. During the strategic stalemate of the Cold War, we suffered a unique affliction: Theorists with little or no military experience flourished, propounding visions of how war should be waged that were so disconnected from reality they resembled unicorn sightings. To its shame, our military establishment embraced one madcap theory after another—especially those that promised easy victories through a "revolution in military affairs" or COIN models "proving" that a bottle of Coke and a smile would win over the poor, benighted natives.

The reality of Somalia and the Balkans, Afghanistan, and now, above all, Iraq, has made inroads against the fantasies of bloodless war and the deadly absurdity that "all men want peace." But the last holdouts among the peace-through-palaver zealots include military intellectuals suffocating our service-college faculties, men so obsessed with defending their theses that they never stop to ask themselves why their COIN templates haven't worked anywhere we've tried them.

The possibility that their prescriptions for COIN operations might be wrong never seems to occur to the Ph.D. gang. Their response to disaster is always, "We've got to try harder." Faced with our strategic and operational failures in Iraq, our theorists cling to a few transitory tactical successes as evidence that their constructs can work, if only, if only, if only we keep reinforcing failure. Confronted with the ultimate collapse of those few tactical successes, they argue that our efforts needed more time, or better funding, or more troops. They justify our casualties with platitudes and miss the fundamental point: We will never operate under perfect conditions. We will always lack something, whether it's time, resources, or even a clearly defined mission. The test of a military doctrine's validity is its effectiveness under imperfect conditions. Any doctrine that requires every star to be in perfect alignment is destined to fail.

The doctrine espoused by the new COIN manual lies between a failed past and a threatening future. The introduction and key chapters now say many of the right things, but they also retain far too many contradictory passages (compromise is the enemy of clarity and utility). Perhaps the gravest omission is the failure to analyze the "combatant" role of the global media, which can determine the outcome of battles, campaigns, and entire wars in the postmodern era. Military leaders admit that they found the issue too politically sensitive and complex to address at this stage of the doctrine's development; nonetheless, any COIN strategy that fails to plan for the media's inherent hostility to any American endeavor sets itself up for unnecessary failures. The insurgents are our open enemies, but many elements within the world's media are their conscious or unwitting allies. Until we force the media to admit its role in shaping outcomes, we will continue to grant our opponents a huge strategic advantage.

Other deficiencies range from the continued insistence that all insurgencies have political goals, even though religion-fueled movements view politics as a means, not an end, to the assumption that all insurgencies focus on the overthrow of a government—this despite the apocalyptic nihilism and transcendental objectives of the Islamist movement. Political grievances sometimes may be satisfied, but the ambitions of a god tend to be insatiable. The manual stresses correctly that "learn and adapt" is an imperative, yet clings to failed Vietnam-era theories of how insurgencies must be understood and treated. Consequently, there's a fatal assumption that all foreign populations ultimately want what we want and can be cajoled into supporting us in their own interests. Yet a crucial lesson from Iraq is that not all foreign populations identify with our vision for their future.

Although the manual correctly stresses the importance of cultural awareness, it fails to warn that an overemphasis on cultural sensitivity—sloppy pandering of the sort we've seen in Iraq—plays into a cunning enemy's hands by allowing him to set the terms of the struggle. For example, our well-intentioned, naive decision to stay out of mosques guaranteed that mosques would become terrorist refuges and insurgent arms depots. Instead we needed to put the onus on our enemies for any violations of holy precincts. Cultural knowledge certainly gives us an advantage—but not if you carry your sensitivity beyond the bounds of common sense and lose sight of the mission.

The Army and Marines will work through these weaknesses in time. As midgrade and junior officers discover for themselves that the traditional COIN wisdom is often dead wrong, our doctrine will improve. The immediate problem is that many nation-building techniques appear to work in the short term, because they function as bribes, but collapse over time—the commander returns from his one-year tour convinced that he's made progress in City X, only to learn that his illusions merely gave the enemy breathing space. To make progress in environments such as Iraq, commanders have to unlearn most of what they've been told about counterinsurgency operations.

BAD HISTORY

Returning veterans are going to have an increasingly tough time with the schoolhouse Army, that tribal refuge of our intellectual Taliban (the Marines are quicker to grasp changed realities). The most troubling indication of how difficult it's going to be to convince the officers, active duty and retired, with too much formal education and too little common sense that their beloved theories don't work lies in the treacherously selective and unscrupulous use of historical examples in the new COIN manual.

Even though the doctrine now admits the necessity of killing at least some of our most fervent opponents while accepting the validity of religion and ethnicity as motivating factors, the authors of the manual ignored the massive body of historical evidence that contradicts their claims in favor of a handful of unique cases that appear to buttress their theories. Bluntly put, the manual lies about history.

The doctrine's authors keep propping the same worn-out hookers up on the barstools: Malaya and CORDS—the Civil Operations and Rural Development Support program in Vietnam—are treated as the definitive examples of COIN warfare, even though they're anomalies from a specific historical juncture (and the latter was, of course, a failure). Other successful COIN operations from the same period go ignored, because the lessons they offer contradict the hearts-and-minds dogmas the drafters treasure. In Kenya, the British destroyed the Mau Mau insurgency—through a combination of hanging courts, concentration camps, and determined military operations—but you won't read about that in the new COIN manual. Because they were bloody and messy, more recent COIN successes in Central America are glossed over, too. Algeria is treated selectively, yet the ferocious French military approach won the Battle of Algiers; a war-weary nation quit because successful military techniques were applied too late. (A key lesson is that, while COIN operations may require years of presence, time cannot be squandered.) Nor does Jordan's savage—and successful—repression of Palestinian unrest merit a mention here. The doctrine writers shun any examples that contradict their politically correct biases.

Reading the manual, it's hard to tell whether the drafters just don't know much history or intentionally rewrote history in the best Stalinist (and American-academic) tradition. Many of the claims made about the historical track record of insurgencies are absurd, and the speciousness of the examples cited reminds one of a quack doctor who, faced with the death of 98 patients, trumpets the miraculous survival of two as proof that his treatment works.

Consider the manual's claim that "killing insurgents—while necessary, especially with regard to extremists—by itself cannot defeat an insurgency." Oh really? Over the past 3,000 years, insurgencies overwhelmingly have been put down thoroughly by killing insurgents. The teething-ring nonsense that insurgencies don't have military solutions defies history—it's campus and think-tank nonsense. Certainly, the military will fail if it isn't used resolutely, but even in our own national history, insurgencies and insurrections have been defeated only with military force, from the Whiskey Rebellion, through a long succession of Indian wars, our Civil War, the Boxer Rebellion, the Moro insurrection, any number of "banana wars," and right down to the 2001 destruction of the Taliban regime.

Critics might respond that some of these military solutions didn't last—but they consistently proved more sturdy than negotiated treaties. We have to accept that there are few permanent solutions in history—those who take a long view recognize that counterinsurgency operations often are about buying time or shifting a regional equation, not achieving ideal end states. But the record is clear that military responses historically have achieved the most durable successes. Our reluctance to face overwhelming amounts of historical evidence is a holdover from that Age of Frivolity, when we could afford to believe comforting nonsense.

Unfortunately, the manual's misleading use of history goes much further. Consider the statement that "Insurgencies and counterinsurgencies have been common throughout history, but especially since the beginning of the 20th century." That would be news to the Roman legions serving from Britain and Gaul, down along the Danube frontier, on to Asia Minor and Palestine, and back to northern Africa (and that doesn't include the slave revolts). There are literally thousands of examples of insurgencies crushed definitively by military force over the millennia, from the revolt of the Zealots in Palestine to the insurrection of the Zanj in Basra, from various Celtic risings down to Nestor Makhno's guerrilla warfare in Soviet Ukraine.

The myopic claim that insurgencies became increasingly numerous in the past century even ignores the other great—and frequent—insurgencies of the Age of Ideology (circa 1789 to 1991). What about the multiple insurgencies that swept Latin America, ultimately driving out the Spaniards? What about the near-endless succession of insurrections and civil wars that ravaged so much of Latin America thereafter—not least tragic Mexico, whose revolution of 1910 remains the greatest unstudied example of multisided insurgency warfare of the last century?

What about the thousands of years of popular insurgencies in China?

That list still ignores the multiple revolutions and insurgencies of 1848 in Europe, as well as the repeated freedom struggles of the Poles, Balkan insurgencies against Turkish rule, tribal insurgencies throughout Africa, multiple uprisings against British rule on the Northwest Frontier, the Mahdist revolt, the Boer uprisings, and on and on. For the serious student of COIN operations, the historical examples are inexhaustible.

Twentieth-century insurgencies that arose in the recession of empires were a mere subset of a subset of history's countless insurgencies. But the common thread running through the sampling above is that those confronted by adequate military forces resolutely employed failed, while insurrections against irresolute foreign rulers or weak domestic governments often succeeded.

Even the rare examples of pre-twentieth-century insurgencies cited in the text are misinterpreted. Although it's true that the "Spanish uprising against Napoleon . . . sapped French strength and contributed significantly to Napoleon's defeat," that Spanish ulcer never healed because British expeditionary forces kept ripping it open; indeed, Britian's policy of supporting anti-French interest groups on the Iberian Peninsula resembles the support

Iran and Syria provide to Iraqi insurgents today—while the Iranians and Syrians have not deployed military formations in Iraq, they have provided arms, funds, training, and above all, encouragement. Without foreign backing, the Spanish uprisings against Napoleon's forces would have failed (as did the anti-French insurgency in the Tirol and partisan-warfare efforts elsewhere in the German-speaking lands). The operative lesson isn't about people-power but about its exploitation by third parties.

BAD MEDICINE

Determined to prove that, in the end, all insurgencies really are the same, the manual offers maxims and prescriptions for global application, contradicting its own claim that all insurgencies have their own unique characteristics that demand a grasp of their cultural contexts. As a result, the drafters muddle together conservative and revolutionary insurgencies; blur religious, ethnic, and political uprisings into a single mass; and confuse struggles to preserve traditions with those that reinvent traditions (as al Qa'eda has done). Yet the medicine for one type of insurgency can be deadly in another. The authors just don't seem to believe that insurgencies really come in different flavors but were forced to sprinkle on some rhetorical toppings to that effect at the last minute.

The default position of the manual is still the Maoist model, with sound bites from T. E. Lawrence tossed in. If a little knowledge is a dangerous thing, then inadequate historical perspective is deadly. Although acknowledging the progress that has been made from the last draft to the final document, one reads this manual asking how many dead American soldiers and Marines it will take before our doctrine writers stop insisting that black is really white, that north is south, that peace is the natural state of mankind, and that foreign populations enduring violent insurgencies just need a bowl of Cheerios.

We need to stop defending the old intellectual order. It's immoral to throw away the lives of our troops in repeated attempts to validate somebody's doctoral thesis. It's time to look honestly at the historical record, to stop saying and writing things we think will make everybody else happy, and to tell the truth about COIN warfare.

The great truth missing in FM 3-24 is that military solutions traditionally have been the only effective tools in defeating insurgencies. To be effective, the military must be used with resolve and boldness—but no other model has a history of consistent success. The implications are obvious: Other branches of government may be of some assistance (or depending on the circumstances, an impediment) to COIN operations, and our endeavors may range from the limited involvement of special operations forces to massive deployments, but if our nation's leaders are unwilling to accept that violence is the currency that pays the serious bills, the insurgents win. After all of the grand academic theories have collapsed, COIN warfare is a fight to the death.

PART II

Iraq and Its Neighbors

What Now, Lieutenant?
Another Day in Iraq

Armed Forces Journal

May 2006

Donkey carts and dented BMWs. Dust. Junked streets and waving children. Shrouded women fingering vegetables at ramshackle stands. Brown slums brightened by Shiite holiday flags, green, blue, red, white, and black. Shoddy construction and rusty metal, an unfinished world. Trash-pile playgrounds. Exhaust. More dust. The stench of raw sewage sickens the air.

Welcome to Baghdad. Romantics may dream otherwise, but there's no greatness left in this city, only a conglomeration of failures and retreats, of spitting hatreds and the dull need to get on with the day's concerns. Ill-tempered, afraid, and warily hopeful, Baghdad suffers not only from its Saddam Hussein decades, but from a general cultural exhaustion.

This is the laboratory of the Middle East's future. In a sprawling labyrinth at Baghdad's southeastern extreme, a U.S. Army first lieutenant is charged to prod the experiment forward.

We linked up at Forward Operating Base Loyalty, a compound notorious for torture under Saddam and now the headquarters of the Army's 506th Infantry Regiment of the 101st Airborne Division. The 506th is the "Band of Brothers" outfit, the "Currahees." The FOB is a testament to the pinpoint accuracy and utter ineffectiveness of the Air Force's precision weaponry. Buildings lean and gape like drunks with their teeth knocked out. Clean, quick, and foreign, American soldiers work around the monuments to the drama and ultimate failure of "shock and awe."

The 506th's commander, Col. Tom Vail, is the unofficial sheriff of Baghdad east of the Tigris. Vail projects enough energy to punch through stone walls bare knuckled, but in conversation he's thoughtful. His missions range from working with the 6th Iraqi Division (whose commander would be assassinated shortly after my visit), through negotiating with clerics and pursuing terrorists, down to warning off two-bit black marketers. A brigade staff meeting addresses dozens of aspects of postmodern conflict, from construction projects to combat.

Vail comes from a military family whose American roots run back to 1648. Yet there's nothing smug about his style of leadership. He stresses the critical importance of keeping subordinates innovative and focused in an environment of long hours and crushing routine—punctuated by sudden violence. He demands that his soldiers out in the streets "notice nuances."

Today the responsibility for investigating the complexities of Iraqi society devolves to 1st Lt. Clenn Frost and his 1st Platoon, Bravo Battery, 4th Battalion, 320th Field Artillery. The gunners have come a long way from entry-level training at Fort Sill, Oklahoma, where the emphasis is on massive firepower. Employed as infantrymen in Baghdad—where infantrymen are always in short supply—they've been mastering new military skills while coping with a culture as asymmetrical to their own as any on earth could be.

The brigade assumed its mission January 5. After not quite two months, the soldiers of 1st Platoon know the layout of the streets, but not the people. They've gotten the general feel of the neighborhoods and made the acquaintance of some Iraqi counterparts, but they struggle with those crucial nuances stressed by their brigade commander. It's an uphill battle, and it would be easy to criticize or even caricature their efforts, but they're doing a terribly difficult job that comes without a blueprint.

All the grand designs and political generalities narrow down to four up-armored Humvees moving gingerly through crowded streets and alleys. The platoon's artillerymen have mastered the discipline of mounted movement, varying the routes to their assigned sector and maintaining the proper tactical distance between their vehicles. They have the drills down to reverse course or clear an area. And they're working out the finer details: In districts judged relatively benign, they slow down to minimize the dust kicked up by heavy-duty tires. In the wretched alleys where Iraqis live out their lives, small gestures make a big difference.

Frost is getting an education no military training institution could provide. Tall and lean, with an all-American face under his helmet's rim, he doesn't waste words or tell jokes. As serious as a church elder, he's a good watcher who thinks before he speaks. The burdens dropped on his shoulders must weigh him down far more heavily than his body armor does. If so, he doesn't let on.

The drive into the day's patrol sector takes a half hour. Trading immediate presence for security, senior leaders consolidated American units on sprawling compounds, instead of establishing more vulnerable (but more responsive and better attuned) dispersed outposts. The media's obsession with casualties drives the practice, which indisputably limits a unit's influence down in the 'hoods. But this is a conflict that ultimately will be won or lost in the media. Iraqi reality is the lesser problem.

Careful in the alleys—not least because of the hordes of children—the platoon covers highway stretches and berm-top roads at a tear. The Humvees race past a dump ideal for concealing improvised explosive devices. Delays in the open are dangerous.

Turning into a far suburban slum near the Diyala River, Frost abruptly halts the patrol. Soldiers dismount and cover the street. They're not yet as crisp as trained infantrymen would be. But they're pretty good. Turret gunners stay alert, scanning the rooftops.

The stop is to tell off a young man selling gasoline from plastic containers. The black market in fuel is lucrative in a city of kilometer-long gas lines—often targeted by car bombs. And unemployment remains painfully high. The kid's trying to make a few dinars. Working through Noah, the platoon's civilian interpreter, Frost has the onerous job of warning the young salesman that his wares will be confiscated if he's spotted hawking them again. The kid pleads that he's only trying to support his family. Frost avoids emotion, telling him, Joe Friday style, that the Iraqi government has outlawed black-market fuel sales, and that's that.

As the discussion proceeds, an excited Iraqi crosses the street— or the gutter that passes for one—to approach a noncommissioned officer providing security. Pointing farther along our route, the local lets go a long stream of Arabic. The sergeant shoos him off. The Iraqi's failure to communicate his message intensifies his tone and enlivens his gestures. Whatever his motivation, he appears to be saying that there's a bigger black-market site not far away.

Suspicious and uncomprehending, the NCO shakes his head. He gestures for the Iraqi to back off. With an expression of disgust, the would-be informant gives up. He's taken a risk and he won't try again. He watches us bitterly from a perch on a broken cinder block—the Iraqi equivalent of a garden gnome. Frost and the interpreter are still engaged with the young black marketer, who's now drawn sympathetic locals and a flock of children to the parley.

The day has barely begun.

FIRST STOP: POB

Our first planned stop is the barracks compound of a Public Order Battalion, a gendarmerie outfit that falls under the Interior Ministry and functions as the punch behind the police. Theoretically. Although the Public Order Battalions and Brigades (POBs) generally have a better reputation than the local cops (still well below the Iraqi army's current standing), there's plenty of variation by unit.

Frost is supposed to pick up a ride-along team from the POB. The Iraqis will help the platoon connect to the local people while learning patrol procedures from the Americans. After a tour of the desolation Saddam Hussein left behind for Iraq's poor—slums amid sewage lakes and endless shoals of garbage—we're waved through the front gate of the POB compound.

The slovenly grounds would give an American sergeant major a heart attack. Most of the unit's vehicles are out on patrol in the wake of the Samarra mosque bombing, but hulks of old passenger cars and odd bits of metal trash litter the parade ground and parking areas. Dismounting, the NCOs joke about the POB commander's dubious hospitality.

"Hey, you going to drink some of that Pepsi this time?"

"Yeah, right. You drink mine."

"Did you see how dirty. . . ."

The barracks hallways echo. Empty. Except for the commander sitting comfortably in his office with a television set blaring. Instead of working the streets with his troops, he's drinking tea with pals in civvies. The lieutenant and his NCOs are intercepted out in the hallway. A meeting of some sort's underway, and the Iraqi commander doesn't want Americans to be part of it. He slips out into the corridor just long enough to offer a perfunctory apology and a Saddam-era smile. No ride-along today. His men are too busy. He reeks of old-school, Middle-Eastern military officer, slothful and self-interested.

Frost isn't in a position to argue with an officer who's technically very much his senior. He pulls out Plan B. The Humvees head down the road to a regular police station, avoiding an M1 tank roaring along in the opposite direction.

The police compound is immaculate. Even given no advance notice, the officer in charge is glad of the opportunity to get his men out into the streets with the Americans. A vehicle's coming in off patrol in a few minutes. The team will head right back out with Frost's platoon.

The formal patrol begins at last. A significant activity, or SIGACT, report comes over the radio as we work back through the labyrinth of slums. An IED exploded in an adjacent sector. No injuries. But the report gets everyone's attention. The platoon is working Mahallas 964 and 966, the first settlement mostly Sunni, the second Shiite, but with mixed transitional neighborhoods. First task: Investigate reports of a mortar position near the Diyala River Bridge. The Humvees erupt from another shabby, identical neighborhood into an expanse of green: Date palms, small plantations of crops—and more automobile carcasses. Then the dust-colored buildings close around us again.

The suspected mortar site—used during the hours of darkness—is hidden in a grove between a boulevard leading out of the city and a strip of crude repair shops and family compounds. Frost sizes up the terrain and gives his orders promptly. His hasty plan is no different from what a veteran infantryman would devise. The dismounts, including the Iraqi police, will scour the grove in a skirmish line while two Humvees provide security on either flank, forming an extended H formation. Visibility's good enough to see from the main road on the left to the open lane on the far right. The machine guns atop the Humvees can overlap fires.

A shell-packing container turns up immediately. But there's nothing else, except a marvelous assortment of empty liquor bottles in the lee of a broken wall. The back side of the grove is the local party central. Broken glass and lurid whiskey labels offer a counterpoint to the muezzin's call from the local mosque.

Mount up. Move. Traffic's congested, locking in the patrol—and immobility's always a security risk. An NCO waves back the Iraqi vehicles to make a hole for the Humvees. Used to such delays, the locals accept the situation with equanimity. Iraqi life involves a great deal of waiting, no matter who's in charge at the top.

Another neighborhood. Time for a foot patrol. "Grip and grin" with the locals. The friendly reception Sunni and Shiite neighborhoods alike display toward our troops is stunningly unlike the situation reported back in the States. Kids are everywhere, flocking to our soldiers whenever we stop.

We walk the lanes of a middle-class neighborhood poisoned with sewage and pimpled with trash. I flash back to India. Smiling women in head scarves hurry their children to their front gates to see the Americans. Alternately timid and cocky, the local teenagers care less about utilities (a top concern to their elders) than about the prospect of a proper soccer field.

A foot patrol in Baghdad can seem almost a ceremonial procession. It would be easy to become overconfident, to drop your guard. But the Iraqi police read differences we can't. Crossing from one block to another, two of the cops (but not their own self-consciously dashing lieutenant) pull balaclavas down over their faces. The reception for the police, who are heavily Shiite in Baghdad, depends on the neighborhood. The locals see lines invisible to us. We can master the externals, as we've done with success from occupied Japan to Bosnia, but a society's innermost dynamics are opaque to those born elsewhere. Which is why Vail stresses nuances. Frost and his soldiers will learn as the months pass.

Where you can't achieve finesse, you settle for effectiveness. You know you've begun to crack the essential code when you react intuitively. Then your unit rotates back to the States. Long-term security for Iraq will depend on Iraqis. We've put the training wheels on the bicycle, and that's all we can do. In the end, they've got to ride it themselves.

We turn a corner, with Humvees creeping behind us in overwatch. Two elderly men in traditional costumes hasten to their compound gate to invite Frost into their garden, the private oasis treasured by every Iraqi family. An old Datsun has been tugged inside for safekeeping. The yard's crowded and half barren, Appalachia on the Tigris. A child sets off at a run to fetch plastic chairs, and one of the old men, who has a bandaged eye and battered eyeglasses, produces local cola, glasses, and a bowl of sesame cookies. He defers to his brother, who's a minor sheikh of sorts. While the rest of the platoon keeps up security along the block, the lieutenant and his interpreter settle in to hear what the old men have to say, to judge whether they exert meaningful influence over the neighborhood or just have their own family agenda.

Our hosts belong to a clan dispossessed of its lands under Saddam. In their youth, the neighborhood had been a village. Their fields had been devoured by the city. They hated Saddam—so they insist—but wonder whether their country can be ruled without a strong hand. They long for the days long ago when sheikhs had real authority. But they don't like the new sheikhs empowered under Saddam, who are only out for themselves. It all begins to sound like the lament of has-beens.

Their complaints are in line with those of other Iraqis, though. They hate the foreign terrorists, who they see destroying their country. And they have no time for the religious militias, who they view as gangsters. Yet a moment later, the sheikh declares that the militias are necessary until the new government can fill the local power vacuum. Iraqis overwhelmingly want the militias disarmed, but they don't want their militia disarmed first. They trust their army to an encouraging degree but don't yet think much of their police.

"Please," the old man asks Frost, "if our houses must be searched, can't you Americans do it? We trust you. But we cannot trust these policemen. . . ." He gestures dismissively toward the men in the ski masks out in the street: Shiite cops on a Sunni block. A number of the sheikh's remarks have been tailored to please his American guest, but the petition comes across as sincere. It's hard to find an Iraqi who trusts the police.

Fingering black worry beads in the shabby paradise of his garden, the sheikh continues, "The Iranians are a problem now . . .

these thugs from outside . . . honest people are killed . . . our government doesn't do enough. We liked it better in the first days, when you Americans were running things."

Frost drinks his flat cola and dutifully crunches a biscuit, listening to Noah's translations. The sheikh watches the lieutenant intently. I feel the request for a favor coming. In the Middle East, there's always a petition at the end of the tea party. Frost responds to the sheikh's complaints with stock answers—exactly as a diplomat would do. He doesn't indulge in self-importance or posturing. Willing to lend a sympathetic ear, he won't make a promise he might not be able to fulfill. American integrity confuses Iraqis, who are used to instant, empty commitments qualified by an "inshallah." Walking the cultural tightrope is a challenge for a junior officer from Bennington, Vermont. If Frost errs, he errs on the side of propriety.

He's on his own in that garden. The interpreter is a conduit, no more. The NCOs take care of security and the strictly military side of things but avoid any part in the parleying. The lieutenant's dependent on his own judgment at the forward edge of American strategy. All day, he's appeared confident and in charge. But the serpentine conversation and Arab tale-telling in that garden—unsettling glimpses of another world—seem to make him uncomfortable.

After refilling our glasses and passing the sesame cookies around again, the sheikh shifts from reminiscences of his family's glory days to the real business at hand.

"This boy's father," he says, pointing to the dark-eyed child flitting in and out of the garden, "has been arrested. Two months ago. By the Coalition. He is in prison in Basra. He has done nothing, he is innocent. Can you help us? Can you have him released, please?"

A bad officer would make empty promises. Frost doesn't. His bearing stiffens slightly. His speech becomes even more measured.

"What's he accused of?"

"Nothing. We don't know."

"Why was he in Basra?"

"We don't know. But he is innocent. Please help this boy's father."

Frost shakes his head. Explaining that, if the man has been arrested, he's suspected of a crime. Justice will have to take its course. He can't interfere in a judicial process.

The Iraqis have been pitching in the dark, seizing a passing opportunity. And they aren't going to burn any bridges. They accept Frost's refusals politely. He and his men are welcome back. Anytime.

BACK ON THE STREETS

More lanes to walk, more black sewage, more garbage, more children. More questions than the interpreter can handle (although he's quite good). Endless pleas for assistance. America's rich, Americans can do anything. The soldiers and Iraqis walk along together, separated by their mutually incomprehensible languages. The Iraqis are curious, the soldiers tired. By the end of the foot patrol, Frost is trailing a pack of children like the Pied Piper.

Time to mount up again. We drive a block on a main drag and spot another cluster of black marketers selling gas. Out of the Humvees again. More no-nonsense orders: Don't be caught out here again or we'll confiscate your goods. You're breaking your country's laws. The young Iraqis fail to see the logic of the matter. They have gas to sell and people want to buy gas. It's a small, befuddled clash of civilizations.

The Iraqi police avoid much involvement. They have to live here. Whether they're corrupt or honest, factional infiltrators or patriots, a kid selling gas from old jugs isn't worth a bullet. They let the Americans be the heavies.

Another traffic jam. In the dusty evening light, markets are thronged and the ovens of shawarma stalls blaze in the early gloom under ragged awnings. It could be any down-at-the-heels city in the Middle East.

As agreed, the police peel off as we pass their compound. Frost's next task is to follow up on the initial investigation at a Sunni mosque where a mullah was assassinated the evening after the Samarra bombing. A Shiite revenge party shot the place up. Far from inviolable, the opposing team's mosques are fair game.

The twilight deepens. The interpreter, a Muslim, takes documentary photos inside the mosque. Frost and two subordinates wait in the courtyard amid locals anxious for justice. Frost does what he needs to do but again avoids making the extravagant promises that adorn Middle Eastern encounters. He hands out chits with rapid-response phone numbers. No guns in the streets—you understand that? If there's trouble, call us and we'll come.

One of the locals claims he called the number and it didn't work. When did he call? The timing doesn't make sense. He's just complaining. All these men can do is complain. Frost lets them have their say, and you can feel the anxiety soften as the light weakens. The lieutenant's restraint and patience are more valuable than superior marksmanship. Amid voluble Iraqis, his taciturn behavior comes off as strength.

Riding toward a linkup with another patrol, we're suddenly cheered by a cluster of teenagers and kids in a Shiite slum. Their parents wave. We're the good guys again. Thanks to Abu Musab al Zarqawi and Muqtada al Sadr, who've given the average Iraqi just enough of a glimpse of hell to convince him of the merits of good behavior.

Another FOB. Weapons cleared. The Humvees grumble through the heavy-vehicle dust that clouds the night. I've been a tourist passing through the collective life of the platoon. Now I've got a ride to another outfit. But Frost still has another set of tasks to complete before his soldiers are done. First Platoon is a small bandage on a vast, wounded country.

It's been a busy day, though uneventful in the grand terms of conflict. Just another patrol in Iraq. "Groundhog Day," as one NCO called it. Far more dust and sweat than glory. Soldiering in the twenty-first century.

Does Iran Want War?

New York Post

April 9, 2006

The most dangerous error we could make in our sharpening confrontation with Iran is to convince ourselves that its leaders will act rationally. Few wars are rooted in dispassionate analysis. Self-delusion sparks most such catastrophes. The power brokers in Tehran may be on the verge of misjudging America's will and resources as profoundly as did the Japanese on December 7, 1941, or al Qa'eda on September 11, 2001.

Stalin misread America's will when he acquiesced in the Korean Communist invasion of the south. So did Castro, when he imagined that he could impose a tyrannical regime on Grenada.

Saddam Hussein misread America, too. Twice. First, when he convinced himself that he could grab Kuwait with impunity and, second, when he did his weapons-of-mass-destruction fan dance. (Bulletin for Iranian President Mahmoud Ahmedinejad: Don't play the I've-got-weapons-you'd-better-be-afraid-of card.)

Given that historical record, what should we expect of a radical-theocrat regime that has no serious grasp of American psychology, that rules an embittered populace it longs to excite and unify, and that believes it's literally on a mission from God?

In recent weeks, Tehran has anxiously publicized its tests of surface-to-surface missiles, of air-to-ground missiles, and, even, of torpedoes. The intended point is that if the shooting starts, Iran can close the Strait of Hormuz to oil tankers—disrupting the global economy—while striking any other target between Israel and Afghanistan. The crucial question is whether the Iranians are still playing at brinksmanship, hoping to spook us into passivity as they build nuclear weapons, or if they've already convinced themselves that a conflict with the United States is inevitable.

Given the closed nature of Iran's ruling clique, it's impossible to know. The most-probable situation is that differing factions within the leadership are at different stages of willingness for war, with some ready to fight and others fearful. Cooler heads may prevail—but "cooler heads" is a relative term in Tehran.

Have the inner-circle Iranian leaders replicated yesteryear's decision-making process of Osama bin Laden and his deputies in their Afghan camps—a hothouse atmosphere in which limited evidence was processed selectively and mutual enablers convinced each other that a few attacks on American landmarks would drive Washington into a global retreat?

Have the Iranians failed to understand the real implications of 9/11? Do they believe that sinking a few oil tankers or even a U.S. Navy ship or two would drive us from the region? Has flawed, impassioned faith led to faulty geostrategic calculations?

The most worrisome possibility is that they may have convinced themselves they can win.

From the Iranian perspective, it may appear that we're fully committed militarily—and they've probably wildly overestimated the "antiwar" constituency in the U.S. Tehran certainly evidences no understanding of the depths of America's military resources, of our decision-making processes—or of NASCAR America's inevitable reaction to attacks on our Navy (or on the fuel supplies for our SUVs).

Whether or not President Ahmadinejad is a madman, he speaks like one. He has no past experience of global statecraft and no grasp of the different mental and moral structures of other civilizations. The extent to which his ability to calculate objectively has been suppressed by a psychological addiction to religious extremism remains an open question. But the portents look bleak. What might the Iranians expect, if brinksmanship fails? Or from an impulsive leap from peace to war?

The extremists in Tehran actually may believe that they could win a military exchange, stymie our Navy in the Gulf, interrupt oil exports, and make any conflict so costly to us and to the world economy that we'd be forced to back down. They doubtless count on support from Beijing and Moscow—much as Saddam did.

Their calculations would be devastatingly wrong.

We can hope otherwise, but Iran's leaders may already have concluded that war is unavoidable—and even desirable, for religious, regional, and domestic reasons. With Tehran pursuing nukes, parading its military, disrupting Iraq, and issuing statements so rabid that they alarm even the regime's foreign backers, it's time to prepare for the worst.

Should Tehran ignite a combat exchange, we need to ensure not only that Iran's nuclear-weapons program is crippled, but that its broader capabilities are shattered.

Militarily, it will be time for our Air Force to prove its worth, with the Navy in support. Iran's recent experience of conflict is of attrition-based land warfare. But there's no need for us to employ conventional ground forces inside Iran (special operations troops are another matter). We'll have to watch the Iraqi and Afghan borders, but our fight would be waged from the air and from the sea.

If we're pulled into war, we need to strike hard and fast—before Iran's allies can make mischief in international forums. We should destroy as much of Tehran's nuclear infrastructure as possible, eliminate its air force and air defenses, and wreck its naval facilities beyond repair—no matter the collateral damage. The madmen in Tehran must pay an unbearable price.

The results within Iran would be unpredictable. Fiercely nationalistic, the country's core Persian population might unify behind the regime, setting back our hopes for an eventual rapprochement with a post-Islamist government.

Alternatively, the regime may be weaker than we think and could topple of its own weight. Or it may continue to muddle through miserably for years. Iran's military could remain loyal to the mullahs or, sufficiently battered, might turn upon them. We don't know what would happen because the Iranians themselves don't know. The variables and dynamics are simply incalculable.

But a half-hearted military response to Iranian aggression would only strengthen the confidence of our enemies and invite future confrontations.

We pulled too many punches in Operation Iraqi Freedom, and now we're paying the price. If Tehran drags us into war, we should make the conflict so devastating and painful that even our allies are stunned.

Blood Borders:
How a Better Middle East
Would Look

Armed Forces Journal

June 2006

International borders are never completely just. But the degree of injustice they inflict upon those whom frontiers force together or separate makes an enormous difference—often the difference between freedom and oppression, tolerance and atrocity, the rule of law and terrorism, or even peace and war.

The most arbitrary and distorted borders in the world are in Africa and the Middle East. Drawn by self-interested Europeans (who have had sufficient trouble defining their own frontiers), Africa's borders continue to provoke the deaths of millions of local inhabitants. But the unjust borders in the Middle East—to borrow from Churchill—generate more trouble than can be consumed locally.

While the Middle East has far more problems than dysfunctional borders alone—from cultural stagnation through scandalous inequality to deadly religious extremism—the greatest taboo in striving to understand the region's comprehensive failure isn't Islam but the awful-but-sacrosanct international boundaries worshipped by our own diplomats.

Of course, no adjustment of borders, however draconian, could make every minority in the Middle East happy. In some instances, ethnic and religious groups live intermingled and have intermarried. Elsewhere, reunions based on blood or belief might not prove quite as joyous as their current proponents expect. The boundaries

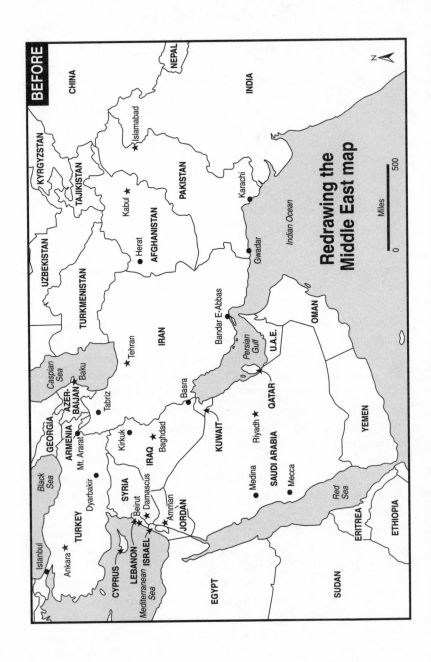

Redrawing the
Middle East map

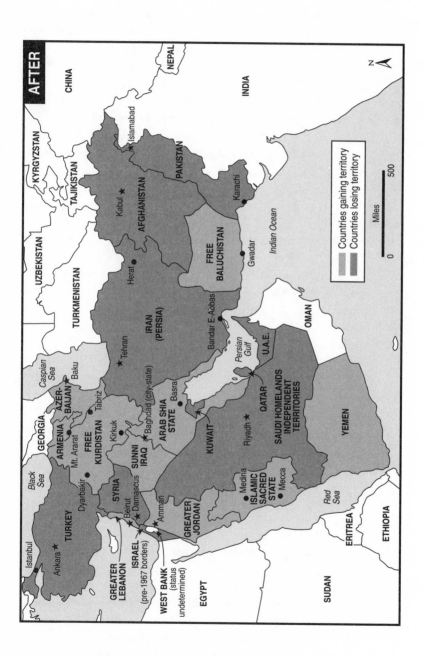

projected in the maps accompanying this article redress the wrongs suffered by the most significant "cheated" population groups, such as the Kurds, Baluch, and Arab Shi'a, but still fail to account adequately for Middle Eastern Christians, Bahais, Ismailis, Naqshbandis, and many other smaller minorities. And one haunting wrong can never be redressed with a reward of territory: the genocide perpetrated against the Armenians by the dying Ottoman Empire.

Yet, for all the injustices the borders reimagined here leave unaddressed, without such major boundary revisions, we shall never see a more peaceful Middle East.

Even those who abhor the topic of altering borders would be well served to engage in an exercise that attempts to conceive a fairer, if still imperfect, amendment of national boundaries between the Bosporus and the Indus. Accepting that international statecraft has never developed effective tools—short of war—for readjusting faulty borders, a mental effort to grasp the Middle East's "organic" frontiers nonetheless helps us understand the extent of the difficulties we face and will continue to face. We are dealing with colossal, man-made deformities that will not stop generating hatred and violence until they are corrected.

As for those who refuse to "think the unthinkable," declaring that boundaries must not change and that's that, it pays to remember that boundaries have never stopped changing through the centuries. Borders have never been static, and many frontiers, from Congo through Kosovo to the Caucasus, are changing even now (as ambassadors and special representatives avert their eyes to study the shine on their wingtips).

Oh, and one other dirty little secret from 5,000 years of history: Ethnic cleansing works.

Begin with the border issue most sensitive to American readers: For Israel to have any hope of living in reasonable peace with its neighbors, it will have to return to its pre-1967 borders—with essential local adjustments for legitimate security concerns. But the issue of the territories surrounding Jerusalem, a city stained with thousands of years of blood, may prove intractable beyond our lifetimes. Where all parties have turned their god into a real-estate tycoon, literal turf battles have a tenacity unrivaled by mere greed for oil wealth or ethnic squabbles. So let us set aside this single overstudied issue and turn to those that are studiously ignored.

The most glaring injustice in the notoriously unjust lands between the Balkan Mountains and the Himalayas is the absence of an independent Kurdish state. There are between twenty-seven million and thirty-six million Kurds living in contiguous regions in the Middle East (the figures are imprecise because no state has ever allowed an honest census). Greater than the population of present-day Iraq, even the lower figure makes the Kurds the world's largest ethnic group without a state of its own. Worse, Kurds have been oppressed by every government controlling the hills and mountains where they've lived since Xenophon's day.

The U.S. and its coalition partners missed a glorious chance to begin to correct this injustice after Baghdad's fall. A Frankenstein's monster of a state sewn together from ill-fitting parts, Iraq should have been divided into three smaller states immediately. We failed from cowardice and lack of vision, bullying Iraq's Kurds into supporting the new Iraqi government—which they do wistfully as a quid pro quo for our good will. But were a free plebiscite to be held, make no mistake: Nearly 100 percent of Iraq's Kurds would vote for independence.

As would the long-suffering Kurds of Turkey, who have endured decades of violent military oppression and a decades-long demotion to "mountain Turks" in an effort to eradicate their identity. While the Kurdish plight at Ankara's hands has eased somewhat over the past decade, the repression recently intensified again and the eastern fifth of Turkey should be viewed as occupied territory. As for the Kurds of Syria and Iran, they, too, would rush to join an independent Kurdistan if they could. The refusal by the world's legitimate democracies to champion Kurdish independence is a human-rights sin of omission far worse than the clumsy, minor sins of commission that routinely excite our media. And by the way: A Free Kurdistan, stretching from Diyarbakir through Tabriz, would be the most pro-Western state between Bulgaria and Japan.

A just alignment in the region would leave Iraq's three Sunni-majority provinces as a truncated state that might eventually choose to unify with a Syria that loses its littoral to a Mediterranean-oriented Greater Lebanon: Phoenicia reborn. The Shi'a south of old Iraq would form the basis of an Arab Shi'a State rimming much of the Persian Gulf. Jordan would retain its current territory, with some southward expansion at Saudi expense. For its part, the unnatural state of Saudi Arabia would suffer as great a dismantling as Pakistan.

A root cause of the broad stagnation in the Muslim world is the Saudi royal family's treatment of Mecca and Medina as its fiefdom. With Islam's holiest shrines under the police-state control of one of the world's most bigoted and oppressive regimes—a regime that commands vast, unearned oil wealth—the Saudis have been able to project their Wahhabi vision of a disciplinarian, intolerant faith far beyond their borders. The rise of the Saudis to wealth and, consequently, influence has been the worst thing to happen to the Muslim world as a whole since the time of the Prophet and the worst thing to happen to Arabs since the Ottoman (if not the Mongol) conquest.

While non-Muslims could not effect a change in the control of Islam's holy cities, imagine how much healthier the Muslim world might become were Mecca and Medina ruled by a rotating council representative of the world's major Muslim schools and movements in an Islamic Sacred State—a sort of Muslim super-Vatican—where the future of a great faith might be debated rather than merely decreed. True justice—which we might not like—would also give Saudi Arabia's coastal oil fields to the Shi'a Arabs who populate that subregion, while a southeastern quadrant would go to Yemen. Confined to a rump Saudi Homelands Independent Territory around Riyadh, the House of Saud would be capable of far less mischief toward Islam and the world.

Iran, a state with madcap boundaries, would lose a great deal of territory to Unified Azerbaijan, Free Kurdistan, the Arab Shi'a State, and Free Baluchistan but would gain the provinces around Herat in today's Afghanistan—a region with a historical and linguistic affinity for Persia. Iran would, in effect, become an ethnic Persian state again, with the most difficult question being whether or not it should keep the port of Bandar Abbas or surrender it to the Arab Shi'a State.

What Afghanistan would lose to Persia in the west, it would gain in the east, as Pakistan's Northwest Frontier tribes would be reunited with their Afghan brethren (the point of this exercise is not to draw maps as we would like them but as local populations would prefer them). Pakistan, another unnatural state, would also lose its Baluch territory to Free Baluchistan. The remaining "natural" Pakistan would lie entirely east of the Indus, except for a westward spur near Karachi.

The city-states of the United Arab Emirates would have a mixed fate—as they probably will in reality. Some might be incorporated in the Arab Shia State ringing much of the Persian Gulf (a state more likely to evolve as a counterbalance to, rather than an ally of, Persian Iran). Since all puritanical cultures are hypocritical, Dubai, of necessity, would be allowed to retain its playground status for rich debauchees. Kuwait would remain within its current borders, as would Oman.

In each case, this hypothetical redrawing of boundaries reflects ethnic affinities and religious communalism—in some cases, both. Of course, if we could wave a magic wand and amend the borders under discussion, we would certainly prefer to do so selectively. Yet, studying the revised map, in contrast to the map illustrating today's boundaries, offers some sense of the great wrongs borders drawn by Frenchmen and Englishmen in the twentieth century did to a region struggling to emerge from the humiliations and defeats of the nineteenth century.

Correcting borders to reflect the will of the people may be impossible. For now. But given time—and the inevitable attendant bloodshed—new and natural borders will emerge. Babylon has fallen more than once.

Meanwhile, our men and women in uniform will continue to fight for security from terrorism, for the prospect of democracy, and for access to oil supplies in a region that is destined to fight itself. The current human divisions and forced unions between Ankara and Karachi, taken together with the region's self-inflicted woes, form as perfect a breeding ground for religious extremism, a culture of blame, and the recruitment of terrorists as anyone could design. Where men and women look ruefully at their borders, they look enthusiastically for enemies.

From the world's oversupply of terrorists to its paucity of energy supplies, the current deformations of the Middle East promise a worsening, not an improving, situation. In a region where only the worst aspects of nationalism ever took hold and where the most debased aspects of religion threaten to dominate a disappointed faith, the U.S., its allies, and, above all, our armed forces can look for crises without end. While Iraq may provide a counterexample of hope—if we do not quit its soil prematurely—the rest of this vast region offers worsening problems on almost every front.

If the borders of the greater Middle East cannot be amended to reflect the natural ties of blood and faith, we may take it as an article of faith that a portion of the bloodshed in the region will continue to be our own.

WHO WINS, WHO LOSES

Winners
Afghanistan
Arab Shi'a State
Armenia
Azerbaijan
Free Baluchistan
Free Kurdistan
Iran
Islamic Sacred State
Jordan
Lebanon
Yemen

Losers
Afghanistan
Iran
Iraq
Israel
Kuwait
Pakistan
Qatar
Saudi Arabia
Syria
Turkey
United Arab Emirates

Kill, Don't Capture

New York Post

July 10, 2006

The British military defines experience as the ability to recognize a mistake the second time you make it. By that standard, we should be very experienced in dealing with captured terrorists, since we've made the same mistake again and again.

Violent Islamist extremists must be killed on the battlefield. Only in the rarest cases should they be taken prisoner. Few have serious intelligence value. And, once captured, there's no way to dispose of them.

Killing terrorists during a conflict isn't barbaric or immoral—or even illegal. We've imposed rules upon ourselves that have no historical or judicial precedent. We haven't been stymied by others, but by ourselves. The oft-cited, seldom-read Geneva and Hague Conventions define legal combatants as those who visibly identify themselves by wearing uniforms or distinguishing insignia (the latter provision covers honorable partisans—but no badges or armbands, no protection).

Those who wear civilian clothes to ambush soldiers or collect intelligence are assassins and spies—beyond the pale of law. Traditionally, those who masquerade as civilians in order to kill legal combatants have been executed promptly, without trial. Severity, not sloppy leftist pandering, kept warfare within some decent bounds at least part of the time. But we have reached a point at which the rules apply only to us, while our enemies are permitted unrestricted freedom. The present situation encourages our enemies to behave wantonly, while crippling our attempts to deal with terror.

Consider today's norm: A terrorist in civilian clothes can explode an IED, killing and maiming American troops or innocent civilians, then demand humane treatment if captured—and the media will step in as his champion. A disguised insurgent can shoot his rockets, throw his grenades, empty his magazines, kill and wound our troops, and then, out of ammo, raise his hands and demand three hots and a cot while he invents tales of abuse.

Conferring unprecedented legal status upon these murderous transnational outlaws is unnecessary, unwise, and ultimately suicidal. It exalts monsters. And it provides the anti-American pack with living vermin to anoint as victims, if not heroes.

Isn't it time we gave our critics what they're asking for? Let's solve the "unjust" imprisonment problem, once and for all. No more Guantanamos! Every terrorist mission should be a suicide mission. With our help.

We need to clarify the rules of conflict. But integrity and courage have fled Washington. Nobody will state bluntly that we're in a fight for our lives, that war is hell, and that we must do what it takes to win.

Our enemies will remind us of what's necessary, though. When we've been punished horribly enough, we'll come to our senses and do what must be done. This isn't an argument for a murderous rampage, but its opposite. We must kill our enemies with discrimination. But we do need to kill them. A corpse is a corpse: The media's rage dissipates with the stench.

But an imprisoned terrorist is a strategic liability.

Nor should we ever mistreat captured soldiers or insurgents who adhere to standing conventions. On the contrary, we should enforce policies that encourage our enemies to identify themselves according to the laws of war. Ambiguity works to their advantage, never to ours.

Our policy toward terrorists and insurgents in civilian clothing should be straightforward and public: Surrender before firing a shot or taking hostile action toward our troops, and we'll regard you as a legal prisoner. But once you've pulled a trigger, thrown a grenade, or detonated a bomb, you will be killed. On the battlefield and on the spot.

Isn't that common sense? It also happens to conform to the traditional conduct of war between civilized nations. Ignorant of history, we've talked ourselves into folly. And by the way: How have the terrorists treated the uniformed American soldiers they've captured? According to the Geneva Convention?

Sadly, even our military has been infected by political correctness. Some of my former peers will wring their hands and babble about "winning hearts and minds." But we'll never win the hearts and minds of terrorists. And if we hope to win the minds, if not the hearts, of foreign populations, we must be willing to kill the violent, lawless fraction of a fraction of a percent of the population determined to terrorize the rest.

Ravaged societies crave and need strict order. Soft policies may appear to work in the short term, but they fail overwhelmingly in the longer term. Wherever we've tried sweetness and light in Iraq, it has only worked as long as our troops were present—after which the terrorists returned and slaughtered the beneficiaries of our good intentions.

If you wish to defend the many, you must be willing to kill the few.

For now, we're stuck with a situation in which the hardcore terrorists in Guantanamo are "innocent victims" even to our fair-weather allies. In Iraq, our troops capture bomb makers only to learn they've been dumped back on the block.

It is not humane to spare fanatical murderers. It is not humane to play into our enemy's hands. And it is not humane to endanger our troops out of political correctness. Instead of worrying over trumped-up atrocities in Iraq (the media give credence to any claim made by terrorists), we should stop apologizing and take a stand. That means firm rules for the battlefield, not Gumby-speak intended to please critics who'll never be satisfied by anything America does.

The ultimate act of humanity in the War on Terror is to win. To do so, we must kill our enemies wherever we encounter them. He who commits an act of terror forfeits every right he once possessed.

Back to Baghdad

New York Post

July 27, 2006

When I visited Baghdad in March, there was no civil war. There is no civil war in Iraq today. But it's beginning to look as if there might be one tomorrow.

Something vital has changed. In Baghdad.

For three years, the violence was about political power in post-Saddam Iraq. Sunni-Arab insurgents and Shi'a militias may have been on opposite sides, but the conflict was only a religious war for the foreign terrorists. And the fighting wasn't between the masses of Sunnis and Shi'as—who were the victims of all sides.

Now it's different. The unwillingness of the Iraqi government to take on the sectarian death squads slaughtering civilians is polarizing Iraq (while the Kurds build up their own peaceful slice of the country as fast as they can).

Political violence with a religious undertone is becoming outright religious violence. The difference is crucial. The earlier fighting was over who should govern. Increasingly, it's about who should define Allah's will on earth. Nothing could be more ominous.

Political struggles may be resolved through compromise. Historically, only immense bloodletting and the exhaustion of one side or both lead to even a bitter, temporary peace in religious conflicts. Leaders may bargain over who runs the ministry of health, but they won't horse-trade over conflicting visions of the divine. When men believe they hear a command from their god, they go deaf to other voices.

Instead of working aggressively toward a solution, key elements within the Iraqi government have become part of the problem. Responsible for the police and public order, the Interior Ministry has failed utterly. Instead of behaving impartially, Shi'a-dominated police units provide death squads to retaliate against Sunni insurgents. As a result, more Sunnis back the insurgents in self-defense. More Shi'as die. More Sunnis die. The downward spiral accelerates.

This is bad news for our troops in Iraq. For the first time, we may face a problem we have no hope of fixing. We can defeat the terrorists. We can defeat a political insurgency. But when our forces find themselves caught between two religious factions, the only hope is to pick a side and stick to it, despite the atrocities it inevitably will commit.

We're not ready for that, psychologically or morally. Yet. We'll try to be honest brokers. But men on a violent mission from God have no respect for mediators.

We helped make this mess. Instead of relentlessly destroying terrorists and insurgents, we tried to wage war gently to please the media. We always let the bad guys off the ropes—and apologized when they showed the press their rope burns. We passed up repeated chances to kill Muqtada al Sadr and break his Mahdi Army militia. We did what was easiest in the short term, not what was essential for the long term.

Now the only way to avoid an outright civil war is for our troops and the Iraqi army to break the sectarian militias in a head-on fight. The media will howl, and we'll see a spike in American casualties. But it's our own fault. We put off going to the dentist until the tooth rotted. Now it's going to hurt.

The alternative would be to let Iraq fail. And we need to ponder that possibility honestly. While it's far too early to give up, we need to "think the unthinkable." We can force the Iraqis to do many things, but we can't force them to succeed. If the jealousy, corruption, and partisanship in the Iraqi government prevent the country's leaders from dealing forcefully with Iraq problems, we should no longer sacrifice our troops.

Here's the brutal reality: If Iraq is destined to become yet another monument to Arab failure, there could be far worse outcomes than a bloody civil war—as long as our troops are out of it. We should be drawing up contingency plans to move a reinforced division and adequate airpower to the Kurdish provinces in the north, to withdraw the remainder of our forces to the south, and then to let Iraq's Sunni Arabs and Shi'as go at it.

Yes, Iran and Syria would be drawn in, through proxies or directly. Not necessarily a bad result, to be frank. At present, Iran and Syria ally against us. An Iraqi civil war would drag them into a military confrontation. Bad news for Hezbollah, not for us.

Let's raise another "impossible" issue: If the Arab world can't sustain one rule-of-law democracy—after we gave Iraq a unique opportunity—might it be a useful strategic outcome to watch Arabs and Persians, Shi'a and Sunni, slaughtering each other again? Just don't try to referee the death match.

Meanwhile, our troops are doing all they can—and our cause remains just and good. Iraq could still succeed. It's too early to walk away. But the Iraqis have to get their act together. We can't keep the training wheels on the bicycle forever. If they won't unite to fight for their own country, we'll have to accept that our noble effort failed.

We should never publicize a timetable for a troop withdrawal, but here's what President Bush should have told Iraq's prime minister, Nouri al-Maliki, yesterday: "You are failing your country. We'll give you six months. If your government can't produce a unified response to sectarian violence that treats all sides impartially, we'll withdraw our troops and our support. Then you can fight it out among yourselves."

Failure in Iraq would be a victory for terror. In the short run. But the terrorists might then find themselves mired in a long and crippling struggle. An Iraqi civil war might become al Qa'eda's Vietnam, not ours. One other thing our president should tell Iraq's top leaders: "If you fail your country, the United States will be embarrassed. But we'll remain the greatest power on earth. Few, if any, of you will survive the catastrophe you brought upon your people."

Arabs' Last Chance

New York Post

August 24, 2006

With the best intentions, President Bush recently declared that it's racist to say that Arabs can't build democracies.

Is it?

I made the same claim in the run-up to the first Iraqi elections, when Western leftists desperate for Iraq to fail tried to block the vote by claiming that the population wasn't ready.

Iraqis deserved their chance. They got it. They voted. Three times. Each time along confessional or ethnic lines. They elected ward bosses, not national leaders. We could have skipped the balloting and apportioned legislative seats by population shares. Iraq doesn't have a democracy in any meaningful sense. It isn't even a nation. Iraqis didn't vote for freedom. They voted for revenge against each other.

In the immediate aftermath of Operation Iraqi Freedom, I argued that the only realistic solution was to break Iraq into three pieces. What we lacked the guts to do, elections have done. The pretense that an Iraqi national identity exists or ever will exist can be sustained no longer.

Iraq doesn't have a government. It has a collection of warlords, demagogues, and thieves with official titles. It's time to put our own politics aside and face reality: If Iraq's elected leaders won't stop looting their country long enough to pull together and defeat the foreign terrorists, internal insurgents, and militias killing Iraqis, we should not ask our troops to defend them.

Iraqi democracy hasn't yet failed entirely. But it looks as if it might. President Bush needs to face that possibility. Managing the regional and global consequences will be his responsibility. We will have to fight on elsewhere—with more realism and, regrettably, less idealism. The fools who hope Iraq will fail will face more wars, not fewer.

Meanwhile, the test for Iraq's elected government is straightforward: Can it excite Iraqis to a spirit of mortal sacrifice in defense of a constitutional system? The terrorists, insurgents, and militiamen will die for their beliefs. If other Iraqis will not risk their lives—in decisive numbers—to seize their unique chance at freedom, there is no hope.

And Iraq is the entire Arab world's last hope.

As for the charge of racism leveled at skeptics of the Arab propensity for democracy, it would be true if the discussion were about individuals. Arabs in the United States are as capable of functioning within a democratic system as anyone else. They're just as American as any other citizens—because their families escaped the Middle East.

Arab states are another story: Their social, political, economic, and cultural structures leave them catastrophically uncompetitive with the developed world. Societies divided down the middle by religion, inhibited by tribal loyalties, and conditioned to accept corruption can't build healthy democracies.

Above all, societies and cultures that refuse to accept responsibility for their own failures can't build democracies.

As difficult as it can be to discern in the hype-and-gripe internet age, our own system works because we shoulder the burden of our errors, seek to understand what went wrong—and fix the problem (the same may be said of Israel, the only successful democracy in the Middle East).

A culture of blame prevents moral, social, and political progress. This is a self-help universe. The nonsensical Arab insistence that all Arab problems are the fault of America and Israel (or the Crusades) ignores the fact that Arab civilization has been in decline for 700 years—and has been in utter disarray for the last 200.

This is a homemade failure. Through their own choices, cherished beliefs, values, and norms, Arabs have condemned themselves to strategic incompetence. No society that oppresses women, denies advancement on merit even to men, indulges in fantastic hypocrisy, wallows in corruption, undervalues secular learning, reduces its god to a nasty disciplinarian, and comforts itself with conspiracy theories will ever compete with us.

The question has been asked before: Despite the massive influx of petrodollars over a half-century, where are the great Arab universities, the research institutes, the cutting-edge industries, the efficient, humane governments, the enlightened societies? The Arab world has behaved as irresponsibly as a drunk who won the lottery, squandering vast wealth and creating nothing beyond a few urban theme parks.

Even the seeming bright spots, such as Lebanon, aren't true democracies. The Lebanese voted for clans, tribes, and faiths, not for policies and programs. The Gulf emirates are mere playgrounds for Saudi debauchees and face the rise of a nuclear Iran. In Saudi Arabia, religious hatred has long surpassed oil as the number one export.

Surely, if Arab societies were capable of producing and sustaining democracies, we would see at least one. Where are the massive rallies in favor of tolerance, that indispensable lubricant of democracy? Where are the militias fighting for constitutional government? Where are the insurgencies demanding female enfranchisement?

It would be racist to claim that Arabs are genetically inferior. It is simply the truth to admit that Arab societies are volatile disasters.

Arab terrorism isn't about redressing wrongs. It's about revenge on a successful civilization that left the dungeon cultures of the Middle East in the dust.

We've done what we could in Iraq, and we've done it nobly. We should not withdraw our troops precipitously, but the clock is ticking. It's now up to the Iraqis to succeed—or become yet another pathetic Arab failure. If Iraqis are unwilling to grasp the opportunity our soldiers and Marines bought them with American blood, it's their tragedy, not ours.

We did the right thing by deposing Saddam Hussein. The Arab Middle East needed one last chance. Iraq is it. If Iraqi democracy fails, there will be no hope, whatsoever, for the Arab world.

Afghan Reality

New York Post

August 31, 2006

It's fascinating to watch Anglo–American leftists (those champions of human rights and freedom) welcoming every Taliban attack and fantasizing of a Western defeat. But the rest of us deal with reality.

And Afghanistan's reality is that things are going as well as any sane person could expect.

The get-Bush-and-Blair partisans who yearn for Afghanistan (and Iraq) to fail, no matter the human or strategic cost, impose impossible standards for success, then insist we're being defeated when their standards aren't met. It's a self-licking ice-cream cone straight from the Stalinist dairy.

The reality is that Afghanistan will always be . . . Afghanistan.

The relevant question is straightforward: "Is it a better Afghanistan today than under the Taliban?" Of course, the answer is an emphatic "Yes!" Afghanistan is never going to resemble the liberal-arts faculty at Columbia. It's a country of jealous clans patched together with uneasy compromises and lubricated with lies (OK, maybe it does resemble a liberal-arts faculty . . .). Kabul long was the refuge of the "enlightened" classes, while the countryside belonged to the mud and the mullahs.

That isn't going to change in our lifetimes. All Afghans, but especially the Pathan majority, will continue to cling to their folkways. Women's liberation isn't scheduled for an early arrival in the faith-choked valleys of eastern Afghanistan, nor will Herat, in the west, soon lead the world in scientific research.

Heroin-poppy cultivation is a serious problem in the south. Warlords—the traditional arbiters of power in the provinces—dominate the north. And yes, the Taliban is a deadly annoyance again—it represents a small but tenacious constituency.

But isn't Afghanistan, urban or rural, better off now than under Taliban rule? In urban areas and even in parts of the countryside, women can at least catch their breath and invoke legal protections—and sometimes the law actually protects them, which is an improvement over the female-hating barbarism of the Taliban.

Afghanistan is still often unjust (to both sexes), but the situation is far better than it was a decade ago in the heyday of public stonings and executions as spectator sport.

Isn't it better to have al Qa'eda's remnants skulking amid remote mountains on the Pakistani side of the border than to have them enjoying the free run of an entire country? Isn't it better if at least some Afghan children (including girls) can get an education that goes beyond rote recitations from religious tomes?

Isn't it better to have the Taliban and al Qa'eda scheming to return to the country's most backward provinces rather than sharing power in Kabul and designing attacks on Manhattan and Washington?

Afghanistan's problems won't disappear in our lifetimes. But the positive changes we wrought or enabled represent an enormous win for decency, dignity, and freedom—despite pestering Taliban attacks on society's edges.

The real worry isn't Afghanistan, but Pakistan, where the Musharraf regime sees no alternative to a two-faced strategy that aims at placating the West (especially America) while continuing to hedge its long-term bets by clandestinely supporting the Taliban.

And this is where it gets interesting: Recently, Pakistani intelligence tipped off the British about the exploding-shampoo plot to bring down multiple transatlantic flights. Why did Pakistan's Inter-Service Intelligence (ISI) boys blow the whistle on the al Qa'eda clones?

For multiple reasons.

First, as Washington and London move closer to New Delhi, Islamabad needs to do all it can to prove itself as an indispensable ally in the War on Terror. Giving up al Qa'eda wannabes in the West is a cheap way to do it, since the Pakistani government has no great affection for al Qa'eda, an interloper with roots on the other side of the Persian Gulf.

If President Pervez Musharraf could hand over Osama today, he'd do it. Al Qa'eda is in the way of Pakistan's long-term policy—a competitor, not an ally. And it draws too much attention to the region.

The Taliban is something else entirely. Experts argue over whether it was created or merely nurtured by ISI operatives, but the consensus is that by the time the Talibs reached Kabul, the group was backed by, equipped by, advised by, and allied to Pakistan's security establishment.

The Pakistanis viewed the Taliban as an ideal tool to achieve two things: First, to bring order to lawless post-Soviet Afghanistan; second, to provide desperately needed strategic depth in the event of a war with India. The Islamist card played well in Peshawar, too.

Today, Pakistan still supports the Taliban, if quietly and within careful limits. The issue of strategic depth hasn't gone away, and the Pakistanis are certain that, sooner or later, America will lose interest and the NATO presence will wither—but India will still be right there on Pakistan's border, big and nuclear (New Delhi has also made overtures to the government of President Hamid Karzai in Kabul). Having the Taliban ready in a back pocket just makes sense to Islamabad.

So Pakistan is playing both a short game and a long one. It cooperates with us against al Qa'eda—and doesn't want to take the rap for another major terror attack in the West. At the same time, it makes sure that the Taliban has "survival rations." It doesn't expect the Talibs to return to Kabul anytime soon, but it does expect to see a Taliban-dominated coalition in Afghanistan eventually.

That mustn't happen. And if we don't walk away, it won't.

Meanwhile, we can be satisfied and proud that our actions have made a dirt-poor, deeply flawed feudal state on the other side of the world a better place for the average human being within its borders.

Oh, and we ripped the guts out of al Qa'eda, too.

9/11: Five Years On

New York Post

September 11, 2006

The biggest story since 9/11 is that there hasn't been another 9/11. According to our hysterical media culture, everything's always going wrong. The truth is that we've gotten the big things right.

On this fifth anniversary of the cold-blooded murder of thousands of Americans by Islamist fanatics, it's tempting to settle for grand rhetoric honoring our dead and damning our enemies. But the greatest tribute to those lost on that September morning is what we've since achieved.

In this vile political season, with those on the left suggesting that our president's a worse threat to civilization than Islamist terror, the rest of us should just review what's happened—and what hasn't: Islamist fanatics have not been able to stage a single additional attack on our homeland. For all its growing pains, our homeland-security effort worked. In this long war with religion-poisoned madmen, the most important proof of success is what doesn't happen—and we haven't been struck again. Wail as loudly as they can, the president's critics can't change that self-evident truth.

Eventually, some terrorists will get through. That's just the law of averages. But we've enjoyed five golden years of safety and prosperity, thanks to our men and women in uniform and those who serve at all levels of government.

Al Qa'eda is badly crippled. While the terror organization and its affiliates remain a deadly threat, al Qa'eda is no longer the powerful, unchallenged outfit it was in the years of Clinton-era cowardice. Instead of holding court, Osama bin Laden's a fugitive. Almost all of his deputies are dead or imprisoned. The rest are hunted men.

And yes, we'll get Osama. Those who whine that we haven't offer no specific solutions themselves—and they'd like us to forget how long it took to apprehend criminals such as the Unabomber here at home. Al Qa'eda can still kill, but its power has been reduced by an order of magnitude.

Terrorists no longer operate in freedom. Even Europeans have begun to awaken to the nature of Islamist fanaticism. One terror plot after another has been foiled. Those that succeeded proved counterproductive, mobilizing antiterrorist sentiment. The world hasn't fully come to grips with the threat, but the progress has been remarkable. The terrorists are now on the defensive.

Our enemies fear our military again. Despite tragic mistakes in Iraq, we've already accomplished one crucial mission neglected for a generation: We've resurrected the reputation of the American soldier.

After our maddening retreats from Beirut and Mogadishu, and the Clinton administration's unwillingness to retaliate meaningfully after terrorist attacks, Islamist extremists concluded—and bragged—that Americans were cowards who wouldn't fight and hid behind technology. Well, Iraq proved that our troops don't run, but fight more fiercely than any other soldiers on earth. Now it's the terrorists who rely on stand-off weapons—roadside bombs. They're terrified of taking on our forces in combat. The importance of regaining our street cred can't be stressed enough.

Iraq has become al Qa'eda's Vietnam. No end of lies have been broadcast about our liberation of Iraq and Afghanistan "creating more terrorists." The terrorists were already there, recruited during the decades we looked away. Our arrival on their turf just brought them out of the woodwork.

As for Iraq, Osama & Co. realized full well how high we'd raised the stakes. They had to fight to prevent the emergence of a Middle Eastern democracy. As a result, they've thrown in their reserves—who've been slaughtered by our soldiers and Marines.

The media obsesses on the price of this fight for us, but the terrorists have been forced to pay a terrible cost in trained fighters—

while alienating fellow Muslims with their tactics. Pundits will argue forever over whether deposing Saddam was a diversion from the War on Terror, but the proof of its relevance—even if unexpected—is the unaffordable cost we've forced on al Qa'eda.

We've achieved new levels of domestic security without compromising civil liberties. Frisking granny at the airport may be silly, but (despite the lies of the left) Americans continue to live in unprecedented freedom. The Patriot Act and other measures worked—without harming the rights of a single law-abiding citizen. The only people who lost out were the terrorists and their supporters. We should be applauding the feds, not running them down.

America is much stronger today than we were five years ago. We have new homeland-security structures up and running, improved intelligence agencies—and the most experienced military in the world.

The dishonest nature of domestic politics and the media's irresponsibility obscure the fact that no one—not even the terrorists—now believes that our enemies can win a global victory. The terrorists are no longer fighting for conquest—they're running a salvage operation.

Does that mean everything's perfect? Of course not. As noted above, some terrorists will manage to hit us again. But if attempt No. 500 succeeds, it doesn't mean it wasn't worth stopping the other 499. Yet, after the next attack, we'll hear no end of trash talk about how the War on Terror "failed."

The truth is that we're winning. Hands down. We just can't afford to revert to yesteryear's weakness and indecision.

What should we worry about? Plenty. First, the unscrupulous nature of those in the media who always discover a dark cloud in the brightest silver lining. They're terror's cheerleaders. Second, the rabid partisanship infecting our political system—when "getting Bush" is more important than protecting our country, something's wrong.

A third concern is the internet's empowerment of fanatics, conspiracy theorists, and all of the really good haters—on both extremes of the political spectrum. If there's one thing all responsible citizens—conservative, centrist, or liberal—should agree on, it's that all extremism is un-American.

On this September morning, let us dedicate ourselves to living for the values the hijackers feared: freedom, tolerance, human dignity—and the invincible strength of our democratic society. The greatest tribute we can pay to the dead of 9/11 is to be good Americans.

Is Pakistan Coming Apart?

Armchair General

September 2006

The comprehensive failure of democracy. Immeasurable corruption. Terrorism, for domestic use and export. Multiple separatist movements. Ethnic and religious strife. Bitter poverty. Mass illiteracy. Rural slavery. A powerful, unsavory intelligence service. A military clamping a collapsing state together. And nuclear weapons.

That's Pakistan. Our (part-time) ally in the war on terror.

The country's boundaries remain intact on the maps, but the central government has ever less control over rebellious provinces. The largest city, Karachi, is a chaos of gangland neighborhoods. The military government presses on with its bankrupting cold war against India in Kashmir while Baluch insurgents rampage at Pakistan's other end.

The Northwest Frontier—where senior terrorists hang their turbans—has never really been under government control. The tribes remain defiant and more closely bound to relatives in Afghanistan than to the radically different cultures of the Punjab and Sindh across the Indus. Sunni Muslims bomb Shi'a mosques. Minority Shi'as assassinate Sunnis. Both murder Christians. In Karachi, Muslims whose elders fled India, at partition, believe the government has betrayed them. Educated Pakistanis flee.

The notorious Inter-Services Intelligence (ISI) agency stages its own shadow plays. The ISI helped create the Taliban in 1990s Afghanistan, and elements within the intel service continue clandestine support of Taliban remnants—and possibly of al Qa'eda. The generals look away, reasoning that America and NATO won't always be in Afghanistan, but Afghanistan will always be next door to Pakistan. The military sees its struggling neighbor as potentially providing strategic depth in a war with India. For its part, the ISI is determined to be the ultimate kingmaker in Kabul.

As for the possibility of another war with India, both countries have come closer than the world realizes to pulling the nuclear trigger. Pakistan has a good early-twentieth-century infantry army that's repeatedly been trounced by India's mid-twentieth-century industrial-age military. Were demagogues on either side of the border to provoke a war, Pakistan would quickly feel compelled to go nuclear.

Meanwhile, the Musharraf regime continues to cooperate fitfully with the U.S. in the pursuit of terrorists. After surviving several assassination attempts, Musharraf doesn't care much for al Qa'eda, but not all of his subordinates share his moderate views. The situation is complicated by the difficulty of hunting terrorists in the rugged backcountry along the Afghan border—some of the world's most difficult terrain and home to tribes whose core competency is killing other human beings.

Pakistan's population has surged to almost 160 million, but its annual GDP of $104 billion remains barely 15 percent of Mexico's—whose 105 million citizens we view as impoverished, although their per capita income is ten times that of the average Pakistani's. Pakistan can't produce enough jobs, enough schools, enough clinics, or enough law and order. Its previous "democratic" governments stole everything in sight (and ravaged the environment) while pandering to religious extremists. Now the country's slowly dissolving, with the military the last functioning national institution.

The military's performance in Baluchistan has been embarrassingly inept to date. Can President Musharraf convince the ISI—the crucial player—to go after tough al Qa'eda targets? Will Musharraf survive? Watch for clumsy moves in Kashmir that attempt to divert popular discontent into a patriotic—and suicidal—face-off with India.

The best we can hope for is that Pakistan will continue to muddle through, avoiding a confrontation with India and cracking down on the worst terrorists. This second-largest–Muslim-majority country—just behind Indonesia—has *no hope* of achieving economic health and little hope of building a rule-of-law democracy. Its ruling class destroyed its future, unchallenged demagogues preach a medieval worldview, and behind a confident front, the military government doesn't know what to do.

Cradle of Hate

New York Post

September 15, 2006

Islamist terror is a deadly threat we have barely begun to address. Yet religion-fueled fanaticism in the Middle East shouldn't surprise us: The tradition predates the Prophet's birth by thousands of years.

Terrorists just have better tools these days.

What should amaze us isn't the terrorists' strength, which has limits, but the comprehensive failure of Middle Eastern civilization. Given all the wealth that's poured into the region, its vast human resources and all of its opportunities for change, the mess the Middle East has made of itself is stunning.

Beyond Israel, the region hasn't produced a single first-rate government, army, economy, university, or industry. It hasn't even produced convincing second-raters.

Culturally, the region is utterly noncompetitive. Societies stagnate as populations seethe. To the extent it exists, development benefits the wealthy and powerful. The common people are either ignored or miserably oppressed—and not just the women.

Operation Iraqi Freedom wasn't so much an invasion as a last-minute rescue mission—an attempt to give one major Middle Eastern state a two-minutes-to-midnight chance to develop a humane, democratic government.

It may not work. But we'd better hope it does.

The Middle East's failure on every front enabled the rise of the terrorists—as well as the empowerment of other religious extremists, secular dictators, and political parties willing to poison electorates with hatred. The popular culprit for the mess is Islam. And there can be no doubt that the faith's local degeneration has been catastrophic for the region. By far the most numerous victims of "Islam Gone Wild" have been Middle Eastern Muslims.

But we can't be content with a single explanation for a civilization's failure, as powerful as the answer may appear. Yes, Islamist governments fail miserably. But so do secular Arab, Persian, and Pakistani governments (whose leaders belatedly play the Islamic card). Yes, the culture is Islamic, even in nominally secular states. But we have to ask some very politically incorrect questions that cut even deeper.

Many of the social, governmental, and psychological structures at the core of Middle Eastern societies predate Islam. Authoritarian government; a slavelike status for women; pervasive corruption; labor viewed as an evil to be avoided; the relegation of learning to narrow castes; economies that rely on trade rather than productivity to generate wealth; even the grandiose rhetoric—all were in place long before Islam appeared.

The repeated failures we've witnessed go far beyond a religion on its sickbed. Instead of Islam being the Middle East's problem, what if Islam's problem is the Middle East?

Were Christianity and Judaism "saved" because they escaped the Middle East? Were these other two great monotheist religions able to master the power of knowledge and human potential because they were driven from their stultifying cultural and geographic origins? Did the Diaspora and the subsequent Muslim destruction of the cradle of Christianity ultimately save these two faiths?

The Middle East is a straitjacket that turns religions mad. We got away.

A dozen years ago, I wrote that "culture is fate." And culture is tied to soil. My travels over the intervening years have only deepened that conviction. Regions have distinct cultures that endure long beyond the shelf life predicted for them by academics.

The stunning conquests Islam made in its early centuries may have been its undoing—a faith secure in its heartlands never had to worry about its survival thereafter. Despite gruesome invasions, Islam remained safely rooted in its native earth.

As "refugee religions," Christianity and Judaism had to struggle to survive—the latter still struggles today. For all of the pop theories blaming the rise of the West on germs, dumb luck, or sheer nastiness, the truth is that Judeo-Christian civilization was hardened by mortal threats—including horrendous internal conflicts.

We got tough. And the tough got going.

It isn't an accident that the industrial revolution took off in resource-poor Britain or that the poverty-ridden continent of Europe invented new means of exerting power.

In exile, the Judeo-Christian civilization grew up on the global mean streets. Middle-Eastern Islam suffered from easy wealth, luxury, and a narcotic regional heritage.

We changed, they froze. An Assyrian tyrant, such as the murderous Ashurbanipal—who reigned over 1,200 years before Mohammed's birth—would understand the governments, societies, and disciplinarian religion of today's Middle East. The West would baffle him.

Since the Renaissance, the West fixed its gaze on the future. Islamic civilization sought to freeze time, to cling to a dream of a lost paradise—part Islamic Baghdad, part Babylon.

Shocked awake over the past few centuries, some Middle Easterners realized they had to change. But they didn't know how. Modernization sputtered out. Pan-Arabism foundered on greed and corruption.

The shah tried to buy the "good parts" of Western civilization, but the pieces didn't work on their own. Next, Iran tried theocracy—government by bigots. Didn't work either.

"Oil-rich" Saudi Arabia has a per capita GDP half that of Israel's (whose sole resource is people). Dubai has shopping malls—selling designer goods with Western labels.

Today's fanatics can hurt us but can't destroy us. Their fatal ability is to drag their civilization down to an even lower level.

The problem is that the Middle East hasn't been able to escape the Middle East.

Kill Muqtada Now

New York Post

October 26, 2006

It was wrenching to listen to President Bush's news conference yesterday. He's struggling to do the right thing. But he's getting terrible advice. He's still counting on a political solution in Iraq. Ain't going to happen. And you can take that to the blood bank.

Our famously loyal president has one grave flaw: He's a poor judge of character. He trusts the wrong people. Then he sticks by them.

Bush met Russia's Vladimir Putin, "looked into his soul," and failed to recognize that the guy is an unreformed secret policeman. He stubbornly defends Defense Secretary Donald Rumsfeld, the Pentagon's architect of failure. Now he's standing up for Iraqi Prime Minister Nouri al Maliki—a man who has decided to back our enemies.

I lost faith in our engagement in Iraq last week. I can pinpoint the moment. It came when I heard that Maliki had demanded—successfully—that our military release a just-captured deputy of Muqtada al Sadr who was running death squads.

As a former intelligence officer, that told me two things: First, Iraq's prime minister is betting on Muqtada to prevail, not us. Second, Muqtada, not the Grand Ayatollah Ali al Sistani, is now the most powerful man in Iraq.

At his news conference, Bush was asked about another statement made by Maliki just hours before. Our troops had conducted a raid in Sadr City, Muqtada's Baghdad stronghold. The Iraqi PM quickly declared that "this will not happen again." He was signaling his allegiance to Muqtada. Publicly.

Oh, Maliki realizes his government wouldn't last a week if our troops withdrew. He doesn't want us to leave yet. But he's looking ahead. For now, Maliki and his pals are using our troops to buy time while they pocket our money, amass power, and build up arms. But they've written us off for the long term.

Does that mean we should leave?

Not yet. Iraq deserves one last chance. But to make that chance even remotely viable, we'll have to take desperate measures. We need to fight. And accept the consequences.

The first thing we need to do is to kill Muqtada al Sadr, who's now a greater threat to our strategic goals than Osama bin Laden. We should've killed him in 2003, when he first embarked upon his murder campaign. But our leaders were afraid of provoking riots.

Back then, the tumult might've lasted a week. Now we'll face a serious uprising. So be it. When you put off paying war's price, you pay compound interest in blood.

We must kill—not capture—Muqtada, then kill every gunman who comes out in the streets to avenge him.

Our policy of all-carrots-no-sticks has failed miserably. We delivered Iraq to zealots, gangsters, and terrorists. Now our only hope is to prove that we mean business—that the era of peace, love, and wasting American lives is over.

And after we've killed Muqtada and destroyed his Mahdi Army, we need to go after the Sunni insurgents. If we can't leave a democracy behind, we should at least leave the corpses of our enemies. The holier-than-thou response to this proposal is predictable: "We can't kill our way out of this situation!" Well, boo-hoo. Friendly persuasion and billions of dollars haven't done the job. Give therapeutic violence a chance.

Our soldiers and Marines are dying to protect a government whose members are scrambling to ally themselves with sectarian militias and insurgent factions. President Bush needs to face reality. The Maliki government is a failure.

There's still a chance, if a slight one, that we can achieve a few of our goals in Iraq—if we let our troops make war, not love. But if our own leaders are unwilling to fight, it's time to leave and let Iraqis fight each other.

Our president owes Iraq's treacherous prime minister nothing. Get tough, or get out.

Last Gasps in Iraq

USA Today

November 2, 2006

Author's note: Writers control the contents of their newspaper columns, but not the headlines, which are chosen by editors. In this instance, I was surprised and angered by the headline chosen, which I did not see before the column went to press. While I believed that Iraq was in crisis, it was not yet at a "last gasp." The headline, intended to shock and entice the reader, gave the piece a defeatist tone several degrees beyond the effect I intended. I stand by the column but reject the inaccurate title foisted upon it.

On Tuesday, Iraqi Prime Minister Nouri al Maliki obeyed Muqtada al Sadr's command to withdraw U.S. troops from Baghdad's Sadr City. He halted a vital U.S. military operation. It was the third time in less than a month that al Maliki had sided with the anti-American cleric against our forces.

President Bush insists that we have no conflicts with the al Maliki government. The president isn't telling the truth—or he himself doesn't support our military's efforts. He can't have it both ways. Bush appears increasingly desperate just to get through the upcoming elections.

I supported the removal of Saddam Hussein. I believed that Arabs deserved a chance to build a rule-of-law democracy in the Middle East. Based upon firsthand experience, I was convinced that the Middle East was so politically, socially, morally, and intellectually stagnant that we had to risk intervention—or face generations of terrorism and tumult. I still believe that our removal of Hussein was a noble act.

I only wish the administration had done it competently.

HOPE IS DWINDLING

Iraq is failing. No honest observer can conclude otherwise. Even six months ago, there was hope. Now the chances for a democratic, unified Iraq are dwindling fast. The country's prime minister has thrown in his lot with al Sadr, our mortal enemy. He has his eye on the future, and he's betting that we won't last. The police are less accountable than they were under Saddam. Our extensive investment in Iraqi law enforcement only produced death squads. Government ministers loot the country to strengthen their own factions. Even Iraq's elections—a worthy experiment—further divided Iraq along confessional and ethnic lines. Iraq still exists on the maps, but in reality it's gone. Only a military coup—which might come in the next few years—could hold the artificial country together.

This chaos wasn't inevitable. While in Iraq late last winter, I remained soberly hopeful. Since then, the strength of will of our opponents—their readiness to pay any price and go to any length to win—has eclipsed our own. The valor of our enemies never surpassed that of our troops, but it far exceeded the fair-weather courage of the Bush administration.

Yet, for all our errors, we did give the Iraqis a unique chance to build a rule-of-law democracy. They preferred to indulge in old hatreds, confessional violence, ethnic bigotry, and a culture of corruption. It appears that the cynics were right: Arab societies can't support democracy as we know it. And people get the government they deserve.

For us, Iraq's impending failure is an embarrassment. For the Iraqis—and other Arabs—it's a disaster the dimensions of which they do not yet comprehend. They're gleeful at the prospect of America's humiliation. But it's their tragedy, not ours.

Iraq was the Arab world's last chance to board the train to modernity, to give the region a future, not just a bitter past. The violence staining Baghdad's streets with gore isn't only a symptom of the Iraqi government's incompetence, but of the comprehensive inability of the Arab world to progress in any sphere of organized human endeavor. We are witnessing the collapse of a civilization. All those who rooted for Iraq to fail are going to be chastened by what follows.

Iraq still deserves one last chance—as long as we don't confuse deadly stubbornness and perseverance. If, at this late hour, Iraqis in decisive numbers prove willing to fight for their own freedom and a constitutional government, we should be willing to remain for a generation. If they continue to revel in fratricidal slaughter, we must leave.

IRAQ NOT OUR VIETNAM

And contrary to the prophets of doom, the United States wouldn't be weakened by our withdrawal, should it come to that. Iraq was never our Vietnam. It's al Qa'eda's Vietnam. They're the ones who can't leave and who can't win.

Islamist terrorists have chosen Iraq as their battleground and, even after our departure, it will continue to consume them. We'll still be the greatest power on earth, indispensable to other regional states—such as the Persian Gulf states and Saudi Arabia—that are terrified of Iran's growing might. If the Arab world and Iran embark on an orgy of bloodshed, the harsh truth is that we may be the beneficiaries.

My disillusionment with our Iraq endeavor began last summer, when I was invited to a high-level discussion with administration officials. I went into the meeting with one firm goal, to convince my hosts that they'd better have Plan B in case Iraq continued to disintegrate. I left the session convinced that the administration still didn't have Plan A, only a blur of meandering policies and blind hopes. After more than three years, it was still "An Evening at the Improv."

Then, last month, as Iraq's prime minister seconded al Sadr's demand that our troops free a death-squad mastermind they had captured, I knew a fateful page had turned. A week later, al Maliki forbade additional U.S. military raids in Sadr City, the radical mullah's Baghdad stronghold. On Tuesday, al Maliki insisted that our troops remove roadblocks set up to help find a kidnapped U.S. soldier. Iraq's prime minister has made his choice. We're not it. It's time to face reality. Only Iraqis can save Iraq now—and they appear intent on destroying it. *Après nous, le déluge.*

Iraq could have turned out differently. It didn't. And we must be honest about it. We owe that much to our troops. They don't face the mere forfeiture of a few congressional seats but the loss of their lives. Our military is now being employed for political purposes. It's unworthy of our nation.

Plan B for Iraq

Armed Forces Journal

November 2006

The odds of Iraq surviving as a constitutional democracy with its present borders intact are down to 50/50. While it's still too soon to give up on the effort to let free elections decide the future of one Arab-majority state, 2007 will be the year in which the Iraqis themselves determine whether our continued sacrifice is justified, or if Iraq is fated to become yet another catastrophic Arab failure.

We have given the people of Iraq an unprecedented opportunity. If they make a hash of it, it won't be our defeat, but theirs. We must make that clear to Iraqis and to the world.

Iraq is a grotesque labyrinth of ethnic and confessional rivalries, and of rivalries within those rivalries. While a minority of Iraqis would like to harm us, a majority would prefer to harm their neighbors. The deep loyalties, legacies of betrayal, and layered relationships are so opaque to outsiders that we cannot be certain even of the leading figures in the Baghdad government. Yet, for all of the country's complexity, one thing is simple and straightforward: The test for the fundamental question (immortalized by The Clash), "Should I stay, or should I go?"

If the people of Iraq are willing to fight for their own constitutionally elected government in decisive numbers, we should maintain a military presence in their country for a generation, if need be. If, however, Iraqi security forces fail to demonstrate a sufficient commitment—by the closing months of 2007—to defeat their government's violent enemies, we must have the common sense to recognize that our dreams for Iraq are hopeless. The Sunni-Arab insurgents, Shiite-Arab militiamen, and foreign terrorists are ready to give their lives for their beliefs and causes. If the remainder of Iraq's population cannot summon an equal will to fight for a unified, rule-of-law state, our troops should not continue to do their dying for them.

The stakes in Iraq are very high, indeed. Yet, an intelligently conducted U.S. withdrawal might be far from the disaster that all-or-nothing partisans predict. Skillfully managed, the removal of U.S. forces from Iraq—except for elements redeployed to Kurdistan—might result, not in catastrophe, but in long-term advantages for the U.S.

The key to making the most of an Iraqi failure to grasp the opportunity we provided is to think imaginatively and ruthlessly, setting aside our political prejudices and middle-brow morality. We should exclude no scenario, however extreme, as we war-game alternatives in Iraq and the Middle East. As for realism, it begins with accepting the Law of Sunk Costs ("Don't throw away additional resources in attempts to recover irretrievable losses") and proceeds to an honest appraisal of the situation in Iraq—something unpalatable to ideologues on both the right and left. Critically, we cannot afford another application of Point No. 1 of the Rumsfeld Doctrine: "Plan only for what you desire and forbid planning for any alternatives."

We require not only a Plan B, but Plans C, D, E, and beyond, as well as constantly evolving variations of each. As former Army Chief of Staff Gen. Gordon Sullivan used to put it, "Hope is not a method." We must not only prepare for the worst, but calculate how to turn it to our advantage.

At present, our enemies—and those of the Iraq we envisioned— have only two advantages over us, but they're powerful ones: They display a greater strength of will, and they dare to think (then do) the unthinkable. Our self-flagellation over media-amplified "war crimes" has trapped us into the far-greater immorality of giving ground to implacable fanatics. We have limited our national imagination to courses of action we hope a global consensus will approve. That's suicidal nonsense. There is no morality—none—in being defeated, however politely we make our troops behave.

We know how to fight. But we must relearn the art of thinking.

We also must shake off the habit of interpreting all developments to our own disadvantage (a media addiction). The most obvious example is the inextinguishable nonsense about Iraq being "another Vietnam" for our military. It isn't. On the contrary, Iraq has turned into al Qa'eda's Vietnam. We could leave tomorrow, lick our wounds, and fight on elsewhere. But whether we stay or go, al Qa'eda's resources will be devoured by Iraq for years to come. Far from profiting from a future Iraqi civil war, al Qa'eda would be its victim.

We also need to recognize when it's time to stop shaking our fists at the sky and commanding the rain to stop. The Shiite-Sunni divide may be unbridgeable and interludes of peace no more than a temporary result of bloody exhaustion or one side's tyrannical supremacy. For all of the fashionable anti-Americanism on the political catwalk, the style of the region is Shiite-Sunni hatred unto death. And fashion is a transient phenomenon, but style endures. Human beings may hate a distant enemy in the abstract, but in practice they prefer to kill their neighbors.

PLAN B

If the Iraqi military and, especially, the police cannot overcome their sectarian rivalries and rally to their government's defense by late 2007, we need to begin an orderly withdrawal of our forces. The decision cannot be based exclusively on the views of our military leaders in Baghdad, since few will see this particular issue with sufficient clarity. The U.S. officer's can-do spirit combines with a loyalty to those he's trained and with whom he's worked that blinds him to their irremediable deficiencies. The generals' line will be, "We can't abandon them now." But we can. And we should, if Iraqis in uniform will not show valor and determination equal to the enemies of their state.

We cannot accept pleas for "just one more year." 2007 should be the last chance. Senior officers will counter that developing a military from scratch takes time, that this is a massive, complex effort. That's true, but, to borrow from Gen.Vo Nguyen Giap, it is also irrelevant. The militiamen, insurgents, and terrorists have not had billions of dollars and years of American military training lavished upon them. Yet they fight hard and often well (if not by our rules). If all of the human capital and material resources we've invested can't arouse an Iraqi will to win sufficient to defeat the elected government's numerically inferior opponents, there is no justification for wasting an additional American life.

Iraqis have to want to fight for their state—and not just a valiant handful of Iraqis. They must be willing to fight in decisive numbers. Yes, those fighters would continue to need American support, from air missions to logistics, for years to come, and the support would be merited. But if Iraqis will not actively and relentlessly carry the fight to their enemies, foreign and domestic, nothing we can do will make up the difference.

If we do leave, we should go out shooting. All antigovernment factions should suffer—the gloves should come off at last. The one thing we cannot afford is a popular view that our troops have been defeated. They haven't been. We will have to make that clear. Our withdrawal should be conducted under conditions that push our enemies bloodily onto the defensive as we make our exit, and we should not worry about collateral damage. If we leave Iraq, we must leave the world with a perception of American strength—and ruthlessness, when required. We can afford being seen as heavy-handed, but we can't afford being seen as weak.

We should leave sufficient forces in Kurdistan to deter foreign interference in that pro-American region, as well as to give us local leverage and emergency bases in periods of crisis. Even after we withdraw from the rest of Iraq, we should be ready and willing to intervene with air power to prolong the subsequent civil war, ensuring that neither Sunni Arabs nor Shiite Arabs gain the upper hand—and that the designs of neighboring states are frustrated.

If we leave Iraq, there will be a civil war. We must accept that and make up our minds to profit from it. Not only would it be al Qa'eda's Vietnam (its cadres hate and fear Shiites far more than they do us), but the strife would inevitably entangle our other regional enemies. Currently aligned against us, Iran and Syria would not be able to sustain their cooperation but would be drawn into backing opposite sides. While we should be willing to use force to prevent the cross-border involvement of Iranian or Syrian regulars, we must accept that their support for rival factions with armaments and "volunteers" is inevitable. Let us turn it to our advantage by bleeding out our opponents and trapping them in a quagmire.

An Iraqi civil war would be a human tragedy. But it would be a tragedy that Iraqis, through factionalism and fecklessness, brought down on their own heads. Given that it cannot be prevented, we should avoid hand-wringing diplomacy in favor of placing no obstacles in the path of Sunni and Shiite extremists anxious to kill each other.

The region is due for another of its periodic bloodbaths and, paradoxically, the exhaustion in the wake of a sectarian war may be the only long-term hope for peace.

As for Iraq's other interested neighbor, Turkey, we should make it explicitly clear that our air power, advisers, special operations forces, and, if need be, regulars will stand by the Kurds if Turkish forces cross the border—but we should do so behind closed doors to avoid a public humiliation for Ankara. As a sop, we should give the Turks a free hand to engage in contiguous regions of Arab Iraq to "protect" the Turkoman minority. (Turkish ambitions will thus prevent any rapprochement with Ankara's Arab neighbors.) We might even offer open support for Turkish efforts and, since Turkey is oil-poor, we should consider a compact that allows Ankara to occupy part of Iraq's oil fields in return for accepting the Kurdish claim to Kirkuk. With their own new oil fields under development, the Kurds can and must be persuaded to share a portion of the Kirkuk area's oil with the Turks in return for security, open trade, and pipeline access.

By offering Turkey a free drink of oil, we might be able to protect the Kurds without fighting. As an insurance plan, we should arm and train the Kurds—who will fight for their freedom—to include applying lessons learned from Hezbollah's strategy against the Israel Defense Forces. Anyway, a Turkish military incursion into Kurdistan might explode the conventional wisdom by failing miserably in the difficult, canalized terrain of northern Iraq. The free Kurds would be the toughest enemy Turks have faced since the Great War, and we might have to intervene with the Irbil government to persuade the Kurds to spare trapped and suffering Turkish units.

Another line of conventional wisdom holds that, should the Iraqi experiment fail, we will lose our influence throughout the region. That is exactly wrong. An Iraq embroiled in civil war would underscore the importance of American goodwill and military power to protect the effete sheikdoms of the Persian Gulf and the hollow Saudi monarchy. Each of these Sunni emirates and states dreads Persian hegemony.

The old Arab-Persian antipathy eventually will reemerge in Iraq, as well. At present, Persian and Iraqi Shiites are religious brothers facing a traditional enemy. But Iran ultimately will insist on exercising too much authority and demand too much subservience. Persian arrogance and racism will undo Tehran's attempts at empire. An eventual Shiite victory in a civil war would lead inexorably to a future Arab-Persian conflict within the Shiite community.

As for securing oil supplies, we have a wide range of alternatives, from a rump occupation that concentrates on Iraq's southern oil fields, through a no-nonsense demand that the Saudis and gulf states maximize their production, to a surprise occupation of Venezuela's oil production sites (most of them conveniently located for military visitors).

We have done our best to help others. The time may be approaching to help ourselves.

Finally, contingency plans to strike Iran's nuclear facilities should be timed for the moment when Iraqi Shiites appear to be gaining the upper hand. With the Sunni Arabs pressed to the wall (which might happen quickly) and Iran pouring resources into the fight, we should blindside Tehran, breaking its nuclear weapons program and preventing an outright Shiite victory in Iraq. The goal would not be to deliver victory to the Sunni Arabs, who could not win a civil war, but to prevent them from losing and keep the confrontation alive. Al Qa'eda's Vietnam could also become Iran's Vietnam.

PLAN C

Make common cause with Iran. Upend the chess board, approach Iran and offer Tehran hegemony over central and southeastern Iraq in return for halting its nuclear-weapons development program and a commitment to defend Kurdistan's independence against all aggressors. Propose an alliance based on noninterference in Iranian affairs (save the nuclear-arsenal issue) and recognition of Shiite ascendancy in the northern gulf.

What if, instead of weakening Iran, we helped it become stronger? Of course, our views on Israel are in direct conflict, but the attempt to assert local hegemony would occupy Tehran and drain its resources for years to come. And, as noted above, the deep conflict in the region isn't between Muslims and Americans or even between Muslims and Israelis, but between Muslims and Muslims. Given the chance to lord it over Sunni Arabs, Tehran might forget about Israel except for intermittent bursts of token rhetoric. And, in the end, an attempt to build a greater Iran will inevitably result in a lesser Iran. Iran's ambitions will be self-defeating, so why not encourage them?

The only way to win in the Middle East is to choose a side and continue to back that side no matter how badly it misbehaves. Our attempts to play the honest broker have failed, preventing resolution and making many a bad situation worse. Sunni-Arab culture is in freefall, and we have to accept the fact. We have bound ourselves to the dead and dying. Perhaps it's time to put our anger over yesteryear's hostages and name-calling behind us—and to ask the Iranians to abandon their own old grudges against us.

As for the benefits of choosing Shiites over Sunnis, we should remember that the worst anti-Western terrorists by far have been Sunnis. Anyway, the odds are better if we back the region's oldest surviving civilization—Persia—over a collection of tribal cultures that do not reach the standard of a civilization.

The formula, in short, would be: Embrace Iran and kill it with kindness; terrify (but continue to embrace) the gulf oil states; isolate Syria and destroy the Assad regime; protect the Kurds, but placate Turkey; and create so obsessive a regional focus on local problems that we can concentrate on future opportunities elsewhere.

Of course, the Iranians would cheat like mad on any such agreement. That's part of the equation. But the loss of the U.S. as a galvanizing bogeyman would foster the conditions for internally driven regime change. Rob the Tehran regimes of its excuses. By making Iran stronger in the short term, we might do more to change its political nature than by striving endlessly—and ineffectually—to weaken it.

Perhaps it's time for the Great Satan to do what devils do best: Seduce.

PLAN D

A variation on Plan C: Cut a deal with Iran to allow it unrestricted influence over the Shiite provinces of Iraq in return for a mutual-support pact that frees American forces to invade Syria (an indirect withdrawal); to provide guarantees for the Kurds; and to raise joint Iranian-Iraqi oil production in return for an American purchasing shift away from Saudi Arabia. The goal would be to lower world oil prices sufficiently (and just long enough) to create a financial crisis in Saudi Arabia, the primary source of anti-Western Islam, of destabilizing policies in the Muslim world, and of terrorists.

By driving Saudi Arabia into a government breakdown, we might dry up the funding for Wahhabi missionary efforts that wreak havoc on states from Pakistan to Nigeria, while diverting Sunni Arab resources and energies to internal struggles in place of the export of fanaticism. At an opportune time, we might occupy key Saudi oil fields, holding profits in trust for a future constitutional state. Let Sunni Arabs fight over Mecca the way Christians once warred over the Papal States.

As for the invasion of Syria, it would be easy militarily, and we would not make the mistake of trying to occupy the country; rather, our goal would be to create "constructive turmoil" that weakened Iraq's Sunni Arabs by depriving them of dependable strategic depth, while embroiling al Qa'eda and its affiliates in yet another Muslim-versus-Muslim struggle that bleeds the movement out. We should never forget that, while we can afford to "lose" Iraq, al Qa'eda can't. Expand al Qa'eda's struggle to Syria, and we create a situation where Arabs do our killing for us. And if al Qa'eda ever achieved unexpected success, we could prevent it from governing: We may have difficulty with postmodern terrorist organizations, but we can take down states with ease (we only have to avoid trying to rebuild them in our own image).

We sought to foster peace in the Middle East. Perhaps it's time to let the Middle East fight itself out. And the best way to protect

Israel is to involve Arabs and Persians in resource-draining struggles within the Muslim world.

PLAN E

Leave. Not just Iraq, but the entire region (except for expandable bases in Kurdistan). Let the region burn, if that's what its populations choose. Put real fear into the lives of our Saudi enemies. Let civil war rage in Iraq and let it expand, if that's the conflagration's natural course. If necessary, intervene just sufficiently to preserve oil supplies. Otherwise, strictly refrain from military engagement in any form, until the various actors have bled themselves out. Let the world get one of its periodic and necessary lessons in the horror of sectarian wars.

Then return and pick up the pieces.

The best-laid plans. . . .

Iraq still has a fighting chance. And if Iraqis will fight for their own freedom and a constitutional government, we should stand by them. But we need to think seriously and creatively about alternatives, in case the Iraqis let themselves down. The Bush administration's cross-your-fingers approach has served us poorly. For their part, the administration's detractors offer no alternatives beyond platitudes and their own brand of wishful thinking.

We cannot afford inane squabbling that elevates short-term political advantage over our strategic interests. It's always up to the incumbent administration to take the lead in pursuing alternatives—simply because it has the power to do so. After actively preventing our military from planning for an unwanted-but-unavoidable occupation of Iraq, the Bush administration must not make the same ideology-driven mistake again. Our efforts in Iraq degenerated swiftly from a nebulous vision to a series of improvisations—none of which convinced the intended audience. After three and a half years, we still don't have a genuine plan, only a loosely connected series of programs and a bucket of fading hopes.

None of the scenarios sketched above would be ideal. The purpose in summarizing them isn't to offer Pentagon planners a blueprint, but to provoke our leaders to think honestly and imaginatively about the wide range of potential outcomes—not all of them necessarily bad for us—should Iraqis lack the will to risk their lives for their elected government. We must smash the self-imposed barriers of political correctness. As we war-game the future, no strategy should be off-limits.

In the Middle East, the closest we can come to certainty is to accept that the one outcome we reject as unthinkable will come to pass.

Iraq's Uncivil War

New York Post

November 30, 2006

You can call her a blond, but she's still a redhead. The endless spitting match over whether Iraq is in a state of civil war is a media-driven grudge fight that ignores the complex reality. It's name-calling, not analysis.

A lot of this is just "get Bush" stuff from journalists whose biased reporting helped shape the dismal reality in Iraq and who now crow that they were right all along— the media as a self-licking ice-cream cone.

The good news—and, unfortunately, the bad news—is that Iraq is not in a state of civil war in the textbook sense. If it were, our military and political mission would be easier.

In a civil war, you have clearly defined sides struggling for political power, with organized military formations and parallel governments. You know who to kill and who is empowered to negotiate with you. You can pick a side and stick to it.

Unleashed, our military could smash any enemy in an open civil war. Even our diplomats would have trouble preventing an American victory. But the violence in Iraq comes from overlapping groups of terrorists, militias, insurgents, death squads, gangsters, foreign agents, and factionalized government security forces engaging in layers of savage religious, ethnic, political, and economic struggles—with an all-too-human lust for revenge spicing the mix.

There is a genuine problem here: The ever-accelerating pace of change since the end of the Cold War has left us with an inadequate vocabulary. Words literally fail us. We don't know what to call things. No military lexicon offers a useful term to describe the situation in Iraq.

This matters. We not only speak, but think, in language. To communicate effectively, we must describe things efficiently. Agreeing upon its name is essential to a deeper understanding of any phenomenon. Nouns are the handles with which we grip reality.

Our troops can kill our enemies no matter what we call them, but our inability to describe our experience in Iraq accurately makes it far harder for our civilian leaders to understand it. (Not that everyone in either party is committed to an honest analysis.) As far as the now-pejorative term "civil war" goes, let's just let activists in or out of the media use it, if it helps them bear the dawning reality that, no, the Democrats in Congress aren't going to bring the troops home for Christmas and declare surrender.

Meanwhile, those of us who care about our country's security and who worry about the futility haunting the Middle East need to face a tougher issue than yo-mama name-calling: Iraq has deteriorated so badly it's hard to imagine a positive outcome unless we're willing to take radical, politically difficult measures.

The administration and Congress have to face a fundamental question: Which result is more important—preserving Iraq as a unified state with a facade of democratic government or protecting our own national-security interests? The two priorities now conflict. Really taking on our enemies—not least Muqtada al Sadr and his legion of thugs—would require us to defy the elected Baghdad government we sponsored. To kill those who need killing to pacify Iraq and reestablish our ascendancy would mean that we would again become an outright occupying power.

Not that it really matters, but doing what it would take to win would also tear up our permission slip from the United Nations.

On the other hand, the prospect of endlessly shoring up a corrupt, divided Iraqi government unwilling to protect its own citizens, and to do so at a cost in American blood, would be a far more immoral course than ordering our troops to kill the butchers who've been assassinating them and tens of thousands of innocent Iraqis.

Let's hope that President Bush will make it hurt-so-bad-he-can't-sit-down clear to Prime Minster Nouri al Maliki at their meeting in Jordan today that Allah helps those who help themselves. Our soldiers and Marines can't continue to serve as human shields for a corrupt, feckless government. Maliki must get serious about Iraq's problems immediately.

And if the prime minister runs back to Baghdad to beg Muqtada's forgiveness for meeting with our president, it will confirm the doubts about Maliki's will, abilities, and allegiance highlighted in National Security Adviser Stephen Hadley's leaked memo—which appears to have wounded the prime minister's vanity.

In his remarks Tuesday at the NATO summit in Riga, Latvia, President Bush stated forcefully that we would not quit Iraq until we had completed our mission. Such tenacity can be admirable, but the mission has to be clear—otherwise, it's just obstinacy.

A fundamental problem is that the mission in Iraq remains vague. And vague mission statements are not conducive to military success.

Generalities won't do. Let's tell our troops precisely what we expect of them: Are they there to defeat our enemies or just to buy time with their lives in the forlorn hope that something will go right? And let's not lose sight of the incontestable fact that, while being liked in the Middle East would be nice, being feared by our enemies is essential.

There's nothing civil about the semichaos defining a new kind of war in Iraq. It's a twenty-first-century phenomenon and our terminology has to catch up. In the meantime, we need to remember that, whatever else our government does or fails to do, its ultimate reason for being is to protect Americans and American interests.

Saving the dubious Maliki government is a secondary concern, at most. The uncompromising defeat of our enemies is what matters.

The Iraq Mutiny?

New York Post

December 3, 2006

The proposal to embed more American military trainers with Iraqi units makes sense, but creates a grave danger: the prospect of a coordinated revolt among Shi'as in uniform who slaughter or take hostage thousands of our dispersed troops.

The best deterrent is the back-up presence of our own Army and Marine combat formations. As long as our cavalry can ride to the rescue, the prospect of a sectarian mutiny to "teach America a lesson" and humiliate us remains low.

Now early word has it that The Fabulous Baker Boys (straight from the political boneyard and known formally as the Iraq Study Group) will recommend withdrawing U.S. combat troops from Iraq by 2008, while leaving behind our embedded trainers and vulnerable support units.

This is the sort of nonsense that sounds great to civilians with no military experience. To veterans, it's nuts. THE problem here is the composition of the panel headed by former Secretary of State James Baker. Not only does it drag yesteryear's Washington insiders out of the crypt, its makeup reveals the disgraceful extent to which our governing "elite" despises those in uniform.

Why on earth wasn't a single retired military officer appointed to the the Iraq Study Group? We're at war, for Heaven's sake. Briefly interviewing a few generals is no substitute for a steadying military voice amid the committee's naïfs.

Washington insiders pretend to respect our troops but continue to believe that those in uniform are second-raters and that any political hack can design better war plans than those who've dedicated their lives to military service. This is arrogance soaring through the clouds—and a disheartening replay of the shut-out-military-advice approach to warfare that got us into such a mess in Iraq.

The administration should've swallowed its pride and asked retired Army Chief of Staff Gen. Eric Shinseki to sit on the panel. Or Gen. Barry McCaffrey, who knows how to think and fight. Or just a lieutenant with a combat patch on his shoulder.

Instead, we got Vernon Jordan (presumably, the token lobbyist) and retired Supreme Court Justice Sandra Day O'Connor. Jordan may know K Street inside out, but he doesn't know a thing about the streets of Baghdad. O'Connor was a terrific Supreme, but she has no background in military matters, the Middle East, or international affairs.

What the Iraq Study Group does have is a staff with long ties to the Saudis. And Baker's own relationship with the Saudi royal family has been so accommodating that he often seemed more of a Saudi lobbyist than a U.S. official. He's got plenty of time for billionaire sheiks and princes but none for American officers.

This is going to be Saudi Arabia's report (and Syria's, too—Baker never met a dictator he didn't like). Even Iran may get a nice slice of the pie. The study's underlying strategy will be to re-establish the sort of phony stability that gave us the Shah of Iran and Saddam Hussein—both horses backed by Baker.

The composition of the study group was just a setup. Baker didn't want experts who could challenge his "experience." And the much-praised bipartisan nature of the panel is meaningless when every member is from the old, failed guard and the youngest member is in his late sixties. Think they're going to produce innovative thinking and fresh ideas?

So we're left with another panel of amateurs designing a military strategy—this one recommending the withdrawal of our combat troops, who constitute the only insurance plan we have in Iraq. Baker would then leave behind embedded trainers and vulnerable logistics bases.

Gee, thanks.

The model for what could result comes from the English-speaking world's history with Islam. In mid-nineteenth-century India, as the British sahibs kidded themselves that their "loyal" subordinates adored them, Muslim (and Hindu) East India Company troops staged widespread, coordinated attacks that butchered "embedded" officers, government officials, and their families.

"Mercy" wasn't in the mutineers' vocabulary. The torture of captives was common. Sound like Iraq to anybody?

The Sepoy Mutiny was a close-run thing. Only the presence of British regiments saved the day. Wherever they had substantial numbers of regulars to call on, the Brits were able to hold off the masses of religious fanatics until additional forces arrived from elsewhere in the empire.

Unlike our politically correct leadership in Iraq, yesteryear's Brits responded to savagery with savagery. The result was six decades of internal peace in India. Of course, not a few American officers would dismiss the possibility that "their" Iraqis could turn on them. That's exactly how the British officers felt.

Our trainers would put up a tough fight against any such revolt. But they could only fight as long as they had ammunition. Even the best Special Forces A-team we've got couldn't hold on indefinitely against a battalion led by fanatics.

Let's not permit vanity-intoxicated Washington has-beens to dictate military policy. If we've learned nothing else from Iraq (and we should've learned plenty by now), it's that the details of military operations must be left to professionals: Tell the generals what you want them to do, Mr. President—then let them figure out the best way to do it.

Only a ship of fools could launch the recommendation that we address the problems of violence-ravaged Iraq by withdrawing our combat troops and leaving behind tens of thousands of hostages in uniform.

From Metternich to Jim Baker: The High Price of Restoring the *Ancien Régime*

The Weekly Standard

December 11, 2006

The superannuated membership of the Iraq Study Group shepherded by former secretary of state James Baker conjures a line from the film *The Sixth Sense:* "I see dead people." Two centuries ago, Europeans dreaming of reform and freedom must have felt just as crestfallen as they watched their continent's ghoulish elder statesmen gather for the Congress of Vienna. Both assemblies symbolize a victory for the *ancien régime,* the bloody-minded refusal to accept that the world has changed profoundly and will continue to change.

If the Baker commission is the K-Mart version of the Congress of Vienna, its influence may prove no less pernicious. Baker is the dean emeritus of a reactionary school of diplomats—inaccurately labeled "realists"—whose support of the shah of Iran, the Saudi royal family, Anwar Sadat, then Hosni Mubarak, and, not least, Saddam Hussein delivered short-term stability that proved illusory in the long run. It was the "realist" elevation of stability above all other strategic factors—echoing Prince Metternich—that gave us not only the radical regime in Iran, but, ultimately, al Qa'eda and 9/11.

The leading modern practitioner of this profoundly reactionary approach to international relations was, of course, Henry Kissinger, whose doctoral thesis championed the diplomats and heads of state who redivided Europe into reform-school states after Napoleon's defeat. A classic revisionist, Kissinger ignored the wisdom of nineteenth-century observers who recognized that the oppression sponsored by the Congress of Vienna created only a mockery of peace. The century of Biedermeier sensibilities and Victorian manners was, in fact, punctuated by a long series of failed—and often grisly—revolutions that radicalized those who found the status quo unbearable. The *Staatsordnung* of the day created the cult of political assassinations that haunts us still. Metternich and his peers induced the social forced labor that gave birth to Marx and all the utopian extremists who came afterward. From the lesser figures, such as Kropotkin or Bakunin, down to Lenin and Hitler, the political distortions of the "orderly" nineteenth century led to the unprecedented bloodbaths of the twentieth century.

The Kissinger school amplified our Cold War support for authoritarian and even dictatorial regimes, deforming the Middle East as Metternich, Talleyrand, Nesselrode, Castlereagh, Wellington, and their lesser contemporaries crippled Europe. For his part, Baker argued—wrongly—that Saddam Hussein should be spared in the wake of Desert Storm; tried to persuade the Soviet Union to remain whole after its comprehensive collapse; and pretended against the increasingly gory evidence that Yugoslavia could be preserved as a unified state. He tolerated Saddam's savage suppression of a Shi'a revolt we incited and only grudgingly—and belatedly— acquiesced in our protection of Kurdish refugees.

One of the many tragedies of our experience in Iraq is that the incompetence of the Bush administration's occupation policy has obscured the necessity of igniting change in the Middle East. Removing Saddam Hussein from power was both an intelligent act and a moral one. But the aftermath was so badly botched that many in Washington now long—as did those powdered cynics in Vienna—for the status quo antebellum. They would renew our commitment to Saudi Arabia and other autocracies, while quietly selling out the Lebanese, the Kurds, and the region's moderates in order to get us out of Iraq. We would return to a version of the old order and *might* gain a brief respite from our troubles in the region. But the greater effects of a renewed stability *über-alles* doctrine would play into the recruitment schemes of the most radical Islamist elements in the region, while instigating human rights violations on a breathtaking scale. We would throw away any hope of a better future for a brief timeout today.

Stability at any price isn't the answer. Stability imposed from above empowered Khomeini and bin Laden as surely as it did the nineteenth-century revolutionaries and nihilists who became the twentieth century's nationalists, demagogues, and mass murderers. Terror is an inevitable by-product of all grand clampdowns.

The statesmen of the Congress of Vienna sought to turn back history's tide, and their philosophical heirs on the Baker panel are trying to do the same. Democrat or Republican, superficially liberal or conservative, the Iraq Study Group is deeply reactionary. Its recommendations, which will be couched in terms of "sensible" *Realpolitik,* envision an impossible restoration of a peaceful Middle East that never existed. No matter the politically correct language in which it may be couched, the group's fundamental recommendation will be to return to a foreign policy in which the quest for stability trumps freedom, ignores human rights, frustrates the will of ordinary people, and violates elementary decency. By resisting change, the study group will only make the changes that do come to the Middle East even more explosive and anti-American.

The Middle East problem was difficult enough when the Bush administration stood for a benevolent revolution in possibilities against a range of reactionary enemies, from al Qa'eda and Shi'a militias to various Ba'athist regimes and the apocalyptic nihilists ruling Iran. For all of the administration's practical ineptitude, its recognition that the Middle East could not continue in its current state was correct. Now we verge on a new clash of civilizations that will oppose our reactionaries to their reactionaries. It is a formula not for stability and peace, but for brutal conflict and spectacular terrorism.

The nineteenth century was far bloodier within Europe than historical glosses pretend, yet the political order the Congress of Vienna sought to preserve in amber did last, more or less, until 1914, when the inevitable explosion came on a massive scale. But history marches double time today, and any attempt to effect a restoration of rigid, top-down order in the Middle East will fail far more rapidly than did the Concert of Europe. Yesterday's solutions—Jim Baker's solutions—didn't work yesterday. They certainly won't work today.

Since the end of the Cold War, every one of our military engagements has come in response to failing states and flawed borders: Desert Storm, Somalia, Haiti, the Balkans, Afghanistan, Iraq . . . we send our men and women in uniform to defend a world designed in Berlin and Versailles according to the macabre political philosophy of Metternich. The greatest democracy in history has been conned by its own political elite into fighting for the cartographic legacy of dead czars, kings, kaisers, and emperors.

The Iraq Study Group's members will assure each other of their conscientiousness, while carefully guarding their legacies for future biographers and historians. And the group's recommendations will suggest, in one form or another, a return to the *ancien régime*.

Of course, the salient difference between the Congress of Vienna and the Iraq Study Group is obvious: The diplomats of the former had just achieved a military victory, while the members of the latter seek to avert a strategic defeat. The freedom of action that the Baker commission might imagine for itself is illusory.

There are no good solutions to Iraq, but some "solutions" are markedly worse than others. Any formula that attempts to extend the lives of dictatorships and oligarchies at the expense of already restive populations will end in disaster—even should it promise us the illusion of a "decent interval."

Why They Got It Wrong

USA Today

December 12, 2006

During my childhood, my favorite cartoon character was Mr. Peabody, the professorial dog whose signature line was "Sherman, set the Wayback Machine!" The bespectacled hound and his young human admirer would then be transported by the time machine to one of history's noteworthy moments.

I recalled those cartoons as I read the Iraq Study Group's recommendations, which promised "a new way forward" and delivered, instead, a dubious blueprint for a return to the days when former secretary of State James Baker's generation blindly supported dictators and authoritarian regimes in the Middle East and beyond.

Those stability-first policies played into the hands of demagogues and the disaffected, enabling terrorist organizations such as al Qa'eda to recruit amid populations deprived of hope. Although the Middle East's core problems are homemade, our embrace—often literal—of mass murderers such as Saddam Hussein and Hafez Assad in Syria exacerbated the region's comprehensive failure.

Now the ISG report, which appears to reflect Baker's world view, resurrects our fateful Cold War-era mistakes with proposals that would reward police states that have promoted chaos in Iraq: By turning to them hat in hand, Baker would further inflate the ambitions of Iran's radical regime while rewarding the cynical—and murderous—behavior of Syria's government. A policy of calculated

171

confrontation would offer more hope—appeasement doesn't work anywhere, but it's especially counterproductive in the Middle East.

The report's capstone recommendations would have little or no useful effect on the security situation in Iraq, but they would penalize our friends to the advantage of our enemies. Arguing that Iraq must be governed by a strong central power and that semiautonomous subregions cannot be tolerated, the report would curtail the freedoms that Iraq's Kurds have enjoyed for the past fifteen years, while outraging Iraq's Shiites.

LIVING IN THE PAST

Astonishingly, the report seeks to tie the future of Iraq to a resolution of the Palestinian issue, thus wedding a terribly difficult problem to an intractable one. With Syria once again implicated in the assassination of Lebanon's democratic leadership, Baker would reward the Damascus government by pressuring Israel to hand over the Golan Heights (with his longstanding ties to Saudi Arabia, Baker appears to accept Riyadh's line that all of the region's problems are Israel's fault).

In another illustration of Baker's priorities—he has close ties to the oil industry—the report's core section devotes one brief paragraph to protecting human rights, women, and minorities, but it features two lengthy recommendations with ten supporting actions to develop Iraq's oil industry.

Much of the report reads as if it had been written in 1976, not 2006. It's not a prescription for success, but an attempted revival of yesteryear's failed policies. Those days of supporting strongmen because they were "ours" remain a black mark on our national history. We paid for them on 9/11. We must not shut our eyes to the necessity of change in the Middle East just because the Bush administration's mishandling of Iraq disappointed us.

The Middle East has changed profoundly since Baker's years in government. Instead of the limited political terrorism of the Palestine Liberation Organization, we face fanatics with global ambitions convinced they're doing their god's will by killing. The past fifteen years also saw the return of genocidal ethnic thugs out to avenge ancient wrongs, real or imagined. And though you might persuade a human being to change his political beliefs, you will not change his religion and he cannot change his ethnicity.

The geopolitical challenges of Baker's heyday were straightforward compared with those confronting us. Yet his generation's solutions didn't work then, either.

THE FATAL FLAWS

The former secretary of state's two primary assumptions are fatally wrong: the belief that stability is the most important international value and the conviction that borders cannot be permitted to change.

Baker is the man who actually tried to persuade the collapsing Soviet Union to remain whole, then insisted that an ever-shrinking Yugoslavia had to be held together. Now, in the interests of "stability," his group's report would deny even limited autonomy to Iraq's long-suffering Kurds and Shiites.

We've been here before.

The United States can no longer afford to stand on the wrong side of history. Borders will change. Yesteryear's brittle stability cannot be recaptured. We will have to live with years of painful instability until this tormented region finds its way to a new "organic" political balance and the appeal of terrorism declines. Young democracies will make choices we deplore but must learn from their own mistakes. As difficult as it is for the American mentality, we must take a long view of the situation: We've failed as a geopolitical architect, but there's still hope for us as a strategic midwife.

Even the report's insistence on the centrality of diplomatic negotiations betrays an obsolete understanding of the world. Diplomacy is uncritically accepted as the answer to all of the Middle East's problems, yet we've been trying it for six decades and the region is arguably worse off today than ever in our lifetimes. You cannot negotiate effectively with interlocutors who either have no interest in talking to you—because they're convinced they're winning—or who view the world as a zero-sum game. Our style of diplomacy presupposes a commonality of interests that simply does not exist in the Middle East.

The traditional wisdom failed us. We need new, innovative ideas, not strategies resurrected from the political crypt. We must deal with the world as it is. Baker's world is gone—and good riddance. We cannot go back to the "golden years" of Saddam and the shah. The Iraq Study Group's report doesn't reflect a "realist" philosophy of international affairs but a destructive, reactionary approach that betrayed us in the past and would be deadly now.

A Lesson for Tyrants

New York Post

December 30, 2006

Saddam Hussein is dead. The mighty dictator met a criminal's end on the gallows. The murderer responsible for one and a half million corpses is just a bag of bones.

For decades, the world pandered to his fantasies, overlooking his brutality in return for strategic advantages or naked profit. Diplomats, including our own, courted him, while the world's democracies and their competitors vied to sell him arms.

Saddam always bluffed—even, fatally, about weapons of mass destruction—but the world declined to call him on his excesses. Massacres went unpunished. His invasions of neighboring states failed to draw serious punishment. He never faced personal consequences until our troops reached Baghdad (a dozen years late).

As long as Saddam paid sufficient bribes and granted the right concessions to the well connected, the world shut its eyes to his cavalcade of atrocities. Even when his soldiers raped Kuwait, the United Nations barely summoned the will to expel his military— and the alliance led by the United States declined to liberate Iraq itself from a tyrant with a sea of blood on his hands.

Everything changed in 2003. For all of its later errors in Iraq, the Bush administration altered the course of history for the better. It may be hard to discern the deeper meaning of our march to Baghdad amid the chaos afflicting Iraq today, but President Bush got a great thing right: He recognized that the age of dictators was ending, that the era of the popular will had arrived. He and his advisers may have underestimated the difficulties involved and misread the nature of that popular will, but they put us back on the moral side of history.

Bush revealed the bankruptcy of the European-designed system of international relations. An unspoken code agreed between kings and czars, emperors, and kaisers, had protected rulers—however monstrous—for centuries, while ignoring the suffering of the masses. The result was that any Third World thug who seized a presidential palace could ravage his country as long as his crimes remained within his "sovereign" borders.

Supported by other English-speaking democracies, Bush acted. Breaking Europe's cynical rules, our forces invaded a dictatorship to liberate its population. And suddenly, the world was no longer safe for tyrants.

No matter the policy failures in the wake of Baghdad's fall, the destruction of Saddam's regime remains a historical turning point. When our troops later dragged the dictator out of a fetid hole, every other president for life shivered at the image.

Tonight, none of those other oppressors will sleep well. They may try to console themselves that America is failing in Iraq, that we've learned our lessons. But no matter what they tell themselves, they'll never feel safe again.

We set a noble precedent, and the critics who insist that deposing Saddam was a mistake are rushing to a very premature judgment.

We did a great thing by overthrowing Saddam. We may have done it poorly, but we did it. We also revealed the hypocrisy of those governments who sold out their professed values for oil money (and pathetically cheaply, too).

From Paris and Berlin through Moscow and Beijing, many will never forgive us. We should be honored.

Was justice done when the trapdoor opened under Saddam's feet? In a clinical sense, yes. But such an easy death was far too kind. He should have been turned loose, naked and handcuffed, in the central square of Halabja, where the survivors of his most notorious poison gas attack could have ripped his flesh with their bare hands.

But we live in a civilized community of nations. Bloodthirsty dictators must be executed humanely—and over the protests of human-rights advocates who insist they shouldn't be executed at all.

Still, Saddam's death was a last humiliation for him. He lived long enough to see his sons die, destroying his dynastic dreams. And long enough to discover that all those Iraqis jumping up and down and crying "We will die for you, Saddam!" didn't really mean it.

Given all of the recent violence in Iraq, it's remarkable how little has been committed in support of Saddam—occasional demonstrations on his home ground and little else. There'll be a hiccup of violence now, but even his fellow Ba'athists have been seeking to regain power for themselves, not for their erstwhile master. (And it's easy to picture their relief at the death of the man they, too, once had to fear.)

The various factions of Iraq are fighting for many things—but Saddam hasn't been one of them. Sycophantic lawyers—Western and Iraqi—doubtless whispered that the people still supported him, that they and his Western friends would never let him hang. (He must have thought ruefully of Ramsey Clark as the noose tightened around his neck.)

Saddam's pathetic grandeur lies in ruins. Millions will celebrate his death; few will mourn. In the end, the all-powerful dictator was just a delusional old man in a cage insisting, "I am the president of Iraq!"

Of course, the Middle East has an ongoing problem with reality. Conspiracy theorists who insisted that the United States was keeping Saddam alive to restore him to power as part of a complex plot will now suggest that one of Saddam's doubles went to the gallows, that the dictator still lives, held in reserve by mysterious forces.

But Saddam Hussein is dead, condemned to death by an Iraqi court. Even the die-hards will figure it out in time.

Again, we can be proud that the United States of America brought him down. And that no dictator can ever feel entirely safe again. President Bush changed the world. For all of today's carnage and confusion, and despite the appalling policy errors after Baghdad fell, the future will show that the change was for the better.

King David Returns

New York Post

January 5, 2007

It's official: Dave Petraeus, one of the U.S. Army's most-impressive leaders, is headed back to Baghdad to take charge. The assignment means a fourth star and the chance to save a desperate situation— or preside over a grim strategic failure.

With back-to-back tours of duty in Iraq behind him and the most-positive image among Iraqis of any U.S. leader, military or civilian, Petraeus is a natural choice. His intelligence, drive, devotion to service, and negotiating skill make the lean, young-looking general seem perfect.

The question is whether Gen. Petraeus is the right choice—or if he'll merely be the final executor of a failed policy.

The general has a winning public demeanor—when he led the 101st Airborne Division in northern Iraq in 2003, he proved such a superb diplomat that the Kurds called him "Malik Daoud"—King David—as a mark of respect. He listened patiently, spent money wisely, used force intelligently, and truly did win hearts and minds.

He went on to tackle the reconstruction of Iraq's security forces—no easy task, given the ruinous legacy of L. Paul Bremer's term as viceroy. Where others had faltered, Petraeus appeared to succeed.

The Pentagon brought him back to Ft. Leavenworth for a breather—formally to imbue the Army's educational system and doctrine production with knowledge from the front but also to give him a break before he worked himself to death.

Petraeus is the sort of soldier who would have stayed on indefinitely in Iraq, setting aside all personal concerns in the interests of the mission. President Bush respects him and even the media admire him. So what could possibly be doubtful about the choice of Gen. Petraeus to take over the leadership of our forces in Iraq?

Having known him—a bit—for years, I have unreserved respect for his talent and dedication, his quality of mind and selfless service. He's the greatest peacekeeping general in the world. But I just don't know if he can win a war.

Regaining control of Baghdad—after we threw it away—will require the defiant use of force. Negotiations won't do it. Cultural awareness isn't going to turn this situation around (we need to stop pandering to our enemies and defeat them, thanks). We insist it's all about politics and try to placate everybody, while terrorists, insurgents, and militias slaughter the innocent in the name of their god and their tribe. Meanwhile, we've been pretending we're not at war. Our enemies aren't pretending. They're not only waging war with everything they've got, but reveling in breathtaking savagery. They're no longer impressed when an American patrol zips by. They know they own the streets, not us. To them, we're just military tourists anxious to go home.

In my contacts with Petraeus, we've sometimes agreed and sometimes argued. But we diverged profoundly on one point: The counterinsurgency doctrine produced under his direction remains far too mired in failed twentieth-century models. Winning hearts and minds sounds great, but it's useless when those hearts and minds turn up dead the next morning.

Gen. Petraeus truly is a brilliant talent. Faced with the reality of Iraq, he may be able to shake off the Pollyanna thinking in which our government and military have become mired. God knows, we all want the general to succeed.

The test will be straightforward: When his tour of duty in Baghdad ends, will unarmed Iraqis—and Americans—be able to walk the streets of Baghdad without fear? Or is our pathetic insistence that compromise can work in the Middle East going to lead to a tragedy beyond the imagination of politicians and pundits.

Will the general fight? Of course, even three- or four-star generals can only do what our civilian leaders order and allow. Half of Petraeus's struggle is going to be with Washington's obsolete view of the world, with our persistent illusions about the Middle East and mankind.

The future of Iraq won't be determined by Gen. Petraeus alone. But his will be the name historians cite when describing our ultimate success or failure in Iraq. I hope Dave Petraeus will go down in the books as the soldier who saved the day. So let me presume to offer a great patriot one piece of advice: Dave, be as tough on our enemies as you are on yourself. And Godspeed.

Eyeing Iran

New York Post

January 6, 2007

Word that Adm. William Fallon will move laterally from our Pacific Command to take charge of Central Command—responsible for the Middle East—while two ground wars rage in the region baffled the media.

Why put a swabbie in charge of grunt operations? There's a one-word answer: Iran.

Assigning a Navy aviator and combat veteran to oversee our military operations in the Persian Gulf makes perfect sense when seen as a preparatory step for striking Iran's nuclear-weapons facilities—if that becomes necessary.

While the Air Force would deliver the heaviest tonnage of ordnance in a campaign to frustrate Tehran's quest for nukes, the toughest strategic missions would fall to our Navy. Iran would seek to retaliate asymmetrically by attacking oil platforms and tankers, closing the Strait of Hormuz—and trying to hit oil infrastructure in Saudi Arabia and the Gulf emirates.

Only the U.S. Navy—hopefully, with Royal Navy and Aussie vessels underway beside us—could keep the oil flowing to a thirsty world.

In short, the toughest side of an offensive operation against Iran would be the defensive aspects—requiring virtually every air and sea capability we could muster. (Incidentally, an additional U.S.

carrier battle group is now headed for the Gulf; Britain and Australia are also strengthening their naval forces in the region.)

Not only did Admiral Fallon command a carrier air wing during Operation Desert Storm, he also did shore duty at a joint headquarters in Saudi Arabia. He knows the complexity and treacherousness of the Middle East firsthand.

Strengthening his qualifications, numerous blue-water assignments and his duties at PACOM schooled him on the intricacies of the greater Indian Ocean—the key strategic region for the twenty-first century and the one that would be affected immediately by a U.S. conflict with Iran.

The admiral also understands China's junkie-frantic oil dependency and its consequent taste for geopolitical street crime: During a U.S. operation against Iran, Beijing would need its fix guaranteed.

While Congress obsesses on Iraq and Iraq alone, the administration's thinking about the future. And it looks as if the White House is preparing options to mitigate a failure in Iraq and contain Iran. Bush continues to have a much underrated strategic vision—the administration's consistent problems have been in the abysmal execution of its policies, not in the over-arching purpose.

Now, pressed by strategic dilemmas and humiliating reverses, Bush is doing what FDR had to do in the dark, early months of 1942: He's turning to the Navy.

As a retired Army officer, I remain proud of and loyal to my service. I realize that the Army's leaders are disappointed to see the CentCom slot go to an admiral in the midst of multiple ground wars. But, beyond the need for a Navy man at the helm should we have to take on Iran, there's yet another reason for sending Fallon to his new assignment: The Army's leadership has failed us at the strategic level.

After Gen. Eric Shinseki was sidelined for insisting on a professional approach to Iraq, Army generals did plenty of fine tactical and operational work—but they never produced a strategic vision for the greater Middle East.

Our Army is deployed globally, but our generals never seem to acquire the knack of thinking beyond the threat hypnotizing them at the moment (the Marines, with their stepbrother ties to the Navy, do a better job of acting locally while thinking globally).

Perhaps the Army's Gen. Dave Petraeus will emerge as an incisive strategic thinker after he takes command in Baghdad, but his predecessors routinely got mired in tactical details and relied—fatally—on other arms of government to do the strategic thinking.

The reasons are complex, ranging from service culture to educational traditions, but it's incontestable that the Navy long has produced our military's best strategic thinkers—captains and admirals able to transcend parochial interests to see the global security environment as a whole. Admiral Fallon's job is to avoid the tyranny of the moment, to see past the jumble of operational pieces and visualize how those pieces ultimately might fit together.

Nor is the Iran problem the only Navy-first issue facing CENT-COM. As you read this, our ships are patrolling the coast of Somalia to intercept fleeing terrorists—and have been hunting pirates in the same waters for years. China's future development (and internal peace) is tied to dependable supplies of Middle-Eastern and African oil transiting Indian Ocean sea lanes, as well as to shipping goods along the same routes. In a future confrontation with China, our ability to shut down the very routes we're now challenged to protect would be vital.

Not least because of the botch up in Iraq, there's a growing sense of the limitations of U.S. ground-force involvement in the Middle East. That doesn't mean we won't see further necessity-driven interventions and even other occupations, only that our strategic planners have begun to grasp that positive change in the region—if it comes at all—is going to take far longer than many of us hoped and won't always be amenable to boots-on-the-ground prodding.

If we can't determine everything that happens in the Big Sandbox, we need to be able to control access to and from the playground—a classic Navy mission.

And in the end, the United States remains primarily a maritime power. As Sir Walter Raleigh pointed out 400 years ago, he who controls the waters controls the world.

General Petraeus is going to Baghdad to deal with our present problems. Admiral Fallon is going to the U.S. Central Command to deal with the future.

W's Last Chance

New York Post

January 11, 2007

Last night, President Bush gave us a candid overview of Iraq and outlined his plan to reverse the bitter course events have taken. The heart of the effort will be a modest surge in American troop strength—to give Iraqis a last chance to save their country.

Will the plan work? Maybe. It's a last-hope effort based on steps that should've been taken in 2003, from providing basic security for the population to getting young Iraqi males off the streets and into jobs.

The added 20,000-plus U.S. troops to be phased in over the coming months will make a tactical difference in Baghdad and Anbar province—but that may not translate into strategic success. Given that we're now committed to a strategy of sending more troops, a larger increase of the sort proposed by Sen. John McCain would make more sense.

Yes, deploying even 20,000 more troops strains our long-neglected ground forces; nonetheless, the number feels like another compromise measure for an administration and country still unwilling to accept that we're really at war.

Given all that, should we support the president's plan? Yes. The stakes are too high to do otherwise—the president's right about that. Iraq deserves one last chance. And I say that as a former soldier well aware of the casualties ahead.

The attempt to reclaim Baghdad from the terrorists, insurgents, and militiamen—to occupy the city, neighborhood by neighborhood—will lead to serious combat. And combat means dead and wounded Americans.

All of this would have been far easier in 2003 or 2004. But we are where we are. And walking away from this fight prematurely isn't a solution.

That doesn't mean our commitment should be open-ended—and the president admits that now. As I've long argued, the Iraqis have to make significant strides in healing and defending their own country by the closing months of 2007. Or we should leave.

Encouragingly, the plan the president outlined was developed in cooperation with the Iraqi government and places far more responsibility on the Iraqis than in the past. If they live up to their part of this compact, we should stand by them no matter how long it takes. But if Prime Minister Nouri al Maliki and Iraq's security forces behave as ethnic partisans, we'll need to leave them to their fate.

Ultimately, it's the Iraqis, not the additional American soldiers and Marines, who'll decide Iraq's future. And the acid test will be their government's handling of Muqtada al Sadr's Mahdi Army.

Paradoxically, a burst of fighting would be a positive sign, indicating that Maliki meant yesterday's disarmament ultimatum to Muqtada's militia. But if the Mahdi Army just goes to ground and the prime minister claims that—poof!—it's no longer a threat, it will mean that he cut another deal with Muqtada.

The crackdown in Baghdad truly has to be nonpartisan, comprehensive, and uncompromising. And the big test isn't going to be the current struggle for Haifa Street—defended by Sunni insurgents and foreign terrorists—but the occupation, disarmament, and ideological disinfection of Sadr City. If we and the Iraqis try to avoid Sadr City's challenges, you'll know the entire effort's a hollow sham.

And there's going to be another major problem that will require great fortitude on the president's part: Destructive fighting lies ahead in Baghdad, and the international media is going to blame us for every broken window and every Iraqi with photogenic wounds. We'll be accused of atrocities and wanton destruction, and the press corps will trot out the Vietnam-era cliché about "destroying the village in order to save it."

Our troops can stand up to any enemy. But I'm not as certain that President Bush can withstand the onslaught of an enraged media—and any prospect that we might be turning the situation around will certainly enrage them. Media pressure will work through our allies, too.

Our troops will never surrender—but I'm afraid the White House might fold.

To a soldier, the most encouraging thing the president said last night was that there had been "too many restrictions" on our troops in the past. Rules of engagement must be loosened. We have to stop playing Barney Fife and fight. And the president has to stand behind our troops when the game gets rough.

As for the Democrats in Congress, they can't continue whining that they support our troops while threatening to cut off funding for those in uniform in wartime. They should be ashamed of themselves for even hinting at such a course of action.

What does the president's plan have going for it? A sound tactical concept for security in Baghdad; significant Iraqi commitments (we'll see what they're worth); an overdue integration of Provincial Reconstruction Teams—the moneybags guys—into our combat units; a core of genuine Iraqi patriots; a refreshingly tough stance with Iran and Syria; and an extremely capable American commander en route to Baghdad, Gen. Dave Petraeus.

There are no guarantees that this plan will work, but it deserves a chance. Surrender isn't a strategy, and cowardice won't save us from the deadly threats we face. The president's new plan will have a painful human cost. But the cost of defeat would be incalculably higher.

Our president deserves our support. One last time.

Talk Is Cheap

New York Post

January 17, 2007

Washington's elite may disdain religious believers, but its own bizarre dogma is far more irrational than faith in God: The D.C. establishment worships the imaginary power of negotiations to make peace in the Middle East.

In the tradition of intolerant believers everywhere, our governing elite rejects all evidence that its faith in diplomacy might be misplaced. Now the pagan priests on the Potomac are chanting, "Only negotiations can fix Iraq."

It's possible that nothing is going to fix Iraq, but "Why can't we all just get along" parleys have about as much chance of bringing the factions together and ending Iranian and Syrian mischief as a rabbi has of being elected king of Saudi Arabia.

There is no hope of pacifying Iraq through negotiations. None. Zero. The country has no tradition of intercommunal compromise—and the fighting factions and foreign governments involved have no incentive to compromise, so there is no way short of the massive use of force to bully them into compromising. Even if we got them all to agree to a patched-together accord, each faction would only honor it as long it seemed to be to its advantage.

But they're not going to agree, anyway, until a great deal more blood has been shed. The window for peace has closed.

Shi'a Arabs are convinced that they're destined to be the winners who take all. Iraq's Sunni Arabs believe they can regain power through violence. The Kurds won't give up what they've gained, and they'd like a bit more, thanks.

Iran believes the United States is ready to quit, leaving Tehran the new hegemon in Iraq and the Persian Gulf. Oh, and the religious fanatics in power will soon have nukes.

The lesson Syria drew from Iraq is that America has forgotten what it takes to win wars and falters when the going gets tough. Even the Israelis have lost their guts. With Hezbollah up and Lebanon sinking, Damascus thinks it just has to keep on making mischief.

The only party interested in a compromise settlement in Iraq happens to be us.

Where have negotiations led to lasting peace in the Middle East? Even the surly accord between Israel and Egypt only came about because both sides were worn out—and the Sinai still requires armed peacekeepers, more than three decades later.

The important point about that one reasonably successful Mideast settlement is that the players on both sides understood that they'd reached the end of the game. That's when Washington-brokered talks can help—when those involved all want an agreement but need a fig leaf they can wear domestically ("The Americans made me do it. . . .").

Otherwise, the fate of negotiations in the Middle East has been consistent failure. Can anyone honestly claim that the region's better off today because of our diplomacy?

Lately, pundits have cited Churchill's line that "to jaw-jaw is better than to war-war." But Winnie was no Neville Chamberlain: He understood that only a position of strength makes jaw-jaw a viable option. And he certainly understood that wars had to be won.

Negotiation only comes into its own when the fighting's essentially over. And this war's barely begun.

So why, despite overwhelming empirical evidence that talks won't solve Iraq's problems, do politicians, diplomats, profs, and pundits unite to insist that "negotiations are the only answer"?

It's not because they're visionaries smarter than the rest of us. The Washington establishment is composed almost exclusively of people who've built successful careers on words, not deeds—on negotiations, not action.

We're all prisoners of our experience to some degree. Stir in the massive egos crowding out common sense in D.C., and personal histories come with titanium bars.

Diplomats, of course, negotiate for a living—but so do lawyers. (Most legal affairs end in compromise settlements, not courtroom fireworks.) And our elected politicians are, overwhelmingly, lawyers. Academics also talk for a living (primarily to each other), while pundits live off words, criticizing the deeds of others. Even political appointees tend to have law or business backgrounds—career paths where successful negotiations lead to wealth and prestige.

And none of these various players believe they need guidance from the janitorial staff or the blue-collar workers down on the production line.

That means they don't want military advice. With no meaningful experience of the world's physical savagery, the Washington elite can't conceive of a problem that can't be solved the way its members always solved problems in law offices, legislatures, corporate offices, and plum embassy jobs: by talking. Those pesky generals just complicate things.

Of course, all of those legislators with law degrees, business execs filling Cabinet posts, career diplomats, think-tank academics, and journalists who kid themselves that they're D.C. insiders all have one other thing in common: They were much too important to serve our country in uniform.

So we're left with the cult of jaw-jaw—which just leads to more (and worse) war-war. For all of the advanced degrees in town, Washington doesn't really think, but accepts the doctrine laid down by the commissars. And the bipartisan party line runs that there's no problem diplomacy can't solve.

Talks won't fix Iraq—indeed, attempts to placate our enemies will certainly make things worse. That doesn't mean that military force will solve Baghdad's problems, either. But unrestricted force has a better chance than a special ambassador's blather.

Talkers dominate Washington, but the world is changed by doers. At present, the doers are on the side of our enemies. Negotiations have no power to fix Iraq or the greater Middle East. The series of debacles ahead, from Beirut to Baghdad and from Tel Aviv to Tehran, is going to prove just that. Again.

Ugly Choices:
Tough Bets in Mideast

New York Post

January 29, 2007

Like plenty of other Americans, I wish we could just be done with the Middle East. Unfortunately, the Middle East isn't done with us. And the situation is going to get considerably worse before it shows a hint of getting better.

Thanks to abysmal policy errors (many predating the current administration), we've caught ourselves between two irreconcilable sides—Sunni and Shi'a Muslims—whose enmity dates back thirteen centuries. And we're now taking fire from every direction.

Dreaming that all Iraqis could get along, we alienated potential friends and empowered deadly enemies. Short of Mongol-quality savagery, the traditional way to win in the Middle East has been to select an ally and stick with him—while avoiding the folly of trying to play honest broker.

The administration has begun to realize that it has to make some hard choices. Yet our leaders still believe they can have it both ways. The result may be bad hard choices.

At the strategic level, Washington is lining up regional allies—Sunni Arab states—to face off with Iran. But in Iraq, the administration continues to tilt toward Shi'a parties—hoping that Iran can be excluded from a decisive role in Baghdad. (Note that we've been fighting hard on Baghdad's Sunni-populated Haifa Street, but we're still avoiding a showdown in Sadr City.)

For their part, our Sunni-Arab "allies" support the Sunni insurgents and dread the prospect of a Shi'a-dominated democratic government or a partition of Iraq.

And now, in the worst American tradition, we're in danger of grabbing at short-term gains at an exorbitant strategic price: Defaulting to our old habit of backing hard-line regimes, we've dropped all pressure on the Saudis and Egyptians to reform their political systems.

Want to recruit more terrorists for another 9/11? Give Sunni-Arab regimes a renewed blank check to shut down all opposition.

True, Shi'a terrorists have attacked us in the Middle East. But the Sunni terrorists attack us globally—and on our own soil. Shi'a extremists think regionally, while Sunni fanatics have universal ambitions.

Yes, Iran is the immediate strategic problem—but it's a far more complex matter than the kiss-the-Saudis'-sandals crowd accepts. A violent rogue with a nuclear-weapons program, Iran backs terrorists in Iraq, Lebanon, and Afghanistan.

Yet Iran also happens to be America's natural ally in the region.

We're in a race against time. The Iranian people have tried religious rule—now they're sick and tired of it. They want to move on. President Mahmoud Ahmadinejad's allies lost the last round of elections and the mullahs are getting nervous about his excesses. Iranians want change but don't know how to get it—and we can't impose it.

Could the Khomeinist regime fall before apocalyptic ayatollahs get the bomb? There's no more pressing strategic question.

If we find it necessary to attack Iran's nuclear program, it's going to be a long and messy process. A thorough effort would kill a lot of Iranians—alienating even the most liberal-minded members of a highly nationalistic population.

Stopping the bad Iranians would cost us the good Iranians. There's no good solution.

The tragedy here is that Iran is farther along in its political development than our Arab "friends." The states to which we're inclined to turn may still have Sunni versions of the Khomeini revolution ahead of them.

Fundamentalist, anti-American regimes could hatch in exactly the baskets where we're tempted to park our strategic eggs.

If we line up with the Sunni-Arab autocracies again, we lose Iran—and perhaps the entire region in the long run. But tolerating the rise of radical Shi'a power in the near term threatens Israel, genocidal conflict in Iraq and beyond, and global economic pain.

In an all-too-real sense, backing either side, Sunni or Shi'a, is just betting on black or red at the roulette wheel—knowing that the house always wins in the end. And the house is the collapsed and vengeful civilization of the Middle East.

But we're locked in the casino; we have to make our bet. So here are the fundamental questions the administration has to ask itself before pushing the chips across the table:

- How do we defeat Iran's government without alienating the Iranian people?
- Do our long-term interests truly coincide with repressive Sunni Arab regimes?
- Are we once again in danger of starting a fight we lack the guts to finish? The administration's less-than-half-hearted military policy in Iraq and Israel's disastrous loss to Hezbollah last summer aren't encouraging models.
- By reinvigorating our "alliance" with Saudi Arabia and other repressive Sunni states, are we just setting ourselves up for another round of "let's you and him fight," with American blood defending Arab oil wealth? Are we still the Saudi royal family's whores?

If our troops do wind up dying to save the House of Saud yet again, we need to recognize that we, not they, are in the power seat. We should demand that they really open the oil taps to bankrupt Iran (and Venezuela's Hugo Chavez) and that they publicly recognize Israel's right to exist.

We're paying a terrible price—and may pay yet a higher one— for the bipartisan failure of one administration after another (and of successive Congresses) to pursue a serious alternative-energy program. Now we're stuck in the kill zone.

There's no easy fix and there are no solid answers to our problems in the Middle East. The region's future has never been so unpredictable and could evolve in a number of startling ways—not all of them bad.

Only one thing is certain: A return to yesteryear's destructive policies and faulty alliances won't solve our long-term problems.

Iraq? That's the easy one.

Sunni Vs. Shi'a:
It's Not All Islam

RealClearPolitics.com

Valentine's Day 2007

Among the worst members of the it's-all-a-conspiracy pack are those who insist that every Muslim is in on a vast jihadi conspiracy to make Natalie Maines of the Dixie Chicks wear a chador (not a bad idea, aesthetically speaking). But those most anxious to condemn Islam in its entirety skip over annoying facts: Overwhelmingly, the victims of Islamist terror have been other Muslims; even the Taliban or the Khomeinist regime never rivaled the Inquistion's ferocity; and Europeans, not Muslims, long have been the heavyweight champions of genocide (with the Turks a distant runner-up).

All monotheist religions have been really good haters. We just take turns.

But the biggest obstacle to establishing the Caliphate in California is that Shi'a "Islam" never bought into the Caliphate at all. At bottom, it's a different religion from Sunni Islam. They're not just different branches of a faith, as with Protestantism and Catholicism, but separate faiths whose core differences are more pronounced than those between Christians and Jews.

Technically, Sunni militants are correct when they label the Shi'a "heretics." Persians and their closest neighbors, with long memories of great civilizations, were never comfortable with the crudeness of Arabian Islam—which the anthropologist Claude Levi-Strauss aptly called "a barracks religion."

The struggle has never ended between the ascetic, intolerant Bedouin faith of Arabia, with its fascist obsession on behavior, and the profound theologies of Persian civilization that absorbed and transformed Islam. While Shi'ism only prevailed in Persia within the last millennium (nudging out Sunni Islam at last), "Aryan"

Islam had long been shaped by Zoroastrianism and other ineradicable pre-Islamic legacies.

Persians made the new faith their own, incorporating cherished traditions—just as northern Europeans made Christianity their own through Protestantism. It's illuminating to hear Iran's president rumor the return of the Twelfth Imam, since the coming of that messiah figure is pure Zoroastrianism, with no connection to the Koran or the Hadiths.

Even the rhetoric of Iran's Islamic Revolution, condemning the U.S. as the "Great Satan," divided the world into forces of light and darkness—Zoroaster again, as well as Mani, the dualist whose followers we know as "Manicheans." Iranians excitedly deny such pre-Islamic influences—then worship at the ancient shrines of reinvented saints, celebrate the Zoroastrian New Year, and incorporate fire rites into social events.

The Prophet's attempt to discipline Arabian hillbillies produced a faith ill fitted to Persia's complex civilization—or to Mesopotamian Arabs, who despised the illiterate desert nomads. Islam was bound to change as it occupied this haunted real estate.

What we've gotten ourselves involved in today is an old and endless struggle between the desert and the city, between civilization and barbarism. Long oppression may have made Shi'ism appear backward, but it's inherently a richer faith than Sunni Islam. With its End-of-Times vision, its founding martyrs and radiant angels, and its mysticism and wariness of the flesh, Shi'ism is closer to Christianity than checklist Sunni Islam ever could be.

Further confounding the strategic situation, there are other, parallel struggles within Shi'ism and Sunni Islam. Over the centuries, *both* faiths developed sophisticated urban classes that are now under assault, as they periodically have been, by intolerant simplifiers preaching the reform-school Islam of seventh-century Arabia.

Simultaneously, there's been some bizarre cross-fertilization: Osama bin Laden, a Sunni who hates the Shi'a more fiercely than he does Americans, has grafted a Shi'a End-Of-Days vision onto Sunni Islam. Meanwhile, the mullahs who locked down Iran obsess about behavior—a Sunni approach to faith—at the expense of Shi'ism's tradition of inner luminosity (in the Sunni world, the persecuted Sufis were the mystics).

We're a fringe player in multiple zero-sum struggles: Persian Zoroastrianism in Muslim garb vs. Bedouin fascism; multiple insurgencies within the Sunni global campaign to reestablish the Caliphate; an interfaith competition to jump-start an apocalypse; an old ethnic struggle between Persians and Arabs; and a distinctly Zoroastrian struggle between good and evil (alert the White House).

Many will reflexively reject this interpretation of Shi'ism and Sunni Islam as two separate faiths with profoundly different inheritances. Blog Bedouins and "scholars" alike will feel threatened. That's part of our problem: We're often as close minded as our enemies. The greatest power in history thinks small.

As I remarked to an Arab-American friend last week, faiths are like bad neighbors—they borrow a great deal and then deny it. There is no such thing as a pure faith today. All have been influenced by their predecessors and peers, by internal evolutions and their historical environments. But even individuals who reject such a view when it comes to their own faith do themselves no favors by refusing to contemplate Islam's complexity.

What does all this mean to us? First, wherever there are irreconcilable differences, there are strategic opportunities. Second, our insistence on seeing the Middle East through the eyes of yesteryear's failed statesmen has been disastrous—we need to reinterpret the Muslim world.

Third, we've entered a new age when all the great faiths are struggling over their identities. As the religions most immediately besieged, Shi'ism and Sunni Islam are the noisiest and, for now, the most violent. But *all* faiths are in crisis—even as every major faith undergoes a powerful renewal.

In my years as an intelligence analyst, I consistently made my best calls when I trusted my instincts, and I was less likely to get it right when I heeded the arguments around me. Today, those surrounding arguments damn Iran.

My instincts tell me our long-term problem is with Arab Sunnis, whose global aspirations have veered into madness. We have a problem with the junta currently ruling Iran but *not* with Persian civilization. Meanwhile, the Bedouin fanaticism gripping so much of the Middle East has no civilization.

PART III

The Home Front

Spies & Lies

New York Post

April 28, 2006

If a street-corner thug knowingly receives stolen goods for profit, he goes to jail. If a well-educated, privileged journalist profits from receiving classified information—stolen from our government—he or she gets a prize.

Is something wrong here?

Media outlets, including the generally responsible *Washington Post,* have had fits over a few retired generals' unclassified criticism of the Secretary of Defense, while simultaneously insisting on their own right to receive and publish our nation's wartime secrets—and to shield the identities of unethical bureaucrats who betray our nation's trust.

Since the Vietnam era, reporters have convinced themselves that they are the real heroes in any story. The archways above our journalism faculties soon may sport the maxim: "The Press can do no wrong."

But the press can do wrong. And it does it with gusto. Let me tell you what the illegal receipt and exploitation of our nation's secrets used to be called: Espionage. Spying. Yet today's "real" spies cause less harm to our national security than self-righteous journalists do.

A nation at war must keep secrets. The media can't plead that classified documents just fell into their hands, obligating them to publish our secrets out of a noble respect for truth. That's bull, and every journalist knows it. Could a punk down on the block claim that, since he was offered a gun, he was obligated to aim it and pull the trigger?

Many in the media not only want to rewrite election results and change national policies—they've been rewriting history, too. On the entertainment-and-propaganda side, George Clooney produced a gorgeous, seductive, and whoppingly dishonest film about journalism last year, *Good Night, and Good Luck.*

Deftly rearranging the fall of Sen. Joseph McCarthy—by slighting the fact that only the Department of the Army had the guts to stand up to Tailgunner Joe at the height of his powers (a civilian lawyer for the Army asked the famous question, "Senator, have you no shame?")—the film leads the viewer to believe that a lone journalist, Edward R. Murrow, broke the senator's evil spell.

Of course, crediting the Army with the courage to defend the Constitution would have played havoc with the left-wing view of civil-military relations. But the greater omission had to do with Murrow's background. He made his bones with courageous radio coverage of the London Blitz. And he didn't feel compelled to tell the Nazi side of the story and help us feel Hitler's pain.

Edward R. Murrow kept secrets. Lots of them. He wanted the Allies to win. He even respected those in uniform. So he—and other journalists—remained silent about the landing exercise that went tragically awry at Slapton Sands and about many another bad-for-morale event that might've made a hot headline. He kept D-Day-related secrets, too.

Do even our most self-adoring journalists really think that Edward R. Murrow would have published secret documents about prisons for senior Nazis during wartime?

None of us wants our media to engage in propaganda. We'd just like them to refrain from harming our country for selfish ends.

Which brings us to the Pulitzer-Prize-winning (and still not confirmed) story that claimed to reveal secret prisons holding a few high-ranking terrorists in Eastern Europe: If such facilities existed, what harm did they do to our country or the world? On the other hand, proclaiming their existence played into the hands of terrorists and America-haters.

That Pulitzer Prize wasn't really for journalism. It was a political statement. No one's going to get a journalism award for reporting on the War on Terror's successes or progress in Iraq. Only left-wing children get a prize.

After laboring in the intelligence vineyards for over two decades, I can assure you of a few things: First, there are no super-top-secret, black-helicopter, kidnap-American-Idol-judges conspiracies hidden since 1776. Second, there are legitimate secrets that must be protected—usually because revealing them would tip our collection methods or operational techniques to our country's mortal enemies (as the secret-prisons story did).

I can assure you of a third thing, too: If an intelligence professional saw a genuine threat to the Constitution or to the rights of his or her fellow citizens, he or she would step forward—and be justified in doing so.

But pique over your presidential candidate's defeat or mere disagreement with a policy does not justify anyone—intelligence professional or political appointee—in passing classified information to a party not authorized to receive it.

This applies to White House staffers, too, no matter how senior. The law should take its course, in every case, from the briefing room to the newsroom. The Washington culture of leaks is a bipartisan disgrace—and a real-and-present danger to our security.

We face savage enemies who obey no laws, honor no international conventions, treaties or compacts, and who believe they do the will of a vengeful god. Under the circumstances, we need to be able to keep an occasional secret.

So I would ask three questions of those journalists chasing prizes by printing our wartime secrets:

- Can you honestly claim to have done our nation any good?
- Did you weigh the harm your act might cause, including the loss of American lives?
- Is the honorable patriotism of Edward R. Murrow truly dead in American journalism?

If you draw a government (or contractor) paycheck and willfully compromise classified material, you should go to jail. If you are a journalist in receipt of classified information and you publish it to the benefit of our enemies, you should go to jail (you may, however, still accept your journalism prize, as long as the trophy has no sharp edges). And consider yourself fortunate: The penalty for treason used to be death.

When a journalist is given classified information, his or her first call shouldn't be to an editor. It should be to the FBI.

Our Strategic Intelligence Problem

Military Review

July–August 2006

Our national intelligence system will never meet our unrealistic expectations, nor can it ever answer all of our needs. No matter what we do or change or buy, intelligence agencies will remain unable to satisfy our government's appetite for knowledge. This isn't defeatism, but realism. We had better get used to the idea.

This does not mean that our intelligence system cannot be improved. It can. Nor does it imply that our leaders should be less demanding. Stressing the system enhances its performance. But our fantastic expectations must be lowered to a level more in accord with our present and potential capabilities.

And we *must* end the decades-old practice of blaming flawed intelligence for broader policy failures. For all of its indisputable shortcomings, the U.S. intelligence community has become a too-convenient scapegoat for erroneous decisions made by a succession of leaders indifferent to the substance of intelligence, but alert to the advantages of politics. If we want to improve our comprehensive security, we need to begin with a sharp dose of realism regarding what intelligence can and cannot deliver. We do not expect our health-care system to return every patient to perfect health. It is just as foolish to expect perfect intelligence.

While there are real, endemic problems within our intelligence system, the greater problem may be with the expectations of the public, the media, and our nation's policymakers. From indefensible defense-contractor promises to the insidious effects of Hollywood's long-running fantasy of all-seeing, all-powerful intelligence agencies, the lack of an accurate grasp of what intelligence generally can provide, occasionally can deliver, and still cannot begin to achieve results in reflexive cries of "Intelligence failure!" under circumstances in which it would have been impossible—or a case of hit-the-lottery luck—for intelligence to succeed.

Despite the political grandstanding over a catalytic tragedy, any probability of preventing 9/11 through better intelligence work was a myth. Our enemies outmaneuvered and *out-imagined* us so boldly that none of those who now insist that they warned us offered any useful specificity before the event. In retrospect, many matters appear far simpler and more linear. We cannot believe that a general was so foolish in battle, forgetting that our privileged view is far different from that confronting the general amid the chaos of war. Looking back, it appears obvious that, by 1999, there was an unsustainable high-tech bubble in the stock market—but how many of us nonetheless bought in near the top? Charges that "They should have seen it coming!" are usually wrong and rarely helpful. The only useful question is "*Why* didn't we see it coming?"

Sometimes the answer is that the system's attention was elsewhere. But the answer also might be that a given event was impossible to prevent without a phenomenal stroke of luck. The problem with luck is that it is not very dependable. September 11 was not only an intelligence failure, it was also a law-enforcement failure, an airline failure, an architectural failure, a fire-and-rescue failure, a long-term policy failure, and a failure of our national imagination. Our enemies told us openly that they intended to attack us. From Langley to Los Angeles, we, the people, could not conceive that they meant it. Even those of us who wrote theoretically about massive attacks on lower Manhattan have no right to claim prescience. We did not truly envision the reality. Our collective belief systems needed to be shaken by images of catastrophes on our soil.

Similarly, our military had to undergo a succession of asymmetrical conflicts to begin to shake its cold-war-era mindset. No succession of briefings, books, or articles could have had the impact of the suicide bomber and the improvised explosive device. Likewise, in military intelligence, we are beginning to see a generational divide between yesterday's technology-*über-alles* managers—who continue, for now, to be promoted—and a younger generation of intelligence officers who have endured the brutal human crucibles of Iraq and Afghanistan and who do not expect a van full of electronics to do all of their work for them. Because it routinely deals with life-and-death issues, tactical intelligence, long a backwater, might improve more profoundly than strategic intelligence in the coming years.

If the events of the past decade (or century) should teach us anything about the relationship between the intelligence community and our national leadership, it is that the more reliant any policy or action is on the *comprehensive* accuracy of intelligence, the more likely it is to disappoint, if not humiliate, us with its results.

Intelligence can help leaders shape their views, but it is not a substitute for leadership. Senior members in the intelligence world must share the blame for our unrealistic expectations. In order to secure funding for ever-more-expensive technologies, too much was promised in return. While technical assets, from satellites to adept computer programs, bring us great advantages in amassing and processing data, even the best machine cannot predict the behavior of hostile individuals or governments.

The salvation-through-technology types do great damage to our intelligence effort. They deliver massive amounts of data, but become so mesmerized by what technology can do that they slight the importance of relevance. And humans are messy, while technology appears pristine. Furthermore, there are massive profits to be made on the technology side (and good retirement jobs for program managers); thus, Congress leans inevitably toward funding systems rather than fostering human abilities.

There is no consistent lobby for human intelligence, language skills, or deep analysis. Despite occasional bursts of supportive rhetoric on Capitol Hill, the money still goes for machinery, not flesh and blood. Recent personnel increases remain trivial compared to our investments in technology. Yet we live in an age when our security problems are overwhelmingly human problems. Despite a half-decade of reorganizations near and at the top of the intelligence system, we remain far better suited to detecting the movements of yesteryear's Soviet armies and fleets than we are at comprehending and finding terrorists. (In Washington, the immediate response to any crisis within a government bureaucracy is to rotate the usual suspects at the top, not to address the pervasive reforms required—and no one in our government understands the concept of "sunk costs.")

Nor do our intelligence difficulties end with our inability to locate and kill Osama bin Laden, who will be eliminated eventually, just as Abu Musab al Zarqawi was. Our high-tech intelligence architecture even failed in many of the spheres in which it was supposed to excel. Consider just a few examples of the system falling short when required to perform:

- During the air campaign to break Belgrade's hold on Kosovo, the Serbian military fooled our overhead collectors with decoy targets composed of campfires, old hulks, and metal scraps. Hundreds of millions of dollars in precision munitions went to waste as we attacked improvised charcoal grills. It took the threat of American ground troops to force a sloppy diplomatic compromise—a six-week air effort hit only a handful of real targets.

- Notoriously, our hundreds of billions in collection systems could neither confirm nor deny that Saddam Hussein possessed weapons of mass destruction as we moved toward war. Our intelligence system proved so weak that it could offer nothing substantial to challenge or support the position assumed by decision-makers. Without convincing evidence to the contrary, the existence of weapons of mass destruction in Iraq became little more than a matter of opinion. Opinion then attained the force of fact in the buildup to war. The lack of reliable sources in Iraq and agents on the ground left the satellites searching desperately for the slightest hint that the Baghdad regime was armed with forbidden weapons. We were no longer collecting—we were conjuring. Conjecture hardened into conviction. And we went to war focused on finding chemical rounds, rather than on a convulsive population.

- None of our technical collection means detected the wartime threat from the Saddam Fedayeen or other irregular forces. As then-Lieutenant General William Scott Wallace, the Army V Corps commander on the march to Baghdad, observed, the enemy we ended up fighting (albeit successfully) was not the enemy the intelligence community had briefed. Commanders learned as they fought, after our best intelligence had promised them a different war. In Iraq, we couldn't see what we wanted to see, so we refused to see what we didn't want to see. We relied so heavily on technical collection means that we forgot to *think*.

- Not a single one of over a hundred attempted "decapitation" strikes with precision weapons succeeded in killing the targeted individual during the initial stages of Operation Iraqi Freedom—even though most of the sites were destroyed. The concept remains sound in theory, but our ability to hit targets has far outstripped our ability to identify them accurately. It's just plain hard to find people who are doing their best to hide. Even now, our successful strikes against terrorists rely far more often on tips, interrogations, and the processing of captured material than on national collection means. On the ground in Iraq, military intelligence personnel diagram the human relationships among our enemies much as their British predecessors would have done eighty years ago (although we can do our sketching on computer screens).

- Satellites famously can read a license plate (and more). But they rarely tell you whether that battered Toyota contains an innocent civilian, a suicide bomber, or a terrorist chieftain. If the enemy declines to use communications technologies, we are back to the human factor to do our target spotting.

The problem with the human factor is that the technocrats who dominate the intelligence community just don't like it. The "metal benders" see technology as reliable (and immune to personnel management problems), even if that reliability isn't germane to our actual needs. The more our security problems take on a human shape, the more money we throw at technology. A retired psychiatrist I know points out that one form of insanity is to repeat a failed action obsessively. By that measure, our intelligence community is as mad as Lear on the heath.

Only human beings can penetrate the minds of other human beings. Understanding our enemies is the most important requirement for our intelligence system. Yet "understanding" is a word you rarely, if ever, find in our intelligence manuals. We are obsessed with accumulating great volumes of data, measuring success in tonnage rather than results. Instead of panning for gold, we proudly pile up the mud.

Two things must happen if our national intelligence system is to improve. Within the intelligence community, we need to achieve a more effective balance between our default to technology and the slighted human factor. At the top of the game, intelligence is about deciphering what an enemy will do before the enemy knows it himself. The very best analysts can do this, if only sometimes. But occasional successes are better than consistent failures. However imperfect the results, who would deny that a better grasp of the mentalities, ambitions, fears, jealousies, schemes, and desires of our opponents would have offered us more in the days before 9/11 or in the buildup to the invasion of Iraq (or now, in dealing with Iran) than any series of satellite photos?

If we want to improve the quality and usefulness of the intelligence that reaches our nation's leaders, we need to accept the primacy of the human being in intelligence. Instead of the current system, in which people support technology, we need our technologies to support people.

The other thing that must be done—and this is terribly hard— is for all of us, from the Oval Office, through military commanders, to the Wi-Fi crowd down at Starbucks, to have rational expectations of what intelligence can provide and how reliably it can perform. The technocrats continue to insist, against all evidence, that machines can solve all of our intelligence problems, if only we develop and buy more of them. But this age of Cain-and-Abel warfare, of global disorientation, and of a sweeping return to primitive identities and exclusive beliefs is characterized by its raw, brutal humanity. Far from bringing us together, the computer age has amplified our differences and reinvigorated old hatreds. A new, global ruling class profits, while the human masses seethe.

Nothing is a greater challenge for the intelligence system than the individual human being who hates us enough to kill us. How do we spot him in the crowd before he acts? *Why* does he wish to kill us—perhaps committing suicide in the process? How do we find him in a city's wretched crowding or amid remote tribes? What happens when he gains access to weapons of mass destruction? The long-term costs to our country from 9/11 proved to be far greater than the 3,000 casualties we suffered that morning. What second-, third-, and fourth-order effects might even a small nuclear blast trigger?

We can defeat states with relative ease. Individuals are tougher. At present, we know approximately where Osama bin Laden is, but we lack the specific awareness to strike him with a single, politically tolerable bomb. To have a reasonable chance of killing or capturing him, we would have to send in a large ground force, potentially igniting all Pakistan and bringing down the military regime that, tragically, is that country's sole hope. So we wait for the whispered word that will tell us what we need to know. After all of the hyper-expensive collection systems have failed, we find ourselves relying on bribes, informers, and luck, and attacking huts and caves rather than command bunkers and missile silos.

Our intelligence system can do more to protect us than it has done, but even reformed, it will not detect or stop all of our enemies. We need to do better, but we will never perform perfectly. Intelligence is, at last, about people—on both sides. And human beings are imperfect. Yet, amid the tumult confronting us today, the imperfect human offers more hope for intelligence successes than the perfect machine.

Decision-makers have to accept that they must live with a large measure of uncertainty. (Generals have had to do so since the Bronze Age.) Even the intelligence estimate that captures today's issues with remarkable acuity might be upended by a single distant event tomorrow. There are few, if any, static answers in intelligence. The problems we face from foreign enemies are throbbing, morphing, living, often-irrational manifestations of human problems that are themselves in the process of constant change. Intelligence *moves.* Even the best strategic intelligence provides only not-quite-focused snapshots and rough-compass bearings, not detailed maps to a pre-determined future. The iron paradox of any intelligence system is that to expand its effectiveness you must recognize its limitations.

Blaming faulty intelligence for policy failures is the ultimate case of the workman blaming his tools. Even the best intelligence can only inform decisions. It cannot be forced to make them.

Secrets for Sale—Cheap

New York Post

September 27, 2006

After more than two decades in the intelligence world, I know a few secrets. Some would merit brief, trumped-up headlines. But keeping those secrets is a matter of honor.

I don't keep secrets *from* the American people. I keep secrets *for* the American people. I took an oath not to divulge classified information. In return, I was trusted. And I never broke my word.

That means that I and all those like me who keep the faith don't fit in Washington, D.C., where leaking our nation's secrets is now a competitive sport—for both Democrats and Republicans.

The climate of leaks-without-penalties must end. But it probably won't. Why? Because senior figures in both parties see political advantages in well-timed leaks. They're willing to betray our nation for a brief partisan edge.

I've already used two out-of-date words that mark me as a patsy in D.C.: "honor" and "betray."

What happened to honor? Among our elected and appointed officials? A sense of honor still prevails within our military and among hundreds of thousands of government employees. Honor still prevails in much of our community life. Many Americans beyond the Beltway maintain a strong sense of personal and professional honor.

But honor's dead in Washington. And at "leading" universities (where patriotism, too, is beneath contempt). And in the media.

Honor isn't hip. It's as pathetic as a powder-blue, polyester leisure suit.

To journalists and members of Congress, the concept of honor is so alien it's incomprehensible. If you can grab a headline, no matter the cost to your country, tell our secrets—and win an award for your "courage."

If you can bump up your poll numbers before the election, spill the beans. If you can stick it to the other party, by all means tell the terrorists what our senior intelligence officers think. Expose our security programs. Exaggerate our military problems. If we're short on bullets, tell the bad guys. Honor's for the chumps, the losers, the average voter who "doesn't have a clue." In other words, for people like you and me.

Of course, reporters and political hacks can't just stroll into a secure vault and walk out with classified documents (well, except for a certain former national security adviser). They need accomplices. So they've created a culture of leaks in which bureaucrats and even military officers convince themselves it's okay to tip our nation's secrets—your secrets—to the media.

What can be done? It's simple: Enforce the law.

Leaking classified information is a crime punishable with prison time. The statutes are on the books, folks. Those who leak classified information and those who publicize it should go to jail. This isn't a matter of creating a police state, for God's sake. We're at war. In war (and in peace, as well), we have secrets to keep. When we fail to keep those secrets, soldiers die, our enemies are encouraged, our allies grow reluctant to share intelligence with us, and our own agencies worry about the danger of sharing information from their top sources. And you, the American people, are betrayed.

"Betrayal" is the other uncool word I used up above. But it's the right word. Whether a senator or a low-level staffer in a government department, the man or woman who intentionally compromises classified information has betrayed you, your family, and your country.

The latest example was a selective leak from a National Intelligence Estimate—a high-level document that reports not only a consensus view, but also dissenting opinions (I know—I read plenty of 'em in the past). According to the media's version of whatever was leaked, we're less secure now than before Iraq was invaded. It was a cynical setup just over a month before national elections: In order to challenge the allegations, the president had to declassify a very sensitive document.

The leak wasn't about some phony "right to know." It was a political stunt performed for political gain. And now our enemies know what our intelligence community thinks. Gee, thanks. We don't need to know what intelligence documents say. What matters is what our leaders do or fail to do.

What will it take to inspire a nonpartisan crackdown on those who betray our secrets, who selfishly expose our country to mortal danger? A punk who robs a convenience store goes to jail, yet an official who passes sensitive intelligence to the press or to the political party he or she favors is rarely pursued at the upper levels of government.

Why? Same answer as above. Your politicians like the culture of leaks. They complain about it, fingers crossed way down in their deep pockets. But they do nothing. Washington's a club—and you're not in it, brothers and sisters.

This shouldn't be a Democratic or Republican issue. It's an American issue. Keeping our country safe is more important than Senator Sweetspot's reelection campaign or a Pulitzer Prize for another self-adoring, America-loathing journalist.

Put 'em in the slammer. Where these criminals belong. Enforce our laws. And maybe—just maybe—folks in Washington will start obeying those laws again.

There's one more reason why I keep old secrets and actively avoid exposure to new ones now that I'm out of the system. In this great, free country, I can figure out anything I need to know from open sources. I don't have to dishonor myself or the United States of America.

And if honor's a joke to those in power, I'm proud to be the butt of it.

Lynching the Marines

RealClearPolitics.com

June 28, 2006

Let's just hang those Marines accused in the Haditha incident. Get it over with. They don't need a court martial. They're guilty. The media already decided the case. A few other Marines and soldiers are also accused of murder in Iraq. Save our tax dollars. Just hang them, too. Forget the stresses of combat. Forget that war really is hell. Whatever you do, don't mention the atrocities committed by the terrorists or insurgents. Those two young American soldiers tortured to death a few weeks ago? Bury that story fast. The terrorists are the good guys. We're the only torturers. Don't close Guantanamo. Put our troops in the cells. There's no surer way to quell the media's outrage over Gitmo than freeing the terrorists held there and filling it with our soldiers. Don't worry about individual charges. Collective guilt applies.

Ignore history. Let's pretend that warfare can be waged with absolute sterility, without so much as giving the enemy a broken fingernail. War isn't about fighting. It's about making people happy. Civilian casualties? The thousands of Iraqis slain by terrorists were legitimate targets. Iraqi civilians are only innocent victims when Americans kill them. And avoid the true potential parallel with the Vietnam War—after we cut and ran those peace-loving Communists killed millions of civilians in cold blood in Cambodia, Laos, and Vietnam. Let's all get on message: America is the real evil empire, American troops are homicidal maniacs, and the world would be a better place if we just surrendered and let a nonpartisan committee of Islamists, Chinese, Russians, and Europeans run it.

Think of how much better off the world would be without us: If American-imperialist thugs had stayed out of World War II, we wouldn't have that nasty Israel problem. The European Union would've come into being decades earlier (speaking German, but what's not to like?). The Japanese would've solved China's over-population dilemma. And the Soviet Union would still be building the workers' paradise.

As for Iraq, not only should we get out now and let all those flower-child terrorists, insurgents, and militias inaugurate the Age of Aquarius, we must get our barbaric troops under control. That means punishing a young Marine if he so much as writes a playful song about the war that turns into an internet hit. Forget the real lyrics to "Mademoiselle From Armentieres," or that old marching song from the Philippines, "The Monkeys Have No Tails in Zamboanga." Forget all those hilarious "Jody" calls and cadences. Just punish that guy with the guitar and the sense of humor (the WWII cartoonist Bill Mauldin should've stood trial at Nuremberg). Thank god we have the media to tell the world how rabid we are. And we won't mention what would happen to every journalist in Iraq tomorrow if our troops disappeared overnight. Bad taste to hint that our enemies might not be champions of free speech. And let's not pile on while the press is still mourning Abu Musab al Zarqawi.

Okay, now let's be serious: I do not condone criminal acts in wartime. If any of our soldiers or Marines charged with murder or other serious crimes are found guilty, they should be sentenced accordingly under the Uniform Code of Military Justice. But let's give them a fair trial first. And let's remember that an act committed in the heat of battle is different from walking into a McDonald's and killing a half-dozen people for meth money.

Isn't it remarkable that, to the media, our troops are guilty until proven innocent, while our enemies are innocent even after they're proven guilty? Compare the media feeding frenzy over Haditha with the utter lack of detailed human-interest reporting on the thousands of victims of terrorist atrocities. And just wait: In no time, we'll hear that those terrorists arrested last Thursday in Miami were unfairly entrapped by the feds.

There is no question: Discipline must be maintained within our military. And discipline is maintained. Anyone who knows anything about wars throughout history has to be astonished at how few criminal incidents our troops have been involved in during their time in Iraq. We have a humane, magnificent military. Given the nature of counterinsurgency operations, we've set a statistical record for good behavior. Our troops will never be given credit, though. To get the media's attention, an American soldier must die, suffer a crippling wound, or commit a crime.

But the media aren't the worst of it, in the end. Who expects responsible, moral behavior from our media any more? No, the worst of it is the cowardice of our political and even military leaders. Four-star generals may be lions on the battlefield, but turn a camera on them and they're jellyfish. Want to send President Bush into a defensive crouch? Mention Guantanamo.

Our leaders need to stand up for those in uniform. While criminal actions must be investigated, when challenged with media exaggerations or outright lies our leaders need to fight back—and to hammer home that there is no such thing as an immaculate war. Instead of blubbering that he, too, wants to close Guantanamo, our president should state manfully that, if necessary, we'll keep Gitmo open for the next hundred years. The United States is history's most virtuous power. Our soldiers are valorous and decent. Our cause is just. Why don't our leaders have the guts to say that? How can they cower while our troops are crucified? Instead of Joshua's trumpets, we get Peter's fretful denials.

At this point, I doubt that any of our accused Marines and soldiers can get a fair trial. I don't want the guilty to go free. But I do think that, if Bill Clinton could pardon his criminal friends, President Bush should consider pardoning any soldiers or Marines convicted of violent crimes under combat conditions.

The hate-America bigots in the media shouldn't get away with lynching our troops.

The New Combatants

Armchair General

March 2007

Deserting the field at Shiloh before the battle ended on April 8, 1862, the *New York Herald's* ambitious correspondent bought his way onto a boat headed north. At Fort Henry, he conned an Army telegraph operator and shot off a lurid, confused account of the fighting. Frank Chapman's brief, rear-area view of the battle, combined with his vivid imagination and ruthlessness, gave him a scoop. His story appeared in print on the second morning after the battle ended, electrifying the Union and interrupting the Senate's order of business.

Accounts that were more accurate soon followed from the half dozen correspondents who remained at the front, but a fateful confusion had been introduced. Authentic battlefield reporting was buried as newspapers back home gave credence to wild rumors and the complaints of the disgruntled. Editors safe in the rear called the Union victory into question, utterly failing to grasp the crippling effect the two-day bloodletting at Shiloh had on Confederate forces in the western theater. Soon, publishers throughout the North were demanding General Ulysses S. Grant's removal for incompetence, setting a precedent for those who have never worn a uniform to make snap judgments about those who do. Had the Yankee media of 1862 had their way, "Sam" Grant would have been given a one-way ticket back to Galena, Illinois.

POWER BROKER

The press had become American power brokers well before the outbreak of the Civil War, with 2,500 newspapers spread across the country by the time the first cannon fired on Fort Sumter. The advent of the telegraph, combined with growing literacy, made "near-real-time" news a commercial commodity. From a business standpoint, press coverage of warfare came of age in the decade between the siege of Sevastopol in the Crimea (1854–55) and Lee's surrender at Appomattox. But problems were evident, too. Reporting was often shamelessly prejudiced in favor of political factions and favored personalities—money sometimes changed hands and access was as important then as it is today.

The media influenced the course of the Civil War, from harassing generals to alarming the public. Lincoln needed a press-acknowledged victory—Antietam—before he could announce the Emancipation Proclamation. William T. Sherman, whose temper made him a popular target, despised journalists and tried to ban them from his area of operations. Ever a stoic, Grant dealt more patiently with the "Bohemian Brigade"—and eventually won the admiration of key journalists. The know-it-all criticism never stopped, though.

If the stories filed by American correspondents were frequently slanted or mistaken in their judgments, the foreign press were worse. *The Times* of London, then considered the world's newspaper of record, yearned for a Confederate victory. When its leading reporter, William Russell (who may have been the best war correspondent in history), warned that the South couldn't win, he was sidelined in favor of reporters willing to interpret every development in Richmond's favor. 1865 was a year of great embarrassment for *The Times*.

Although the press could agitate governments even then, they remained far from their present-day power to overturn the verdict of the battlefield. The road was a long one, with plenty of ups and downs, from Shiloh to the First Battle of Fallujah—where the global media stopped a battle a few days short of an American victory, handing terrorists a triumph they had not earned.

RISE OF MASS MEDIA

The history of popular journalism in wartime really begins with the Protestant Reformation and the religious wars it spawned. Just over a half-century after the invention of movable type for the printing press, broadside sheets attacked opponents in language fiercer than today's worst hate speech. From pamphlets prefiguring today's internet extremism to gory woodblock prints for the illiterate, cheap products of the printing press allowed the Reformation to survive but exacerbated religious hatreds and bloodshed. Mass printing didn't make wars, but it made wars worse: Information's destabilizing effects resembled those of the internet in today's Middle East (another realm of superstition, ignorance, and hatred).

The first true newspapers appeared in English just over a century later, during the "other" Civil War (England's bloody struggle, 1642–46). With Parliament's abolition of the inquisition-like Star Chamber, writers were suddenly free to write and printers free to print. They chose sides—throne or parliament bench—and went at it with glee and venom. Parliament got off the mark first, publishing the text of its debates in an early effort at "transparent government," while Puritan pamphleteers catered to the fervent believers who filled the ranks of Oliver Cromwell's Ironsides and the other forces arrayed against the cavaliers of King Charles II.

Royalists responded with a clever newssheet, *Mercurius Aulicus,* which poked fun at the "Roundheads." But wit proved no match for religious passion and the desire for liberty. The papers issued by the Parliamentarians and their colorful (sometimes fanatical) supporters won the allegiance of the "swing voters" of the day. Overall, the media battle between Cavalier and Roundhead bore an uncanny resemblance to the opposing national security stances today of *The New Yorker* magazine, with its sly appeals to a cultural elite, and Fox News Network's vigorous populism. In the end, numbers trump art.

By the time of the American Revolution, newspapers shaped public opinion, and masters of the pen—such as Thomas Paine—shook thrones. The French Revolution's lasting symbol is the guillotine, but the struggles that led to the Place de la Concorde were waged in print. From 1776 to 1793, blood and ink ran together.

BATTLEFIELD REPORTERS

The art of *reporting* matured from the 1850s onward. *The Times'* William Russell filed dispatches from the Crimea (1854–56), the Sepoy Mutiny (1857–58) and the Austro-Prussian War (1866) that still read wonderfully today. Russell had a keen eye backed by a good mind, and he drove Army reforms, foresaw that British supremacy in India must ultimately end, and recognized the impact of technologies such as the Prussian "needle-gun" (a breech-loading rifle) on the future of warfare. It won him no friends in the North, but his eyewitness account of the pell-mell Union retreat from Bull Run is a classic—brilliant and scrupulously honest. Russell saw clearly, wrote well, and judged fairly. Needless to say, he was as much the exception to the rule in his own day as he would be today.

Russell's downfall as the dominant military correspondent of his age resulted from growing fogeyism: He didn't like the telegraph and used it reluctantly. By the Franco-Prussian War, he was scooped routinely by correspondents for other London papers—despite remarkable access to the Prussian general staff and court. It was as if a twenty-first-century journalist refused to use satellite communications.

Phillip Knightley, whose classic *The First Casualty* tells the wartime-coverage story from the journalists' side, calls the half-century after Lincoln's assassination a "golden age." Well, it was, and it wasn't. Undersea telegraph cables and swifter steamships undercut the tyranny of distance—but the period was also the heyday of jingoism, when the sharp eye and skilled pen of a Russell gave way to yellow journalism. Notoriously, the newspaper magnate William Randolph Hearst deserves at least partial credit for igniting the Spanish-American War in 1898. When the Hearst-employed artist Frederick Remington arrived in Cuba before the outbreak of hostilities, he cabled home complaining that there was no war to cover. Hearst responded that if Remington supplied the pictures, he would supply the war.

The era of the World Wars made journalism a serious endeavor again, and the quality of American military coverage peaked between 1938 and 1945. It would never be equaled thereafter. The best correspondents of the day genuinely sought to understand their subject, cared about their integrity—and still managed to be patriots. No one doubted which side our reporters were on during World War II, and none of them spilled wartime secrets that could have helped the enemy.

Edward R. Murrow and William L. Shirer essentially invented the medium of radio at war in the years between the Austrian Anschluss (1938) and the London Blitz (1940). Richard Tregaskis lived beside the Marines he covered on Guadalcanal, sharing their hardships. Ernie Pyle found a uniquely American voice to report on GI Joe—until he was killed by Japanese machine-gun fire in the closing months of the war. Cartoonist Bill Mauldin didn't mock Army grunts; rather, he loved and respected them. His Willie and Joe were wonderfully, hilariously American—a celebration of the dog Soldier's ordeals, common sense, and resigned fortitude.

None of those journalists was a patsy—each simply *respected* the soldiers fighting under our flag. In those days, reporters still "came up through the ranks" of society instead of arriving, journalism degree in hand, from Ivy League colleges and privileged back-grounds. World War II journalists understood the troops they were covering because they shared the same working-class and small-town roots.

The immediate postwar years saw more good conflict journal-ism, from Korea to the brushfire wars that scorched Europe's dying empires. Media veterans of World War II were still doing the report-ing, and they understood what they saw.

The generations, and journalism, changed just a decade later in Vietnam.

ACTIVISM AND AGENDAS

In 1968, the "us" generation gave way to the "me" generation. With ever fewer exceptions, reports from the war in Indochina were filed by young, ambitious, self-consciously hip journalists, not by the aging veterans of previous wars. Some fine reporting came out of Vietnam, but the fashion of the day was "attitude." Patriotism was uncool. All authority figures, from platoon leaders to generals, were bad. Journalists sought out embittered and unmotivated soldiers. Classic reporting gave way to activist journalism.

The most lauded journalist's book to emerge from Vietnam was Michael Herr's *Dispatches*. Read today—and it's still worth a read—it feels more dated than William Russell's account of the aftermath of Bull Run. Written by a physically brave reporter, Herr's work in Vietnam is nonetheless spoiled by his "I'm-hip-to-this" tone. He was out looking for bad news—and there's plenty of it on any battlefield.

The Tet Offensive of 1968 was a milestone for war coverage. The media establishment had turned against the war and Tet was written up as a Vietcong victory. It didn't matter that Tet was a disaster for the VC and broke the movement forever, forcing North Vietnamese forces to intervene openly and massively. American combat competence and battlefield triumphs went ignored. The media, not reality, decided what the story of Tet would be.

The Vietnam era saw the emergence of anti-American journalism among American reporters and editors. It wasn't cool—or a wise career move—to question the media's emerging party line that the military was evil, that U.S. policies were inevitably wicked, and that we, the people, didn't deserve to win. Vietnam was also the first "television war," with combat images broadcast into the land of TV dinners. The immediacy and breadth of the new medium supercharged the power of the press. While reporters, editors and cameramen could not yet change the course of tactical combat—the reporting time still lagged—the media could influence the outcome of a war more profoundly than ever before. American troops won on the ground, but the media declared defeat and convinced the public the effort was hopeless. The result was communist tanks in Saigon in 1975.

In the wake of Vietnam, a new elitist media emerged whose practitioners came from families that belonged to country clubs, not from parents who worked in steel mills and cleaned other people's houses. There was a sharp break in background, privilege, and experience between the Americans who covered wars and the Americans who waged them. The fighters drank Bud; their judges drank Bordeaux.

The media's Indochina hangover lasted for decades, resulting in whopping misjudgments by "distinguished" journalists such as James Fallows, whose book *National Defense* portrayed the M-1 tank as a hopeless, wasteful folly. (M-1 series tanks quickly proved to be the world's best, and they still maintain their supremacy a quarter-century later.) On the eve of Desert Storm (1991), journalists regarded military coverage as a down-market beat and had missed the revolution in the quality, doctrine, and capabilities of the U.S. armed forces. The media warned of a bloodbath at the hands of "battle-hardened" Iraqi troops.

The American military's performance in our first Gulf War stunned the world. For a time, it bought the military some respect. But it wasn't long before reporting from the Balkans concentrated on a river crossing the media condemned as too slow (few reporters have ever commanded a bridgehead) or the problems with an attack helicopter unit deployment. Good news wasn't news. If something could be construed as a military screwup, then that got the headlines. Any vehicle with tracks was a tank, and any operation that wasn't a perfect success was a failure. Under increasing pressure from 24/7 news networks, reporters from every medium no longer bothered to ask *why* something happened as it did. They filed their stories and moved on.

Increasingly, both the global media and the American media picked sides—with the American media's stance often dictated by political bias. President Clinton's weakness on terrorism received a pass, as did his "I-see-nothing" approach to the genocide in Rwanda. When his administration went to war halfheartedly in the Balkans, criticism focused on the military, not on the administration. Kosovo was a "good war" because a president the media liked had waged it.

The worst was yet to come.

"GOTCHA!" JOURNALISM

The tragedy of September 11, 2001, should have rallied American journalists behind their country. And it did—for about a week.

By the time U.S. forces struck the Taliban/al Qa'eda condominium in Afghanistan a month later, pundits were back to predicting a bloodbath since "no one had ever conquered Afghanistan" and "Afghans were the toughest fighters in the world." When a relative handful of U.S. special operations forces and CIA teams backed by airpower helped the primitive Northern Alliance topple the Taliban in a matter of weeks, the disappointment in some media quarters was palpable.

A too-cool-to-be-a-patriot attitude that placed journalists above their own country not only prevailed but also was strengthened by media hostility to the presidential administration of George W. Bush. By the time deployments began for the campaign to topple Saddam Hussein, journalism had returned to its "gotcha" mode. A fair-minded analysis of media biases suggests that, had President Clinton toppled Saddam, he would have been hailed by the press as the greatest liberator since Abraham Lincoln. President Bush, however, was attacked for deposing the living dictator with the most blood on his hands.

During Operation Iraqi Freedom, a rift emerged in the media that would have serious repercussions for subsequent reporting on the occupation of Iraq. With a growing awareness of the power of the media, the U.S. military embarked on an "embedding" program that placed journalists with units in the fields—in some cases, with tactical outfits headed for direct-fire combat. For years, reporters had complained about "lack of access." Now the gates were open, but few of the celebrity journalists wanted to go in. With a few exceptions, hungry, younger reporters were the ones who witnessed blind firefights during sandstorms, chaotic urban combat, and armored rampages.

The reporters who risked their lives got the airtime and column space—to the chagrin of the members-of-the-club careerists who stayed behind at the theater headquarters in Qatar. With blitzkrieg speed, journalists who lacked the courage to emulate Pyle or Tregaskis spread the calumny that the "embeds" had lost their objectivity, that they'd been seduced by the military, and that their coverage "wasn't balanced."

Since journalism fosters a socialist environment where jealousy of the success of others rules, the charges took root. In the early days of the occupation, embeds were already regarded with suspicion and, by my last trip into Iraq in 2006, the military was having serious difficulty attracting journalists to go out and remain with the troops to *really* see what was happening. Most journalists preferred to stay in heavily guarded hotels or compounds, relying on Iraqi stringers (who have their own agendas) and visits to the Green Zone in Baghdad. Their most frequent contacts were with each other, and—predictably—a "herd" mentality prevailed.

Some journalists in Iraq were physically brave, but few had the moral courage to challenge the party line. By 2004, the global and domestic-American media had decided that the experiment in democracy had to fail—and they did their best to portray it as a failure. Elections were impossible. When one ballot after another succeeded, the voting was written off as meaningless. Every misstep by American troops was exaggerated. Abu Ghraib equaled Auschwitz. The handful of Soldiers and Marines accused of crimes elsewhere in Iraq were convicted in the press long before they faced the first court-martial. Reporters gave more credence to claims put forth by terrorists and insurgents than to military briefings.

But the fatal shift in the media's battlefield role came in April 2004 in Fallujah.

THE ENEMY WITH THE CAMERAS
The First Battle of Fallujah began when terrorists led a crowd in seizing, torturing, mutilating, and killing four U.S. contractors and then leaving their charred body parts dangling on a bridge. Outraged, President Bush ordered the Marines responsible for the area of operations to free the city of terrorists and insurgents—immediately and with whatever force was necessary. Marine commanders would have preferred more time to allow for a methodical, prepared attack, but they saluted and went into battle. Gnawing their way into the city, the Marines slaughtered their enemies until they were two or three days away from gaining complete control of Fallujah.

The president stopped the attack. Over the next six months, Fallujah became a terrorist city-state. In November, American troops had to go back and finish the job.

What happened?

I was in Iraq during First Fallujah, traveling with the Kurds up north. Every night we did our best to get to a television and tune in al Jazeera and other regional channels. The Kurds just shook their heads. Arab-world networks broadcast an avalanche of lies, inventing atrocities, doctoring footage, and claiming that American forces were killing indiscriminately, violating mosques, attacking hospitals and schools, raping women, and executing children. With their own veteran intelligence operatives reporting from Fallujah, the Kurds knew that none of it was true.

But the truth didn't matter. The Western media didn't challenge the wild lies. Instead, the BBC and other European channels accepted the Arab media's line. Even U.S. reporting portrayed First Fallujah as a needlessly harsh attack. Inside of a week, global media pressure had become so unbearable that Prime Minister Tony Blair, as well as Iraqi leaders allied with the Coalition, begged Bush to stop the offensive. The political risks, in their view, outweighed the benefits of defeating terror.

President Bush folded, and history was made. For the first time, the media had been able to reverse the course of *battlefield* events, deciding the outcome of direct-fire combat.

That turning point in media-military relations should chill every Western military commander. It confirmed that American generals, for example, would never again face only the enemy shooting at them but would also face a third party to every conflict—the media—at which our forces cannot fire back.

Long a power in war, the media became a *decisive* power in Fallujah.

Some military leaders got the message. When a return to Fallujah became inevitable, the second-time-around plan relied on massive firepower, shock, and—above all—speed. Where a generation earlier commanders sought to "operate inside the enemy's decision cycle," the new imperative was to operate inside the media cycle.

A 12,000-man force of Marine battalions and Army armored cavalry squadrons (and special operations teams) took down Fallujah within a week, before the global media could muster sufficient opposition to rescue the terrorists. (The attack's timing proved opportune, too, since a recent wave of terrorist videos showing the grisly beheading of captives had embarrassed their media supporters, leaving them slower to respond during Second Fallujah.)

U.S. forces scored a swift, lopsided victory before the media could intervene. Still, the media had their revenge. Instead of reporting the skill and courage of American troops, the media selected an image of a Marine shooting a wounded prisoner—under murky circumstances—as the symbol of the battle.

The bottom line for future campaigns and battles: Plans can no longer focus exclusively on the enemy with the guns when the enemy with the cameras may be even more powerful. The media are a new form of combatant, and we will have to formulate new rules that prevent them from decisively aiding our opponents.

Much thinking remains to be done on this subject. The power of the formal media and their internet auxiliaries has grown so swiftly that laws, rules and practices that long sufficed have now become outmoded. The U.S. military, which handles the media cautiously, will have to develop new levels of sophistication in its dealings with journalists. In some cases, "new" might mean a return to old forms—censorship, exclusion (for journalists and organizations proved hostile), and imprisonment for violating security. To date, journalists have gotten away with depicting themselves as above all laws, even when reporters and camera crews collaborated with terrorists to cover and publicize car bomb attacks, ambushes, and suicide bombings. *The media are now a tool of warfare and must be treated as such.*

And we'll have to decide whether reporters' lives are really more valuable than the lives of our troops.

WINNING THE WAR THAT MATTERED—LEBANON, 2006

If the media won the First Battle of Fallujah, they also won the recent miniwar between Israel and Hezbollah. During the first week of the conflict, the media's pilot fish decided that the "narrative" of the war was going to be Lebanese suffering. Doctored photographs, faked casualties and video footage, and outright lies were accepted without question (except in a few cases where internet detectives exposed the manipulation). Day after day, the world saw exactly the side of the conflict that Hezbollah wanted it to see: Israel was an aggressive bully indiscriminately bombing women and children.

Except that it wasn't and it didn't. Covering the war from the Israeli side in the conflict's latter phases, the situation I saw for myself contradicted the agreed media line. While the Israeli Defense Forces and their civilian superiors made plenty of strategic and tactical errors, it was visually evident, day after day, that the IDF was taking extreme care to minimize civilian casualties on the other side. I stood on a kibbutz roof watching a wide sweep of the battle unfold—a dozen engagements were underway before my eyes. I went to the front repeatedly. Yet for all of the Israeli artillery deployed, I never saw or heard a single battery firing all of its guns in a unified volley. Those self-propelled howitzers shot one to two rounds at pinpoint targets in response to calls for fire. On some days, the shelling was heavier than on others—but there was *never* an artillery barrage.

Air strikes also sought to avoid civilian casualties, but Hezbollah purposely built command facilities and bunkers in residential neighborhoods. Some had to be destroyed. Yet for all of the bombs dropped, Israel's restraint was remarkable—it had the capability to inflict far more damage on Lebanon than it did. Repeatedly, targets were spared because of the projected cost in civilian lives, and the IDF spent its own lives to avoid striking noncombatants. In one incident, IDF SEALs went ashore behind the lines to take out a rocket command-and-control cell in downtown Tyre. The terrorists had established their post on one floor of a crowded apartment building. Instead of flattening the building, which would have been simple enough (and justified under the laws of war), the IDF special operators landed from the sea, penetrated several blocks into the city, successfully hit the command post, and withdrew—but not without a firefight and friendly casualties.

Another largely unreported story was *Israeli* suffering. While networks rebroadcast images of destruction in Lebanon, northern Israel endured more than 4,000 rocket strikes. Those rockets were unguided—true terror weapons—ranging from basement-built, low-caliber "Katyushas" to 220mm and 302mm imports from Syria and Iran. The rockets were just launched in the general direction of Israeli towns and cities. They were *meant* to kill civilians. And they did. Kiryat Shmona, a town in northern Galilee, was struck by nearly 400 missiles, with 1,500 buildings destroyed or damaged. Tens of thousands of Israelis became refugees. Tens of thousands more spent a month in bomb shelters. But the media's party line had been agreed, and the media stuck to it.

Of course, there were journalists in Israel, too. Israelis I met at the front laughed bitterly over the TV stand-ups filmed on safe hotel terraces down south. Reporters broadcast in flak jackets and helmets while, just off camera, civilians were calmly eating dinner and relaxing over drinks.

In the end, the global impression was that Israel was the aggressor, that Hezbollah was valiant, and that the Lebanese people were

Israel's intended victims. Especially in the Middle East where perception is usually far more important than fact, Hezbollah won the media war. And that just may have been the war that mattered.

LETHAL REPORTING—OVERTURNING THE BATTLEFIELD'S VERDICT

In this multimedia age, an American journalist's insistence that he or she is responsible to no one but an editor or producer, and that he or she is above national loyalty, combines with ruthless competition for airtime or column space at any price. Too often, the price is the *truth*. Some journalists are simply ignorant and uninterested in learning about military affairs. Others know better but have predetermined political agendas. Friends serving in Iraq often complain to me about journalists who arrive for a quick visit with their stories prewritten in their heads—they don't really want to learn what's happening; they just want the dateline that says "Ramadi," "Samarra," or "Baghdad." Some journalists try, and fail. Others don't really try, but succeed. For some, it's a matter of on-camera presence; for others, it's a party line that appeals to their readership.

And then there are the real journalists. Fortunately, we always have some of them covering our troops, and some of their stories get through. Great journalists may well be critical of our policies or actions, but they base their criticism on thoughtful observation, not on prejudice or a desire to pander. Sean Naylor of *Army Times* leaps to mind—without a doubt, he is our finest combat correspondent and a courageous man. His criticism can be tough, but it's always constructive. CNN had Jane Arraf in Baghdad for years—a tiny woman who almost disappeared under her helmet but whose integrity and personal valor are enormous. Robert Kaplan, the magazine journalist and author, has covered the military services superbly and thoughtfully. His work ranges from outstanding direct reporting to speculations on a philosophy of war. Rick Atkinson, now at work on the second volume of a grand trilogy on the Army in World War II, has produced wartime journalism that rises to the level of literature. At his best, Tom Ricks of *The Washington Post* is the equal of the great war correspondents of the past. But these serious correspondents don't have critical mass.

There are no easy remedies to a situation in which a biased global media and their political-activist domestic counterparts can overturn the verdict of the battlefield and decide the outcome of wars. But of two things we may be certain: The media are now full-blown participants in the wars of the information age, and "lethal reporting" will prove to be one of the greatest battlefield challenges facing generals and privates alike.

PART IV

Israel's Struggle

Kicking Out Corruption

New York Post

January 27, 2006

In Wednesday's Palestinian elections, Hamas, a fundamentalist party that sponsors terrorism and denies Israel's right to exist, won an outright majority. It was a victory for democracy.

While supporting Israel's legitimate security needs, we have to analyze what happened without prejudice: Why did Hamas win? Why did Fatah, the movement that dominated the Palestinian cause for more than a generation, suffer a stunning defeat?

After all, the Palestianian Authority had established a fledgling government—with broad international support. Aid was flowing. Israel left Gaza—and began to admit that its West Bank posture is unsustainable.

Why did the Palestinian people overwhelmingly vote for terrorists?

They didn't. Fatah lost because of the party's disgraceful corruption and neglect of the practical needs of its constituents. If not all politics are local, most are. Hamas won by providing basic services slighted by the Palestinian Authority and by avoiding the blatant corruption of Fatah's old guard.

Did Hamas's hard line on Israel help it? Yes, with a minority of voters. But most Palestinians voted for a better quality of everyday life, not for a doomsday confrontation with Tel Aviv. Disgust had more to do with the outcome than militancy.

This isn't meant to whitewash Hamas's history of mass murder. On the contrary, the lesson we need to take from this election is one we should have learned years ago: Corruption is the greatest plague on the developing world, opening the door for fanatical movements insightful enough to offer children a semblance of education and to provide the neglected poor with running water.

In country after country, Islamic parties gained power by filling the vacuum left in urban slums by corrupt governments. Westerners made excuses as Turkish, Pakistani, Egyptian, Algerian, Palestinian, and an array of African governments looted their national patrimonies, stole aid funds, and behaved with utter disdain for their fellow citizens. The bills come due.

No human being likes to live in squalor while his leaders splurge on London real estate. The wretched of the earth—to use that still-valid phrase—simply want their basic needs addressed. Above all, they want hope for their children.

If the desires of the global poor could be summed up in three words, they'd be "work, education, pride." Throw in electricity and sanitation, and you've got a winning electoral program.

Too often, we remain on the side of the corrupt and powerful, instead of standing up for the hurt and humiliated. If America won't defend the poor, who will? Extremist parties with bigoted agendas.

So, what does the Hamas victory mean for us?

First, the era of strong-man rule is ending. Democracy is on the march. Yet, from sheer inertia we often find ourselves on the side of the old, collapsing order—while our enemies grasp the potential of the ballot box better than we do. Second, we must be far more aggressive in spotting, publicizing, and fighting corruption around the world—no matter the short-term costs. Corruption is the most insidious enemy of rule-of-law democracy. Third, we have to avoid knee-jerk reactions. By reflexively condemning electoral outcomes we don't like, from Venezuela to the Middle East, we only make heroes of our opponents—while sounding like hypocrites ourselves. President Bush's comments yesterday struck about the right note, accepting the results and praising the positives, while staying noncommital on future relations.

Fourth, democracy requires patience. Whether in Iraq or Bolivia, we can't force voters to make the "right" choices. Electorates need to make their own mistakes—and learn from them.

Give Hamas time to discover how much harder it is to govern than to oppose a government. See if the movement evolves—or defaults to violence. In power, Hamas will have to deliver the goods. And better lives for Palestinians can't be achieved through terrorism.

The ball's in Hamas's court. If we don't like their serve, we've got a powerful backhand.

Tragedy of Errors

New York Post

July 16, 2006

The violence that scorched the Middle East this time didn't result from a sly Iranian plot. It was the product of emotion, miscalculation, impulsiveness, and folly. On all sides.

Here's a sound rule in analyzing problems anywhere between Cairo and Karachi: Never ascribe to a calculated strategy what can be blamed on passionate incompetence.

Another iron rule that applies to this and every Israeli attempt to strike back at Islamist terrorists is that, just when the Israeli Defense Forces really start to hurt the enemy, the world community—including the United States—intervenes to save the terrorists from destruction.

Europeans have more sympathy with Iran's nuclear program than they do with Israel's attempts at self-defense. But, then, the only thing continental Europeans regret about the Holocaust is that they didn't get to finish the job. Even as Europe suffers its own attacks by Islamist terrorists, Europeans defend the selfsame terrorists against Israeli retribution.

Meanwhile, the flare-up that began last week resulted from bad judgment on the part of every organization and state involved—as well as producing some spectacularly bad analysis by our herd-like media.

As soon as Hezbollah commandos snatched two Israeli soldiers from northern Israeli, we were told Iran was behind it. Utterly wrong. That raid was a Hezbollah-conceived copy-cat operation launched impulsively to piggyback on the Hamas seizure of an Israeli soldier in Gaza the week before. The Iranian government was as surprised as anyone.

Iran was dragged into the mess thereafter. But—while President Mahmoud Ahmedinejad is always delighted to give we-will-bury you speeches—Iran's best interests just now are served by avoiding violent confrontations with Israel while Tehran tries to persuade the world that its nuclear program is strictly for peaceful purposes. Iran's fanatics don't just want to capture or kill six Israeli soldiers. They want to kill six million Jews.

The Iranians were blindsided but had to back their clients (as Germany had to back Austria in 1914).

Because it offers an easy sound-bite explanation, journalists consistently misrepresent Iran's degree of control over Hezbollah, insisting that Tehran pulls all the strings. Just not true. Iran's relationship with Hezbollah is a dark mirror image of our own relationship with Israel: We support Israel, providing funds and weapons, and we can influence Israel. But we don't control Israel. Sometimes Israel surprises us—and not always happily.

Iran's in the same situation with Hezbollah.

Despite drawing vital support from Iran and Syria, Hezbollah has its own goals, tactics, and internal dynamics. And since it was allowed to defy U.N. resolutions calling for it to disarm in the wake of Israel's withdrawal from southern Lebanon, Hezbollah has been able to build the most effective and best-motivated Arab military, man-for-man.

But Hezbollah got this one wrong. Whoever green-lighted the raid on Israel didn't anticipate the ferocity or scale of the Israeli reaction.

Then the Israelis began to miscalculate—reacting impulsively and emotionally themselves. Attacking Hezbollah was fully justified and necessary, but Israel's frustration with the Lebanese government's toleration of terrorists boiled over into folly. Israeli aircraft attacked Beirut's international airport and other targets around the city, doing both Israel and Lebanon's fragile democracy far more harm than good.

Israel hopes to pressure the Lebanese government into taking action against Hezbollah. But Lebanon's leaders can't do that. If they ordered their work-in-progress military to attack and disarm Hezbollah, some Lebanese Armed Forces units would mutiny; others would disintegrate—and any outfits that attempted to take on Hezbollah would be badly and swiftly defeated. And the action would reignite the country's dormant civil war.

After the Israeli strikes in Beirut, Hezbollah then raised the stakes again by raining rockets down on Israeli cities—making it impossible for Israel to limit its offensive. The global media nonetheless portrayed Israel as the aggressor, highlighting Lebanese casualties, rather than the suffering in Israel.

For its part, Israel picked the wrong fight by striking Beirut's infrastructure while its deadly enemies sat comfortably in Damascus.

Israel should've hit Syria. It had nothing to lose and far more to gain. No matter what Israel does and no matter how many concessions Israeli governments make, its enemies prove implacable and the "global community" will condemn it.

Returning Gaza to Palestinian control was a noble attempt at making peace. Fanatics made sure it failed. Likewise, withdrawing from southern Lebanon was a risky attempt at compromise and international cooperation. We've seen the rewards. The heart of the problem beats in Damascus, not Beirut. Israel should've gone for it.

As for world opinion, it's saved the terrorists, time and again. Does any reader believe that the United Nations or more than a handful of its member states would act to save Israel? Israel's in a ceaseless fight for its life, and we, at least, have to stop intervening to save its enemies.

The situation in the Middle East has no good or clear solution. The struggle will continue beyond our lifetimes (unless, of course, the Iranians get their nukes). This is just the latest round, if a particularly ugly one. The ultimate amount of blood that will be shed is unknowable. But we can be certain that Israel's genocidal enemies will always be saved by the bell.

Israel's New Fear

New York Post

July 17, 2006

Something big hasn't happened in the current round of fighting between Israel and its terrorist foes. That absence represents a potentially fatal change in Israeli policy.

For all of the air attacks on targets in Lebanon, the Israeli Defense Force has not sent in ground troops. If IDF tanks don't thrust across the border in force in the next few days, it will reflect the greatest crisis of will in Israel's history.

Israel is signaling its enemies that it's afraid to risk its soldiers' lives. And the terrorists read the message clearly. This caution will only encourage Israel's enemies—just when the seemingly inevitable advent of Iranian nuclear weapons poses the greatest threat to Israel since 1948.

Israel never squandered the lives of its soldiers. It couldn't afford to. But in past crises a sense of necessity prevailed. The IDF did what it had to do and did it well for two generations. Then came the long involvement in Lebanon, "Israel's Vietnam." It broke something inside the IDF.

Is Israel's spirit of sacrifice dying? If so, it may prove fatal. Once brilliant in the attack, the IDF has declined into a defensive mindset that air strikes can't camouflage. Meanwhile, the ruthlessness of Israel's enemies has increased horrifically. They would sacrifice millions of their own people to destroy Israel.

Perhaps the air campaign to date is only meant to prepare the battlefield for a strike by ground forces. For Israel's sake, let's hope so. Because Israel's enemies will only be unified—and never defeated—by attacks from 15,000 feet.

Precision munitions can't turn the tide in struggles of the soul. And the souls of men are Hezbollah's center of gravity.

Israeli decision-makers appear to have learned nothing from the failure of our "shock and awe" air campaign against Saddam's regime. After all the ludicrous claims that a sound-and-light show over Baghdad would drive Saddam to surrender, the war had to be won the old-fashioned way, with the Army and Marines battling their way to Baghdad.

If the U.S. Air Force, with all its resources, couldn't break Saddam's regime, IDF jets won't defeat Hezbollah—an organization with genuine popular support—by blowing holes in runways in Beirut and humiliating the Lebanese people. But that's about all that air power acting alone can do.

One of the many frustrating aspects of Hezbollah is that, while it's increasingly a potent, disciplined military force, it doesn't present many conventional military targets. It's maddeningly difficult to find dispersed clusters of terrorists—and it's impossible to corner and kill them in significant numbers without boots on the ground.

Israel is making the American mistake of betting on technology to defeat primal beliefs. The result is the opposite of the one desired: Stand-off attacks only convince religion-fueled terrorists that we—Americans or Israelis—lack the courage to "face them like men."

This time, it seems they're right. Israel's refusal to fight in the spirit of Dayan and Sharon will boost the morale of Hezbollah fighters, unify their supporters—and serve as a recruiting tool. In the Muslim world, this round of fighting will count as a terrorist win.

At present, Hezbollah is embarrassing Israel with its rocket attacks, while Israel has yet to wound Hezbollah.

For all the capabilities of high-tech weapons systems, this is a new age of Cain-and-Abel warfare, of vicious close-in fighting in villages, apartment blocks, and olive groves. No reconnaissance system can locate enemy warriors hiding in an urban labyrinth or a shaded village courtyard. The grunts have to do it. As in the age of Joshua, David, and Solomon.

No one wants to pay a price in blood. But postponing the payment of an unavoidable blood price in war only raises the ultimate cost (another lesson of Iraq). Without defeating Hezbollah on the ground—no matter what it takes—Israel can't win.

Israel faces enormous challenges and metastasizing threats. Like cancer, those threats will only grow worse if not treated aggressively. By trying to establish "psychological leverage" over the Lebanese government and population with attacks on the country's civilian infrastructure, Israel played into the hands of its enemies and came off as a bully in the eyes of the world. Attempts to wage "war-lite" have a heavy price.

Israel is in a fight for its life, but looks irresolute for the first time in its history. It appears shockingly weak where it counts most, in strength of will. And will is one thing Israel's fanatical enemies do not lack.

If, in the coming days, we do not hear the roar of IDF tanks pursuing Israel's enemies, we may one day hear a new lament for the children of Zion.

Can Israel Win?

New York Post

July 22, 2006

Israel is losing this war. For a lifelong Israel supporter, that's a painful thing to write. But it's true. And the situation's worsening each day.

A U.S. government official put it to me this way: "Israel's got the clock, but Hezbollah's got the time." The sands of the hourglass favor the terrorists—every day they hold out and drop more rockets on Israel, Hezbollah scores a propaganda win.

All Hezbollah has to do to achieve victory is not to lose completely. But for Israel to emerge the acknowledged winner, it has to shatter Hezbollah. Yet Israeli miscalculations have left Hezbollah alive and kicking.

Israel has to pull itself together now, to send in ground troops in sufficient numbers, with fierce resolve to do what must be done: Root out Hezbollah fighters and kill them. This means Israel will suffer painful casualties—more today than if the Israeli Defense Force had gone in full blast at this fight's beginning.

The situation is grave. A perceived Hezbollah win will be a massive victory for terror, as well as a triumph for Iran and Syria. And everybody loves a winner—especially in the Middle East, where Arabs and Persians have been losing so long.

Israel can't afford a Hezbollah win. America can't afford it. Civilization can't afford it. Yet it just might happen.

Israel tried to make war halfway and only made a mess. Let's review where the situation stands:

- By trying to spare Israeli lives through the use of airpower and long-range artillery fire instead of ground troops, the IDF played into Hezbollah's hands. The terrorists could claim that Israel feared them. Meanwhile, Israeli targeting proved shockingly sloppy, failing to ravage Hezbollah, while hitting civilians—to the international media's delight.
- The IDF is readying a reinforced brigade of armor and 3,000 to 5,000 troops for a "limited incursion" into southern Lebanon. Won't work. Not enough troops. And Hezbollah's had time to get locked and loaded. This is going to be messy—any half-hearted Israeli effort will fall short.
- Famed for its penetration, Israeli intelligence failed this time. It didn't detect the new weapons Iran and Syria had provided to Hezbollah, from antiship missiles to longer-range rockets. And, after years of spying, it couldn't find Hezbollah. This should set off global alarm bells: If Hezbollah can hide rockets, Iran can hide nukes.
- The media sided heavily with Hezbollah (surprise, surprise). Rocket attacks on Israel were reported clinically, but IDF strikes on Lebanon have been milked for every last drop of emotion. We hear about broken glass in Haifa—and bleeding babies in Beirut.
- Washington rejoiced when several Arab governments criticized Hezbollah for its actions. But the Arab street, Shi'a and Sunni, has coalesced behind Hezbollah. Saudi and Egyptian government statements are worth about as much as a greeting card from Marie Antoinette on New Year's Day, 1789.
- Syria and Iran are getting a free ride. Hezbollah fights and dies, Damascus and Tehran collect the dividends.
- Israel looks irresolute and incapable—encouraging its enemies.
- The "world community" wants a cease-fire—which would only benefit the terrorists. Hezbollah would claim (accurately) that it had withstood Israel's assault. Couldn't get a better terrorist recruiting advertisement.

- A cease-fire would be under U.N. auspices. Gee, thanks. No U.N. force would protect Israel's interests, but plenty of U.N. contingents would cooperate with or turn a blind eye to the terrorists. Think Russia's an honest broker? Ask its Jews who fled to Israel. Would French troops protect Israeli interests? Ask the Jews Vichy bureaucrats packed off to the death camps. (The French are more anti-Semitic than the Germans—just less efficient.)

- One bright spot: The Bush administration continues to resist international attempts to bully Israel into a premature cease-fire. Secretary of State Condoleezza Rice is flying off to the big falafel stand as a token gesture, not to interfere with Israel's self-defense. But the clock's ticking. Washington can only buy Israel so much time.

- Every rocket that lands in Israel is a propaganda victory for Hezbollah. After 1,000-plus Israeli air strikes, the rockets keep falling, and Israel looks impotent. The price of sparing Israeli infantrymen has been the elevation of Hezbollah to heroic status through the Muslim world.

- The Olmert government tried to wage war on the cheap. Such efforts always raise the cost in the end. Olmert resembles President Bill Clinton—willing to lob bombs from a distance but unwilling to accept that war means friendly casualties.

- Israel needs to grasp the power of the global media. Long proud of going its own way in the face of genocidal anti-Semitism, Israel now has to recognize that the media can overturn the verdict of the battlefield. Even if Israel pulls off a last-minute win on the ground, the anti-Israel propaganda machine has been given so big a head-start that Hezbollah still may be portrayed as the victor.

The situation is grim. Israel looks more desperate every day, while Hezbollah appears more defiant.

This is ultimately about far more than a buffer zone in southern Lebanon. In the long run, it's about Israel's survival. And about preventing the rise of a nuclear Iran and the strengthening of the rogue regime in Syria. It's also about the future of Lebanon—everybody's victim.

The mess Israel has made of its opportunity to smack down Hezbollah should be a wake-up call to the country's leadership. The IDF looks like a pathetic shadow of the bold military that Ariel Sharon led into Egypt three decades ago. The IDF's intelligence, targeting and planning were all deficient. Technology failed to vanquish flesh and blood. The myth of the IDF's invincibility just shattered.

If Israel can't turn this situation around quickly, the failure will be a turning point in its history. And not for the better.

Target: Hezbollah

New York Post

July 28, 2006

Yesterday, Israel's government overruled its generals and refused to expand the ground war in southern Lebanon. Given the difficulties encountered and the casualties suffered, the decision is understandable. And wrong.

In the War on Terror—combating Hezbollah's definitely part of it—you have to finish what you start. You can't permit the perception that the terrorists won. But that's where the current round of fighting is headed.

For the Israelis, the town of Bint Jbeil is an embarrassment, an objective that proved unexpectedly hard to take. But the town's a tactical issue to the Israeli Defense Force, not a strategic one. For Hezbollah, it's Stalingrad, where the Red Army stopped the Germans. And that's how terrorist propagandists will mythologize it.

Considering only the military facts, the IDF's view is correct. But the Middle East has little use for facts. Perception is what counts. To the Arab masses, Hezbollah's resistance appears heroic, triumphant—and inspiring. We don't have to like it, but it's true.

So why is defeating Hezbollah such a challenge? Israel smashed one Arab military coalition after another, from 1948 through 1973. Arabs didn't seem to make good soldiers.

Now we see Arabs fighting tenaciously and effectively. What happened?

The answer's straightforward: Different cultures fight for different things. Arabs might jump up and down, wailing, "We will die for you Saddam!" But, in the clinch, they don't—they surrender. Conventional Arab armies fight badly because their conscripts and even the officers feel little loyalty to the states they serve—and even less to self-anointed national leaders.

But Arabs will fight to the bitter end for their religion, their families, and the land their clan possesses. In southern Lebanon, Hezbollah exploits all three motivations. The Hezbollah guerrilla waiting to ambush an Israeli patrol believes he's fighting for his faith, his family, and the earth beneath his feet. He'll kill anyone and give his own life to win.

We all need to stop making cartoon figures of such enemies. Hezbollah doesn't have tanks or jets, but it poses the toughest military problem Israel's ever faced. And Hezbollah may be the new model for Middle Eastern "armies."

The IDF's errors played into Hezbollah's hands. Initially relying on air power, the IDF ignored the basic military principles of surprise, mass, and concentration of effort. Instead of aiming a shocking, concentrated blow at Hezbollah, the IDF dissipated its power by striking targets scattered throughout Lebanon—while failing to strike any of them decisively.

Even now, in the struggle for a handful of border villages, the IDF continues to commit its forces piecemeal—a lieutenant's mistake. Adding troops in increments allows the enemy to adjust to the increasing pressure—instead of being crushed by one mighty blow.

This is also an expensive fight for Israel in another way: financially. The precision weapons on which the IDF has relied so heavily—and to so little effect—cost anywhere from hundreds of thousands of dollars to seven figures per round. Israel has expended thousands of such weapons in an effort to spare its ground forces.

Theoretically, that's smart. But we don't live in a theoretical world. Such weapons are so expensive that arsenals are small. The United States already has had to replenish Israel's limited stockpiles—and our own supplies would not support a long war. In Operation Iraqi Freedom, a relatively easy win, we were running low on some specialized munitions within three weeks.

Precision weapons also rely on precision intelligence. It doesn't matter how accurate the bomb is if you can't find the target. And Israel's targeting has been poor. It even appears that Hezbollah managed to feed the IDF phony intelligence, triggering attacks on civilian targets and giving the terrorists a series of media wins.

The precision-weapons cost/benefit trade-offs aren't impressive, either. Killing a terrorist leader with a million-dollar bomb is a sound investment, but using hundreds of them to attack cheap, antiquated rocket launchers gets expensive fast.

Just as the U.S. military learned painful lessons about technology's limits in Iraq, the IDF is getting an education now: There's still no replacement for the infantryman; wars can't be won nor terrorists defeated from the air; and war is ultimately a contest of wills.

Those of us who support Israel and wish its people well have to be alarmed. Jerusalem's talking tough—while backing off in the face of Hezbollah's resistance. Israel's on stage in a starring role right now, and it's too late to call for a rewrite.

As a minimum, the IDF has to pull off a hat trick (killing Hezbollah's leader, Hassan Nasrallah, would be nice) in order to prevent the perception of a Hezbollah victory—a perception that would strengthen the forces of terror immeasurably.

If this conflict ends with rockets still falling on Haifa, Israel's enemies will celebrate Hezbollah as the star of the Terrorist Broadway (Ayman al Zawahiri's recent rap videos were an attempt to edge into Hezbollah's limelight). Israel—and the civilized world—can't afford that.

Yes, Israel's casualties are painful and, to the IDF, unexpected. But Hezbollah isn't counting its casualties—it's concentrating on fighting. In warfare, that's the only approach that works.

Israel and its armed forces are rightfully proud of all they have achieved in the last six decades. But they shouldn't be too proud to learn from their enemies: In warfare, strength of will is the greatest virtue.

The Road to Qana

New York Post

August 1, 2006

The airstrike on the Lebanese village of Qana has been a tragedy for Israel. A publicity debacle, the deaths of fifty-seven civilians united Israel's enemies, complicated American support—and may lead to a cease-fire that rewards Hezbollah.

The Qana attack can't be excused. But it can be explained.

The images of children's bodies dug out of an apartment building's rubble were a gift to Hezbollah, Syria, and Iran—and a direct result of the Olmert government's attempt to wage an "easy" war.

All efforts to make war easy, cheap, or bloodless fail. If Israel's government—or our own—goes to war, our leaders must accept the price of winning. You can't measure out military force by teaspoons. Such naive efforts led to the morass in Iraq—and to the corpses of Qana.

Despite one failure after another, the myth of antiseptic techno-war, of immaculate victories through airpower, persists. The defense industry fosters it for profit, and the notion is seductive to politicians: a quick win without friendly casualties.

The problem is that it never works. Never.

Even the Kosovo conflict—frequently cited as an airpower victory—only climaxed after we threatened to send in ground troops. Prior to that, we'd spent billions bombing charcoal grills the Serbs used as decoy tank engines. (Our sensors read hot metal, and bombs away!)

Without boots—and eyes—on the ground, you just blast holes in the dirt. Or hit the targets your enemy wants you to strike. That's what happened in Qana.

Anyone who's ever served on a military staff or at the upper echelons of government during a crisis can tell you what happened: The pressure to obtain results grew ever heavier as it "rolled downhill." The prime minister and his Cabinet pressured the generals. The generals pressured the staffs. Staff principals pressured the intelligence officers and targeting analysts.

When Israel's version of "shock and awe" failed, Prime Minister Ehud Olmert froze like the proverbial deer in the headlights. Committed to a model of war that couldn't work, the stunned Israeli government insisted on "making" it work. Day after day, the pressure increased—until a desperate system dropped its safeguards.

Hezbollah sized up the situation perfectly. It already had succeeded in feeding the Israelis false intelligence about various sites and vehicles, gulling the IDF into attacks on civilian buses and buildings—followed up by prompt hate-Israel orgies in the media. But Hezbollah needed a "name" event, an apparent atrocity that would echo across continents.

Qana was the perfect setup. Hezbollah fired rockets from a position near the building that the terrorists wanted the IDF to bomb. This time, Hezbollah probably didn't "shoot and scoot" but let the launcher linger as bait. Hezbollah also may have fed the Israelis phony info about the doomed building serving as a terrorist safe house.

As for the women and children occupying the target, Hezbollah wrote them off as a necessary sacrifice. The terrorists would have sacrificed 570 innocents as readily as they did 57. Their will to win—at any cost—is their most formidable weapon.

Within the Israeli headquarters responsible for green-lighting the strike—where staffers are undoubtedly weary after weeks of war—the targeting data didn't get the "Are we sure?" grilling that doctrine demands. And—because of the Olmert government's unwillingness to commit serious numbers of ground troops (or even a heavy special-operations presence)—there were no Israeli eyes on the scene to confirm the target's validity.

Anxious to hurt Hezbollah, a chain of command grown tired and careless ended up by harming Israel terribly. The consequences are grave. At Qana, Israel lost the information war beyond all hope of recovery. It's losing the war on the ground, too. After ill-judged claims a week ago that the Israeli Defense Forces had eliminated 40 percent of Hezbollah's military capability, more rockets rained down on Israel last Sunday than on any previous day of the conflict.

The Olmert government chose war but didn't want to pay war's price. The cost of fighting half-heartedly has been Hezbollah's transformation from a middleweight sparring partner into the Middle East's new heavyweight champion. This woefully mismanaged war strengthened America's enemies, too. Away from the microphones, you can bet that plenty of profanity has been aimed at Israel in the West Wing—and it wasn't just Mel Gibson calling to chat. (Secretary of State Condoleezza Rice probably ain't too thrilled, either, after being blindsided by Qana—her multicountry diplomatic effort turned into a trip for brunch in Tel Aviv.)

Our support for Israel has always been costly to our foreign policy, yet it was justified on several grounds: morally imperative backing for a Jewish homeland after the Holocaust, moral and practical support for a fellow rule-of-law democracy and the knowledge that Israel would fight to win.

But Israel isn't fighting to win this time: It's been tossing bombs and hoping for a miracle.

With the Muslim world infuriated and Hezbollah reaping the benefit, the Olmert government's fecklessness has boosted the cost to Washington of supporting our old ally. We can't help Israel if Israel won't help itself.

So far, the Olmert government has been a disastrous aberration in Israel's history of wartime Cabinets—and a gift to Hezbollah. Israel needs leadership, not Clintonesque equivocation. President Bill Clinton's weakness led to 9/11. Olmert's weakness led to Qana.

The problem isn't Israel's people—who overwhelmingly support the effort to destroy Hezbollah. And the IDF knows how to do the job. But the Olmert government seems terrified of finishing what it started. Now, with global cries for a cease-fire, it may be too late. This may be the first "shooting war" Israel loses.

War is never a cheap date.

Defying Terror

New York Post

August 6, 2006

TEL AVIV—They sunned themselves on the beach where Richard the Lionheart fought. Rockets fell thirty miles up the coast. But these Israelis played volleyball.

They weren't callous. They simply refused to let terror control their lives.

Some of the swimmers had been displaced by the rocket attacks (although most Israelis refused to leave their homes). Others had relatives fighting Hezbollah in Lebanon.

Even the children knew war. Their country had been under siege every day of their lives. Genocidal neighbors dreamed of butchering them. Safe in Malaysia, Iran's president preached that the "elimination" of Israel would solve the Middle East's problems.

But on the beach at Tel Aviv, the kids yelled and splashed, watched over by parents determined to frustrate those who wanted their blood for a vicious god. Eight hundred years after a blood-spattered English king swung his sword by Jaffa's walls, kids ate dripping ice cream bars in the sun. The scene had changed profoundly over the centuries.

But the enemy remained the same: Those who believe Islam is destined to subjugate all other faiths and races.

The struggle may never end. In the meantime, one of the many ways to defy the Islamo-fascist enemies of joy is to go to the beach— no chadors, thanks—and laugh. Of course, there's a war on. It's harsh, and it's hard. The worst fighting is only a few hours up the highway. Behind the front, Israelis argue about the government's errors, failed strategy, and dubious tactics.

But even those debates, in a cafe or in Israel's tough-minded media, are another act of defiance. The terrorists would like to put an end to all of the world's debates forever.

The Israeli genius for argument, which can seem comical to an outsider, is one more source of the nation's strength. And all debates aside, Israelis overwhelmingly support their troops and the battle with Hezbollah.

Terrorist rockets may kill Israelis, but they can't even make a dent in Israel's spirit.

We Americans do not know what it's like to live surrounded by those who long to see our children lying dead, who cannot accept the fact of our survival. Even in this Age of Terror, we live in remarkable safety. And I pray that we will never be threatened by such hateful foes as Israel must face.

But Israel must live with hatred and jealousy on its borders. Its many successes humiliate its neighbors—just as its freedom alarms them. It's long been a cliche to note that Israel "made the desert bloom" after long centuries of Arab abuse of the soil itself and the destruction of the biblical landscape of "milk and honey." But the settlers and their children who built Israel did more than irrigate orange groves. They built a civilization where there had been only neglect, decay, and oppression.

Above all, the Israelis planted democracy and the rule of law in fields that had been hostile to elementary human decency and dignity for thousands of years.

And on the seventh day, they went to the beach.

Soldiers' Grit in
"Organized Mess" of War

New York Post

August 8, 2006

ON THE LEBANESE BORDER—Nobody flinched. A pair of Katyusha rockets struck just outside of the bunkered command post. The reserve infantry brigade's staff calmly continued directing their war.

Israeli howitzers returned fire, making the air tremble. Dug into forward slopes, Merkava tanks shot straight into Lebanon.

Note to self: Outgoing rounds are preferable to incoming rounds.

The headquarters pressed up against the border, controlling a war that moved in and out of rifle range. The staff were running "dig and scratch" operations against Hezbollah terrorists who'd had years to prepare for this fight.

The combat was slow and grinding. But the battlefield casualties were overwhelming on the enemy's side. As I stood talking to an Israeli army officer, word came over the communications net that a dismounted antitank company had just killed six terrorists up close and personal. With no Israeli Defense Force losses.

Asked how the fighting was going, an operations officer said, "It's going pretty well. It's an organized mess."

You couldn't get a better description of warfare.

I had gone forward with Maj. Manny Socolovsky. Raised in Upper Darby, Pennsylvania, Manny's a former competitive wrestler and a karate devotee. You could do a lot worse for your road dog in a shooting war.

Manny plugged us into his old brigade. The comradeship within the IDF was evident immediately. The reservists included physics professors and businessmen, mechanical engineers and farmers. All with shared experiences of combat. It's a first-name army.

It certainly isn't a spit-and-polish outfit. The "area police" would make a U.S. Army sergeant major faint. But the IDF knows how to fight.

At least at the tactical level. Israel's current strategy is another matter. Despite superb efforts against Hezbollah, to some extent the IDF appears to be fighting the wrong war: Too slow, too measured and, frankly, too gentle. The Israeli dread of casualties plays into Hezbollah's hands.

The day Manny and I were up on the border, one of the rockets Hezbollah had stockpiled got lucky—killing twelve IDF soldiers. That evening, rockets rained down on Haifa again, deep inside Israel. And the Israelis end up chasing ghosts, since the terrorists can set up the rockets, then trigger them with timers or by remote control while watching television and waiting to see them hit.

Even on the ground, Hezbollah was given a pass for much too long. As a result, every village near the border has been turned into a haunted fortress. In the stronghold of Bint Jbeil, the terrorists had developed a complex network of bunkers and connecting tunnels, with huge arms caches and even disguised video cameras to monitor approaches and fields of fire. And, of course, civilians are used routinely as human shields. As one young IDF veteran of the fighting in Bint Jbeil put it, "Every building we went into was part of their network."

The really bad news is that Hezbollah isn't a ragtag outfit anymore, but a postmodern military—cellular, dispersed, and better equipped than the Iranian army, since the newest and best equipment goes straight from Tehran to the terrorists. This is a new kind of war.

Faced with well-prepared strongholds and preset ambushes, the Israeli approach has been to avoid massed rushes of armor that would allow Hezbollah to fire volleys of antitank guided missiles and claim dramatic kills. Instead, infantry and engineers—supported by artillery, tanks, and air power—clear the way, then cordon off the villages, penetrating them with raiding forces as necessary.

Makes sense. Saves friendly lives. But it might be too damned slow in the age of media-driven war. The IDF must be in a position of unchallenged strength when the clock runs out. And after the Olmert government's slow start, the army's playing catch-up on the ground.

None of that's meant as criticism of the troops who are fighting. They're doing a superb job of executing the mission their government gave them. The question is whether or not they were given the right mission (sounds eerily familiar to American ears). Meanwhile, those soldiers, young and old, are tough, efficient, and impressive—they know they're fighting for the ultimate survival of their homeland.

Leaving the brigade headquarters between Katyusha volleys, we drove along the front to the east, with Israeli howitzers booming from their defilade positions in the valleys. The occasional pop of a Hezbollah rocket added a bit of excitement to the route. I drove, while Manny rode shotgun—with an M-16. Caught in the open once, we sheltered in someone's carport until the rockets were done.

That was when I gave Manny fair warning: If I went down, there wouldn't be any consequences. But if those Hezbollah SOB's damaged my rental car, they'd have to answer to Hertz.

We finished the day by falling back from the tanks and personnel carriers to climb to the top of Mount Adir.

The sweeping view made the difference between the warring civilizations as stark as could be: On the Israel side, the world was green. Then, abruptly, at the border, the landscape went brown—neglected for centuries, wasted, trashed by a suicidal value system. It wasn't hard to figure out who would triumph in the end.

As we stood on that mountaintop watching the Israeli fields ignited by errant Katyushas and the IDF artillery rounds smacking down in Hezbollah-world, I told Manny the secret of how to watch other people's wars: "No need to be afraid until the guys with the guns look afraid."

The one thing I never saw in the faces of the IDF was fear.

Watching the War

New York Post

August 9, 2006

KIBBUTZ SASA, ISRAEL—In the battle's lulls you hear the wind sweeping the hilltop. Scented with pine, it chases the heat, reminding the skin on your forearms that you're alive. For a few silent minutes, the only hint of war is the smoke drifting across a pasture or rising from a valley behind a ridge.

Then the sounds come back. Howitzer rounds impacting to the north, the quivering of a giant metal sheet. A village across the border appears deserted, but bursts of automatic weapons fire signal combat in an alley.

Long bursts, heavier caliber now. The woodpecker taps of a machine gun. A self-propelled 155mm battery down in the valley snorts out two rounds—the Israelis shoot precisely, not in indiscriminate volleys. Seconds later, the shells strike near Bint Jbeil. Brief scream of an incoming rocket. Close enough to snap my head around. Just in time to see it impact down the slope to my right, in an apple orchard. It explodes with the snap of an English Christmas cracker.

Much ado about nothing. Just Hezbollah saying hello.

More friendly rounds grump in the distance. A hamlet on a ridge begins to smoke. Another position near Bint Jbeil gets a pounding.

Sirens. This side of the border. Ambulances evacuating the wounded. Fast. An enemy rocket misses the Israeli town it targeted

257

and sets fire to a patch of scrub. Crows caw, a mean audience. More and more small arms join in the firefight to the north. For thirty seconds, it's the most even firing I've ever heard, a drumbeat you could march to. Then it breaks down into the normal disorder of war.

Helicopters throb. Medivacs? Gunships? Can't see. They're flying low behind a ridge, wary of shoulder-fired missiles. Excited by the overpressure from the big guns, a rooster crows in a barnyard just below me. He's answered by a bird that sounds like a deranged whippoorwill.

A convoy of tracked vehicles grinds along the road that hugs the valley. Tanks, the pale horsemen of modern war. You can follow the pattern of the wind by the battle smoke. Where the blow gets into a temper, it draws the smoke across the landscape, a gray curtain. Where the wind pauses, black smoke rises straight toward heaven—in this biblical landscape of groves and terraces, stones and death.

The quiet returns. The wind falls and the sun presses down on my shoulders. It's the strangest of wars. I just drove up to it in a rental car, with a loaf of Russian rye bread, a block of cheese, and a few cans of beer in the back seat. I feel like the postmodern version of the spectators who rode their carriages out to watch the First Battle of Bull Run.

From my vantage point, the view runs for tens of miles, from the ridges above Tyre to Mount Hermon. Another rocket screams overhead, but it's traveling deeper into Israel. And I'm watching not only a war but a race against time as the Israeli Defense Forces gnaw into southern Lebanon—Hezbollah's fortress—while the "international community" does all it can to rescue the terrorists.

The high ground always matters. I can see the telltale signs of a dozen separate engagements that take turns providing the overall battle's soundtrack. And the oddest thing of all is that it's spectacular—not the sort of thing we're supposed to admit. It's a beautiful summer day in the Holy Land. Where there happens to be a war.

But it's only appealing because I'm not really "danger close." From the rooftop where I stand scribbling, I can't see the faces. And the faces make war real and terrible—the faces of the dead and wounded, the faces of men fighting each other to a bitter death.

I only hear the big, dramatic sounds, not the moaning of gut-shot boys or the urgent cries of their friends, the young officer's excited voice calling for fire support, or a last unintelligible whisper.

But I see what I do because the Israeli Defense Forces have made no effort to hide this war away. Although I'm bunking in a building full of soldiers, I have no minder telling me what message I'm supposed to carry away, what I'm "really" seeing. Despite the lies in all too much of the media, the Israelis are struggling to fight a moral war—against enemies who know no morality, fanatics who trot out the same dead baby repeatedly for sensation-hungry cameras.

So I'm alone with the war for a little while, counting the time to impact of outgoing rounds and ranging detonations by ticking off the seconds between the flash and the follow-on bang.

What's striking is that every Israeli round is aimed at a military target. Even though the intensity of the firing increased today, as the IDF intensify the offensive, there's no wanton destruction—just the ugly necessity of war.

But Hezbollah's rockets aren't aimed. They're merely pointed. In the general direction of Israeli cities and towns. Simply put, the Katyushas are terror weapons. That difference sums up this war for any decent human being.

Ghost Towns of War

New York Post

August 10, 2006

KIBBUTZ SASA, ISRAEL—Driving north to the war from Tel Aviv, the traffic thins gradually—until you realize abruptly that your car is the only one left on the road.

Cities and towns beyond the range of most of the rockets carry on as normally as possible. As far north as Nazareth, it feels—almost—like peacetime.

But as you climb the hills of Galilee, you meet ever fewer vehicles on the roads. A short convoy of Humvees heads toward the fighting, followed by a pair of old Willys jeeps painted olive drab—the Israeli Defense Forces don't all have state-of-the-art gear, but make do with many leftovers from past wars.

A military flatbed loaded with 155mm artillery shells labors up a curling mountain road. In a sheltered pass, a last, defiant gas station remains open.

Then, suddenly, you're alone among the ghost towns. The city of Safed is empty, a scene from a 1950s science-fiction film. A few residents remain, but I did not see a single one. Just a lonesome dog. In town after town, it's as if a plague has struck. And one has: the plague of terrorist rockets, whose only purpose is to butcher indiscriminately.

Another sort of plague hasn't hit: There is no looting. The empty houses of the refugees are safe. Israel pulls together, and no police patrols are needed to protect these businesses and homes.

Remaining behind in the north, emergency personnel do what must be done. Hospital staffs work underground in bunkers and bomb shelters, treating military casualties and victims of the terror rockets. Utilities function. The water runs.

But hundreds of thousands of Israelis have been driven away from their homes. You don't hear much about that. Journalists love to think of themselves as bold individualists—but the truth is that they're herd animals.

And the herd has decided that the big story of this war is the suffering of Lebanese civilians—misery exaggerated skillfully by Hezbollah's propagandists. They work the complicit international media like veteran hookers playing a pack of drunk conventioneers (Sure I love ya, sure you're the best. . . .).

Dead or displaced Jews? Who cares? That's yesterday's news. Today's hot fashion statement is to champion Israel's genocidal enemies. And every ambitious journalist wants to be in style.

If the year were 1939, our media would be trumpeting every note provided by Joseph Goebbels.

And then there are the chickens. Not cowards. Real chickens. Thousands and thousands of them, cackling away. Still in their coops. Untended, they'd die quickly. So farmers stay on the front, putting out feed between Katyusha barrages. One of the oddest images I'll carry away from this war is of tanks positioned to fight on either end of a long, noisy chicken barn: The Chicken-Coop War.

Vineyards need tending, but grow unkempt. Summer crops rot. Terror rockets burn the fields and set fire to painstakingly reforested hillsides. (Where's Greenpeace when you need them?) It's as if Israel's enemies are jealous even of this reborn earth.

On another "patrol," I passed through more deserted towns—and was startled by the sight of two old women in headscarves. Often, it's the old who refuse to leave their homes and the only lives they know. Kibbutzniks stay at the front, as well. The spirit of the founding generation lives on—despite Israel's phenomenal progress and hard-earned wealth. Villagers from the hills hang on, too, protective of their animals. And those villages suffering under the rain of rockets are not only Jewish but Muslim, Christian, and Druze. Of course, Hezbollah rockets killing Muslims wouldn't make a politically correct story. So you don't hear about that, either.

Driving south to file this series of columns, I gave a lift to a naval officer candidate—even in the most desolate spots, you see military hitchhikers. The IDF moves largely by private vehicles, buses, and the thumb. The young man in the carefully pressed uniform told me that he'd been permitted a quick trip home because thirty-five Katyushas had slammed into his little village.

The media didn't report that, either. They were posing on hotel terraces in Haifa, wearing flak jackets for the camera, fifty miles from the war.

No innocents should die on either side. But they do. That's war. Yet the one-sided coverage of this conflict is disgraceful. The truth is that all of the dead or wounded, on both sides of the border, are Hezbollah's victims.

Israel longs to live in peace with its neighbors. Can anyone honestly claim that for Israel's enemies? Where is humanity's fellow feeling for Israel? Where is the sense of justice?

The sorry answer is that a bigoted world couldn't care less. Nobody gives a damn.

Except you, my fellow Americans. Except you.

NYer Hangs Tough

New York Post

August 10, 2006

KIBBUTZ SASA, ISRAEL—After fifty-six years in Israel, he still compares the height of the local mountains to the Catskills. Now eighty, Bill Selah—formerly William Silverman of the Bronx—is one of the men who built Israel. And he won't let terrorists' rockets drive him away.

Smack on the border with Lebanon, Kibbutz Sasa has been Bill's home since 1950, when he left the Merchant Marine to join his older brother in Israel. Founded in January 1949, only months after Israel's birth, Sasa was an American-Jewish vision, drawing idealists from Los Angeles, Chicago, Milwaukee—and, above all, New York City.

Utopian dreamers, well-educated city kids trained for agricultural work on a farm in New Jersey. World War II put their plans on hold for a bit, but after Germany's defeat, they flocked to Britain's Palestine Mandate territory, entering illegally.

The kibbutz's early years were marked by backbreaking work and a struggle just to survive. A pioneer outpost on Israel's front line, Sasa had poor land and little water. Faced with harsh conditions, some of the founders gave up. It was only after a quarter century that the kibbutz gained a firm footing—thanks to capitalism's rescue of the old socialist vision.

Bill hung in there through all of it. (When a guy from the Bronx starts something, he finishes it.) Today, Sasa's a lovely garden on a hill, surrounded by orchards and vineyards. A tourist lodge—all are welcome—overlooks a biblical landscape. The kibbutz is booming financially, thanks to two factories that fund the old back-to-Eden dream. One of the plants has had a series of $100 million contracts with Oshkosh Trucks to make armor plating for U.S. military vehicles headed for Iraq. The factory continues working, despite the war.

As for the proud kibbutzniks, Bill Saleh embodies their attitude toward terrorism: He won't run, and his wife, Nurit, is staying put, too. After all, Bill first faced "Katyushas" on leave in 1944 as the Nazi buzz bombs streaked the skies over London. He was relaxed and full of life as we shared a dinner in his home on Sunday night—while artillery boomed down in the valley.

The kibbutz's children have been evacuated deeper into Israel. But the old guard stands fast—the community dining hall proudly displays the scraps of a Katyusha that just missed. The hearts of Sasa are stronger than any rockets.

Sasa's a living monument to the spirit that built Israel from the dust. Helped by Bill from the Bronx.

Destination: Stalemate

New York Post

August 11, 2006

TEL AVIV—No one knows exactly how or when the war in Lebanon will end. U.N. resolutions could interrupt hostilities—or the guns still may be blazing a month from now.

The big-picture outcome's already apparent, though: No clear winner, a practical stalemate—and both sides declaring victory.

A day spent listening to Israeli generals, active and retired, was just plain discouraging. Most were in denial, convinced that they're winning. They're right—if you only count war's physical effects. The Israeli Defense Forces have wounded Hezbollah deeply. But not one of those generals grasped the importance of the media war—which Hezbollah has mastered.

Even with 30,000 more reservists called up and IDF forces pushing toward the Litani River, the Israelis aren't turning tactical wins into strategic effects. In the combat zone, they've "taken the sea, but not the islands." Controlling much of the countryside, they've hesitated over rooting Hezbollah fighters out of their town and village strongholds. Fear casualties, lose wars.

In the air, the IDF has flown over 10,000 sorties, dropping more than 13,000 bombs and launching over 2,000 air-to-ground missiles. Yet the terrorists keep firing "junk" rockets—they're shadow targets airpower can't hunt.

Embodying a brave military's strategic blindness, a retired major general remarked dismissively that "a missile strike on Tel Aviv wouldn't matter, because it wouldn't do any serious damage."

That's nuts. If one Hezbollah missile reached Tel Aviv and knocked over a trash can, it would be perceived as an electrifying triumph by the Muslim masses in the Middle East.

The problem isn't that the Israeli generals are "fighting the last war." The problem is that they haven't been fighting seriously—as if Israel's future depends on it. The stakes are huge, and they've been fighting small. Now they'll have to hit very hard to make up for lost time.

A lone general put the situation bluntly: "Hezbollah prepared for exactly the war we're fighting."

Now let's look at who's winning from the Hezbollah's perspective—something senior IDF intelligence officers seem unable to do. Here's the terrorists' take on what they've achieved:

- They've won a huge propaganda victory among the Muslim masses by standing up to Israel—and surviving (Sunni-Arab leaders are terrified, but Mo' down on the block is thrilled by Hezbollah's toughness).
- They've endured a month-long Israeli offensive—and they still hold most of their fortress towns near the border.
- Despite the IDF's technological advantages, the terrorists are still raining their crude rockets down on Israeli territory.
- They've forced the evacuation of northern Israel's civilian population and driven still more Israelis into bomb shelters—for Arabs, it's grimly satisfying to turn Israelis into refugees.
- The Israeli army's tactical caution during the first four weeks of war convinced Hezbollah that the IDF fears its fighters.
- Hezbollah even managed to hit an IDF vessel at sea— another symbolic score.

For the bad guys, all that adds up to a win.

The practical outcome of this conflict remains obscure. There are plenty of moving parts. And, ultimately, the Lebanese will make the decisions that determine the long-range results.

Weakened militarily, Hezbollah could nonetheless be perceived as the moral victor in the region—attracting support and encouraging Syria and Iran to cause more trouble. Or, if its charismatic leader, Hassan Nasrallah, were killed, the movement could deteriorate. Israel's security could be strengthened—or the decades-long bloody muddle could drag on.

But let's stand way back: Picture a minority people in the Middle East. They're outnumbered and outgunned but willing to fight to the death for their dream. Once, that was Israel.

Now, in the Muslim narrative, it describes Hezbollah.

Facts hardly matter in the Middle East (for Arabs, especially, facts are too terrible to contemplate). Beliefs trump all else. And tens of millions of Arabs and Persians already believe that Hezbollah's the victor.

Israel has got to learn to see the world through the eyes of its enemies.

Bloody Border

New York Post

August 12, 2006

MISGAV AM, ISRAEL—This landscape bears so massive a weight of history it's astonishing it doesn't sink into the earth. And now another war increases the load.

Pressed against the Lebanese border and high above the Upper Galilee Valley, the Israeli settlement of Misgav Am is obviously a strategic point. Countless armies must have used it as an outpost down the centuries.

Now Israeli tanks blast terrorist positions from the heights. Ranked across mountain meadows, howitzers fire in support of the infantrymen gnawing their way forward. The northern horizon of this ruptured landscape is bounded by the ruins of a Crusader castle. To the east, a Saracen fortress guards a pass onto the Golan Heights. In historical terms, they're all newcomers. Blood was shed here before history was recorded, when battles were wrapped in myths.

Officially, the war has been on hold while U.N. delegates quibble. But the Hezbollah rockets don't stop. Kiryat Shmona, a compact Israeli town down on the valley floor, has been hit by 360 Katyushas since this war began. 1,500 houses have been destroyed or damaged. The residents who haven't left have lived in underground shelters for a month.

And the world turns up its nose at Israel's suffering. Killing Jews is still a sanctioned sport.

So Israel's guns shoot back as the politicians bicker and blunder. Along the high road that runs along the military crest, lines of tanks and armored personnel carriers wait for the order to join the 20,000 Israeli troops already in southern Lebanon. Every soldier waits for the signal to go. And artificial delays only hurt morale.

Engineer vehicles roll off flatbeds below the border fence. In this war of rocky hillsides, narrow roads, concrete towns, and mines, combat engineers are the unsung heroes. One bulldozer can be worth two dozen tanks. And it takes a brave man to drive it under fire.

But there are negatives, too. The Israeli Defense Forces are good—great at some things—but their reserve system is growing obsolete. As a former soldier, it pains me to see combat vehicles just behind the front lines crowded together as if the front were a Manhattan parking garage. One lucky rocket strike could cause a tactical catastrophe.

And not one unit—not one—has security out. Maintenance seems poor, with too many tank engines being replaced by the roadside (a nasty job even in peacetime). Israel's best combat outfits are superb— but these reservists don't look ready by American standards.

Allowed to fight, they'll beat Hezbollah. An army only has to be better than its enemy. But the IDF needs to think harder about its future foes. The neighborhood gets tougher every decade.

The fighting obviously hasn't stopped— although it's slowed a bit as foreign diplomats work to save Hezbollah. At some points, the IDF is ten kilometers inside Lebanon. At other spots, combat still erupts a hundred yards from the border. At Misgav Am, the war is all around us. Sirens, rockets, and jets. Tanks and howitzers. Heavy firing. Officers checking their assigned terrain against their maps on the high ground, waiting for the green light. Orchards and fields burning below in Israel.

History echoes again as the afternoon fades. The IDF captures more Iranian equipment every day—including a sophisticated missile-control system preprogrammed to fire on cities throughout Israel. And the Israelis know that Iranian officers are present on the battlefield—they're anxious to kill or capture them.

It's a long way from fighting West Bank punks with rusty Kalashnikovs.

And yet, how little changes. Iran's been here before, in its Persian-Empire incarnation. After twenty centuries, Jews are once again defending their homeland. In the twilight, I can almost see a Roman legion marching below. The last rays of the sun spark off the armor of Crusaders riding into a Saracen ambush. Babylonians, Assyrians, Phoenecians, Greeks, Arabs, Ottomans, Mamlukes, British gunners, and Australian cavalry. All have passed by.

Now, in a fight that will shape Israel's future more profoundly than its abysmal politicians realize, the IDF awaits orders and tension thickens the air. If U.N. shenanigans halt the fighting, Hezbollah wins—despite its battlefield losses.

And much of the world wants the terrorists to win. In this contest between a twenty-first-century civilization and medieval fanatics armed with postmodern weapons, even our own secretary of state now seems willing to give Hezbollah a pass.

Israel has made a number of mistakes, but one has been fateful, if not fatal. It didn't fight hard enough when it had the chance. Now it's ready to fight seriously— but the window may have closed.

Let's hope not. Israel must smash the terrorist presence in southern Lebanon. Beyond dispute. It has to create a new reality on the ground.

By the time you read this, the IDF may be approaching the Litani River with 40,000 combat troops and hundreds of armored vehicles. Or the diplomats and politicians may have handed victory to the advance guard of the latest Persian satraps.

In this beautiful, tormented land, history doesn't repeat itself. It accumulates. It's hard to believe there will ever be true peace.

Lessons So Far

New York Post

August 13, 2006

TEL AVIV—Israel's war against the Middle East's first true terrorist army provides tough military and strategic lessons—old, new, and all too often disheartening. Israel's been winning on the ground. And still losing the war.

This bitter conflict—in which most casualties on both sides of the border are civilians—raises troubling questions, too. Some are identical to those confronting us in Iraq. Many have troubling answers. Others have no real answers at all.

The elementary fact—which far too many in the West deny—is that our civilization has been forced into a defensive war to the death with fanatical strains of Islam—both Shi'a and Sunni. We may be on the offensive militarily, but we did not start this war—and it's all one war, from 9/11's Ground Zero, through Lebanon and Iraq, and on to Afghanistan. Until that ugly fact gains wide acceptance, we'll continue to make little decisive progress. American or Israeli, our troops are trying. But the truth is that we're really just holding the line.

We have not yet begun to fight. And many among us still dream of avoiding this war altogether. It can't be done. Because our enemies—Hezbollah, al Qa'eda, Islamist militias, regimes in Iran, Syria, and elsewhere—are determined to confront us.

We're going to learn the hard way. But we're going to learn. Meanwhile, here's what the latest battlefield has to say to us:

271

Lesson 1: You can win every tactical engagement and still lose at the strategic level. Israel's fought well. But its forces did a polite minuet, while its enemy's danced madly in the streets. The Israeli Defense Forces have done what their government asked of them. But the Olmert government asked them to do the wrong things—and to do too little for too long.

On the ground, in the air, and at sea, the IDF or our own forces can't be beaten. But without sound strategic planning, our tactical wins will not add up to victory. We have to relearn this lesson again and again: Vietnam, Somalia, Iraq—and now Lebanon.

Lesson 2: The global media can overturn the verdict of the battlefield.

Too many politicians and generals still don't get it. This new truth about war slapped us in the face during the First Battle of Fallujah. Now, facing a hostile global media, the Israelis are learning it.

Lesson 3: If you start off on the wrong foot in war, you may never recover your balance. This old rule never changes. The Israeli government dreamed of fighting a short, clean war on the cheap. Now they're playing incremental catch-up. It's a formula for stalemate, if not defeat. If you must go to war, go with everything you've got. From Day One. In war, the only bargain at any price is victory.

Lesson 4: Technology alone can't win twenty-first-century wars. You've heard it before and, sadly, you'll hear it again. These asymmetrical, brutal human conflicts require flesh-and-blood solutions—boots on the ground, not just airpower.

Lesson 5: Never underestimate your enemy. Another timeless rule. The Israelis did it in 1973, and now they've done it again. They undervalued Hezbollah's preparedness for a serious war, its armaments, its training—and its tenacity. And we ourselves did it after Baghdad fell.

This is one of the worst mistakes any government and military can make.

Lesson 6: In war, take the pain up front, and the overall suffering will be far less. A policy of casualty aversion—in Israel or in the United States—results in more casualties in the end. Because the IDF wasn't permitted to wage a serious war from the first day (and it remains severely restricted even now), the rockets continued to rain down on Israel—while Hezbollah won the propaganda war.

Lesson 7: Terrorism is no longer a limited, diffuse, disorganized threat. Hezbollah has an army, if of a new and innovative kind. Iran and Syria supply, support, and succor it. It has strategic depth and startling resilience.

With Hezbollah on point, Shi'a terror is now better-prepared to wage postmodern war than Sunni organizations such as al Qa'eda. We're witnessing the rise of transnational terrorist armies.

There are many more lessons, especially down at the soldier level. But let's turn to two critical questions:

Can a military that relies heavily on reserve call-ups win this new kind of war? For Israel, it's an existential question. My own conclusion is that the IDF, as currently structured, is living on borrowed time. Having seen our own forces operating in Iraq and the IDF at work along the Lebanese border, my frank assessment is that Israel's brave reserve brigades would crumble in fights such as those in Fallujah or Ramadi. This isn't the West Bank anymore. This is war to the death. The IDF must stop looking backward toward its proud heritage and look honestly at the future of war.

Can we win "Eastern" wars with Western values? I doubt it.

This question is going to eat at our consciences for years to come—even as we learn to do what must be done.

Despite media lies about Israeli "atrocities," the IDF has been doing all it can to spare civilians. For example, the Israelis repeatedly risked commando teams deep in hostile territory to take out Hezbollah command-and-control cells—instead of just leveling the crowded apartment buildings where the terrorists were hiding. But, ultimately, all of the special operations in the world will fall far short of delivering decisive, crushing victories. We are going to have to learn to fight by the enemy's rules. And we aren't going to like it.

The wars of the future will be won by those with the greater strength of will. And boundless determination is one weapon that Islamist extremists unquestionably possess.

Do we?

Hezbollah 3, Israel 0

New York Post

August 17, 2006

Israel's rep for toughness in tatters. Hezbollah triumphant. Iran cockier than ever. Syria untouched. Lebanon's government crippled. An orgy of anti-Semitism in the global media. Anti-Americanism exploding among Iraqi Shi'as inspired by Hezbollah.

Thanks, Prime Minister Olmert. Great job, guy.

The debacle in Lebanon wasn't even a war. It was only round one of a war. And Israel's back in its corner, dazed and punch-drunk.

Israel got in a gut jab, but Hezbollah landed three ferocious haymakers:

- Despite the physical damage the Israeli Defense Forces inflicted, Hezbollah's terror troops were still standing (and firing rockets) when the bell rang.
- At the strategic level, Hezbollah's masterful manipulation of the seduce-me-please media convinced the region's Shi'a and Sunni spectators alike that Hassan Nasrallah is the new Great Arab Hope. He's got a powerful Persian cheering section, too.
- While Israel couldn't plan or execute a winning campaign, it also failed to think beyond the inevitable cease-fire. But Hezbollah did. The terrorists had mapped out precisely what they had to do the moment the shooting stopped: Hand out

Iranian money, promise they'll rebuild what Israel destroyed—and simply refuse to honor the terms of the U.N. resolution.

Israel couldn't wait to throw in the towel and start pulling out troops. Then Hezbollah's fighters emerged from the rubble of towns Israeli leaders lacked the courage to conquer—and the number of terror soldiers who survived shocked the Israelis.

Politicians and generals everywhere, repeat after me: "Air power alone can't win wars; you can't defeat terror on the cheap with technology; and (in the timeless words of Nathan Bedford Forrest) War means fighting, and fighting means killing."

The U.N. resolution called for Hezbollah to disarm—a fantasy only a diplomat could believe. As soon as the refugees began flowing southward and packing the battlefield, Nasrallah told the international community to take a hike. He knows that U.N. peacekeepers won't try to disarm his forces—if they ever show up—and the Lebanese military not only won't try, but couldn't do it.

The world's response? The French (who talked so boldly) took a cold swig of Vichy water: Now they say they won't send in their peacekeepers until Hezbollah is completely disarmed—which isn't going to happen. And Lebanese leaders stated openly that not only wouldn't the Lebanese army attempt to take away the terrorists' weapons, it wouldn't even confiscate caches it stumbled on.

Sucker punched (well, don't fight with your eyes closed), Israel's complaining to the ref. While staring around in bewilderment.

Want more good news? After finally calling our enemies by the accurate name of "Islamofascists," President Bush backtracked so fast the White House lawn was smoking. Then he declared that Israel had won.

That's about as credible as insisting the *Titanic* docked safe and sound.

And that ain't all, folks. If you're an Israel supporter—as I proudly admit to being—get ready for some tough love: Not only did Israel's abysmally incompetent government start a war impulsively and prosecute it halfheartedly, the country's military leadership failed, too. Chief of Staff Lt. Gen. Dan Halutz, who was going to destroy Hezbollah from the skies, reportedly put his main effort on the eve of war into selling off his stock holdings before his bombs could weigh down the market. Now that's insider trading!

But that was just one jerk general dishonoring his uniform. The serious news is that the IDF's reserve forces were a shambles when they mobilized. Information from an inside source reveals that, when the reserves' warehouses and depots were opened, key stocks were missing—stolen.

What was gone? Fuel, weapons, ammunition, food, spare parts—all that a modern military needs to go to war. And I doubt it ended up in Iceland.

The IDF has great combat leaders and brave soldiers. But Hezbollah's boys proved tougher—and we can't pretty it up. The terrorists were willing—even eager—to die for their cause. Israeli leaders dreaded friendly casualties. And IDF troops—except in elite units—lacked the will to close with the enemy and defeat him at close quarters.

Israel tried to fight humanely. Hezbollah was out to win at any cost. The result was inevitable.

On the ground in southern Lebanon, the IDF was able to muster a ten-to-one advantage around contested villages. But its leaders lacked the guts to do what needed to be done. And Hezbollah's frontline fighters survived.

You can't win if you won't fight.

The IDF needs pervasive reform. Still structured to defeat the conventional militaries of Syria and Egypt, it faced an enemy tailored specifically to take on the IDF. Historical reputation isn't enough—the IDF must rebuild itself to take on postmodern threats. As one senior American general put it, "The IDF's been living on fumes since 1967."

Hezbollah cleared the air.

All this is heartbreaking. I wish it were otherwise. I wish I could back up our president's surreal claim that Israel won. I wish Israel had won. I wish it had the leadership the Israeli people deserve.

And that's what's tragic: Israel's politicians turned out to be even more profoundly out of touch with their people than the pols in Washington. Israelis were willing to fight. They wanted to win. The rank and file of the IDF would have done what needed to be done. And their leaders failed them.

There will be consequences. Iran's convinced it's on a winning course. Syria got away with murder (literally). And Hezbollah will come back more determined than ever.

Oh, I almost forgot those two IDF soldiers whose kidnapping triggered all this. But I can be forgiven, since Israel's leaders forgot about them long before I did: The U.N. resolution Olmert welcomed makes no binding and immediate demand for their return.

And the world is going to let Iran build nuclear weapons.

Get ready for Round Two.

Moment of Truth

New York Post

August 20, 2006

Where will it lead? Iraqi men wailing as they carry the coffin of a victim of ongoing bloodshed in Baghdad. It's not just Iraq, but the entire region whose future hangs in the balance, with the key players plotting new moves. One somber possibility: a revival of the West's thirst for blood.

In the wake of Israel's strategic setback in Lebanon, where's the Middle East headed? (Hint: The road sign doesn't read "Age of Aquarius.")

Powerful emotions intoxicate all sides. In the Middle East, only the Israelis have intellectual and moral integrity. Arabs and Persians rely on a culture of blame. The media obscure as much as they illumine.

So what should truly concern us? Bad news first.

Within the forces of terror, the balance of power has shifted. Sunni fanatics, such as al Qa'eda's supporters, have suffered severe losses in Afghanistan, Iraq, and around the world. Still capable of doing serious damage, they're nonetheless being eclipsed in importance by state-backed Shi'a terrorists, with Hezbollah in the lead and Iran providing arms, money, training, and strategic depth.

- A postmodern terrorist army—Hezbollah's—just achieved the first terrorist defeat of a powerful state on a conventional battlefield. The strategic echoes will embolden extremists throughout the Middle East and beyond.

- Iran, a state that openly sponsors terrorism, is well on the way to possessing nuclear weapons. And the world community pretends it doesn't really matter. Worse, military action to destroy Tehran's dispersed and bunkered nuclear program would require a massive, sustained effort—and still might fail. Iran's been playing poker while the West plays Old Maid.
- Iraq could fail—if the Iraqis fail themselves. It's still too early to pack up and leave, but if the people of Iraq will not seize the opportunity we gave them to build the region's first Arab-majority–rule-of-law democracy, it won't be an American defeat, but another self-inflicted Arab disaster. Iraq is the Arab world's last chance—and the odds are now 50-50 they'll throw it away.
- Lebanon, the region's other "almost" democracy, is in shambles, thanks to Hezbollah's ruthlessness and Israel's misjudgments. By failing to take Lebanon's complex group psychologies into account, Israel's air campaign converted Hezbollah opponents into Hezbollah supporters.
- Syria escaped the recent fighting with just a few tactical nicks. Now Bashar Assad appears stunningly unaware of his odious regime's vulnerability. And overconfident dictatorships do very stupid things.
- The region's Sunni-Arab autocracies—on which we have relied, to our great shame—are terrified and unstable. Egypt, the Gulf city-states, and even Saudi Arabia expected Israel to make short work of the Shi'a-Hezbollah problem. Instead, Hezbollah won—and the subjects of those sheiks and kings and eternal presidents have been cheering.
- Crucial oil producers on the Arab side of the Persian Gulf grow more vulnerable each day. Iran intends to exert hegemony over the region through nuclear threats and the exploitation of Shi'a discontents. The world's worst real-estate investment is luxury property in Dubai.

There's more, of course, from the Islamist takeover in Somalia, at the region's southern edge, to the Dorian Gray decomposition of the Pakistani state at its eastern extreme. So what on earth might give us cause for hope?

- Israel's recent defeat, for one thing. Yes, you read that right. The truth is that Israel got a relatively cheap, if embarrassing, wake-up call. And Israel's a part of Western civilization, not of the Middle East's decaying cultures. That means that Israel doesn't just wallow in blame—like Americans, Israelis figure out what went wrong and then fix it. After the postwar soul-searching and investigations are finished, failed leaders will be replaced and Israel will reemerge with a renewed sense of mission, a stronger government, and a powerfully reformed military—the next time the IDF goes to war, watch the way it devastates its enemies.

- The "unity of Muslims" confronting the West is history (it was always a bogus, ramshackle affair). Sunni-Arab leaders increasingly grasp that the real threat isn't from the United States or Israel, but from the explosion of Shi'a ambitions, prowess, wealth, and desire for vengeance. The future of the Middle East could go a number of ways, but we may find ourselves as bemused spectators, while our sworn enemies and phony friends kill each other. Afterward, we'll pick up the pieces.

- Iraq still could muddle through—but even if it doesn't, our stock in the region is headed up, not down. The paradox is that a future civil war between Iraq's Sunnis and Shi'as makes our military protection more essential than ever to the effete Gulf emirates and the cowardly Saudis. Avoid linear analysis and reflexive predictions of doom for American interests: The Middle East will always do more harm to its natives than it does to foreign powers. Human beings may hate a distant enemy in theory, but they generally prefer to kill their neighbors.

- Terrorist groups with global aspirations continue to pursue grand, counterproductive gestures rather than effective actions. Plots to blow up a series of airliners, lesser strikes on subways or trains in the West, and even the eventual "big one" they'll pull off won't convince the West to surrender. Despite intermittent left-wing lunacy, our debates and disagreements are about how best to solve the problem—not how to capitulate. Bit by bit, the Western mood is turning from disbelief regarding the "terrorist threat" to hard-knuckled realism about extremist Islam. 9/11 taught the terrorists little of use and many wrong lessons. It may be hard for some of us to discern what's really happening, but the Islamists are resurrecting a militant, ruthless West.

The florid American master of horror fiction, H. P. Lovecraft, warned his characters, "Do not raise up what ye cannot put down." Islamist terrorists are reviving the West's thirst for blood. And this time it won't be slaked in Flanders.

Things are going to get uglier east of Suez. And we're going to win.

Lessons from Lebanon:
The New Model Terrorist Army

Armed Forces Journal

October 2006

Much has been written about Israel's strategic errors in this summer's conflict with Hezbollah, from the embrace of the long-since discredited notion that a war can be won with air power alone to the fateful indecisiveness of political and military leaders whose plans had gone awry. Israel lost the media war and squandered combat opportunities because of a dread of friendly casualties. Wretched though it was to watch, all of that simply reprised the postmodern Western Way of War, which begins with absurd expectations and ends with a whimper, not a bang.

In short, nothing new. *Im Osten nichts Neues.*

Far more interesting and instructive were the battlefield developments that went largely unremarked—not least because of the paucity of reporters with military experience on the scene. If the conflict in Lebanon and northern Israel merely replayed earlier American and European errors at the strategic level, the tactical fighting proved to be a laboratory of the future.

Hezbollah fielded an impressively innovative military force incisively tailored to meet a specific foe on particular terrain. While it could not match Israel's overall technology, professionalism, or number of troops, that didn't matter. Hezbollah fought with alternative means for asymmetrical goals. On its own terms, it succeeded, adding a new model terrorist army to the already-daunting range of twenty-first-century asymmetrical threats: the army without a state.

At the mention of stateless military organizations, historians flash back to Renaissance-era companies of mercenaries or the armies for rent during the Thirty Years' War, but Hezbollah's ground forces were of a different order: They were not for sale and, while they did not serve a state, they served a multifaceted organization with a unifying vision. Hezbollah's front-line fighters were the new version of the holy warriors of the Mahdi in the Sudan, the Scottish Covenanters, or the Bohemian Hussites. Such forces have taken anywhere from decades to a century to defeat.

WHAT HEZBOLLAH DID

Force Tailoring. Hezbollah is the antithesis of the U.S. armed forces, which must be ready for any form of military activities anywhere in the world. Hezbollah faced a known enemy on predetermined terrain. In consequence, the well-funded terror organization was able to organize, equip, train, and deploy a force specifically tailored to stand against the Israel Defense Forces (IDF). Hezbollah wasn't interested in building a versatile force—it put all of its energies and thought into fighting a single enemy in a specific manner.

With decades of experience in low-intensity conflict with the IDF, Hezbollah understood its enemy's strengths and vulnerabilities. The IDF's ground forces remain structured for swift, conventional thrusts toward Damascus or Cairo. So Hezbollah leaders didn't attempt to build traditional brigades or battalions equipped with armored vehicles—the classic Arab error. Instead, they concentrated on stockpiling the most sophisticated defensive weapons they could acquire, such as the Kornet, a lethal late-generation Russian antitank missile, as well as a range of rockets, from long-range, Iranian-made weapons to man-portable, point-and-shoot Katyushas. Thanks to the Katyushas, an Arab military force was able to create a substantial number of Israeli refugees for the first time since 1948.

Clear, Realistic Goals. Hezbollah had no intention of invading Israel and occupying territory—it recognized its limitations. Instead, it assigned its front-line forces the achievable mission of holding out in towns, villages and small cities that had been turned into virtual fortresses. Attuned to the Israeli fear of friendly casualties—as well as Israel's reluctance to inflict high numbers of civilian casualties among its enemies—Hezbollah structured its defenses to make it forbiddingly expensive for the IDF to seize, sanitize, and hold urbanized terrain.

To be perceived as the victor, Israel had to shatter Hezbollah and drive it from southern Lebanon. But to be declared the winner by regional populations, Hezbollah only had to frustrate the IDF and survive. In the event, Hezbollah turned out to be the first Arab army with a credible claim to having defeated Israel's armed forces.

The Ascendancy of the Defense. Historically, the military advantage has shifted between attackers and defenders based upon various factors, from new technologies to innovative tactics or asymmetric organizational skills. At the outset of the 1973 Yom Kippur War, the Egyptian operational offensive relied on a tactical defense with Sagger antitank missiles to defeat Israeli armor. After suffering startling initial losses, Israeli ground forces commanders quickly devised tactics for overcoming the Sagger threat: The missiles were difficult to steer, crews were vulnerable to airburst artillery, and, above all, the terrain in the Sinai made it impossible for Egyptian formations to hide from aerial observation and strikes after Israel took control of the skies.

Three decades later in Lebanon, Hezbollah recognized that it had several important advantages that favored the defense. First, late-generation fire-and-forget missiles were faster, more accurate, and easier to wield. Second, the broken, mountainous terrain of southern Lebanon, with its towns and villages crowded within supporting distance of one another, strongly favored a prepared defense. Third, Hezbollah's tactical defense was also a strategic defense, and the terrorist army had years to prepare fixed bunkers and connecting passages. Designed by Iranian engineers, the most formidable of the bunkers proved impervious to Israeli precision weapons—and Hezbollah also took care to embed its defenses amid civilian populations, preventing the Israelis from applying devastating area fires. (I personally witnessed the IDF's carefully controlled use of artillery as calls for fire were answered with a single round or a pair of rounds—in several days at different points along the front, I never heard a battery fire full, repeated volleys.)

Defense in Depth. IDF spokespeople repeatedly claimed to have broken through Hezbollah's defenses—only to have Israeli troops encounter additional ambushes, mines, and bunkers. Hezbollah designed its defenses to kill tanks if the IDF tried armored thrusts along traditional movement corridors—but also prepared to take on infantry and engineers. Hezbollah made no attempt to construct a Maginot Line; instead, it built weblike defenses that could absorb penetrations and continue to fight, harass and hold. By the cease-fire, fighting continued at several points immediately adjacent to the border. The small city of Bint Jbeil, population 20,000, which IDF leaders prematurely and repeatedly claimed to have cleared, never fell completely to the Israelis.

Hezbollah also fielded more trained fighters and auxiliaries than Israeli intelligence predicted, allowing them to cover secondary and tertiary avenues of approach. Repeatedly, Israeli forces blundered into ambushes, as in the battle of Wadi Saluki, when eight Merkava tanks tried to negotiate a path through a steep gorge. In another wadi (ravine) fight, an officer unaccountably ordered a tank platoon into a narrow passage between steep banks—without infantry support to secure the high ground. When an ambush crippled the tanks, a para-recon platoon was inserted to rescue the crews. Overconfident and careless, the paratroopers bunched up. A short-range rocket landed in the middle of the platoon, killing nine IDF soldiers and gravely wounding four more. The mission then became a rescue of the para-recon platoon.

Modular Units and Mission-Type Orders. Hezbollah had a more developed, robust chain of command than the IDF expected. It also displayed impressive flexibility, relying on the ability of cellular units to combine rapidly for specific operations or, when cut off, to operate independently after falling in on pre-positioned stockpiles of weapons and ammunition. A Hezbollah antitank hunter-killer team had more autonomy than an IDF squad or platoon—and could operate for much longer periods without support from a higher echelon. Although Hezbollah used redundant communications, from cell phones through land lines to messengers, each front-line team of fighters was a machine that would go of itself. Hezbollah's combat cells were a hybrid of guerrillas and regular troops—a form of opponent that U.S. forces are apt to encounter with increasing frequency.

Low-level commanders operated under mission-type orders—not the looser sort meant by the U.S. military but the more restrictive form employed by the Bundeswehr (and, earlier, by the Wehrmacht), in which a tactical leader could not alter his mission but called the in-sector plays to accomplish that mission. It's impossible to gauge how much initiative local Hezbollah commanders exercised, but it appears that some were more creative and adventurous than others—typical of any military. Hezbollah's front-line units proved resilient, however—and they had to be killed. Few surrendered.

Innovative use of weapons. When the IDF failed to take the bait and led with infantry and engineers rather than tank formations, Hezbollah used its arsenal of antitank missiles against dismounted infantrymen—to deadly effect. Accustomed to fighting the ill-equipped and anarchic Palestinian groups in the West Bank and Gaza, dismounted IDF troops assumed that the masonry buildings of southern Lebanon provided adequate cover. When infantrymen bunched inside, Hezbollah hit the houses with double-charge–double-penetrator AT missiles that punched through reinforced walls to kill everyone in the targeted room. The missiles were also used against IDF troops in the open—evidence both of the extent of Hezbollah's stockpiles and a willingness to invent solutions on the spot.

Notoriously, Hezbollah also achieved strategic effects with tactical weapons—the Katyusha rockets it rained down on northern Israel. Armed with excellent strategic targeting data, the Israeli Air Force succeeded in hitting nearly all of Hezbollah's long-range (and more easily detected) rockets on the first night of the war: eighteen out of twenty Iranian-built Zilzal 2 and 3 launchers, as well as virtually all Fajr 4 and 5 weapons, were destroyed, ensuring the safety of Tel Aviv and Jerusalem.

But the terrorist army had stockpiled at least 14,000 short- and mid-range rockets in calibers ranging from less than 100mm through 122mm and 220mm, up to 302mm. Designed seven decades ago as area-suppression and psychological weapons to support tactical assaults against entrenched defenders, the rockets gained a new lease on life as terror weapons with strategic resonance in this summer's conflict. The higher-caliber rockets were used to strike deep into Israel, repeatedly hitting and closing down the vital port city of Haifa and landing halfway down the coast to Tel Aviv (as well as straying into the West Bank). Notoriously inaccurate, the rockets nonetheless achieved multiple strategic goals when employed by a force that had no qualms about inflicting civilian casualties—indeed, killing civilians and terrorizing Israel was a key Hezbollah objective. By midwar, driving through the cities and settlements of northern Israel was eerily reminiscent of science fiction films from the 1950s in which nuclear war or alien invasions turned cities into ghost towns. Arabs and other Muslims found it grimly satisfying that this time Israelis, too, were refugees or driven to huddle underground as the bombs fell.

Israel had no adequate answer to the problem. Its air force achieved an impressive target-identification-to-kill time of less than five minutes—a task eased by the small size of the operational sand box—but the technique only worked against larger-caliber weapons delivered by formal launchers. The man-pack Katyushas that rained down on Israel day after day proved too elusive for technical collection means. Nor were most of the rockets very powerful, as I can attest from watching them strike. But delivered in sufficient numbers, they did the job. Israel's total casualties remained low (117 soldiers killed and 41 civilians dead), but a new sense of vulnerability stunned the population.

As an Israeli general commented during the last week of the conflict, "Hezbollah prepared for exactly the war we're fighting."

And when the fighting stopped, IDF forces on the scene were bewildered by the numbers of Hezbollah fighters who emerged alive from forward bunkers. For the first time, an Arab army had stood up to the IDF and held much of its ground—the attacking Israelis took the sea but feared the islands, punching into the countryside and approaching the Litani River but unwilling to do more than conduct in-and-out raids on the bunker network in the area's urbanizing terrain; viewed from high ground along the border, the villages and towns in southern Lebanon reach out to one another with tentacles of new construction.

Fear casualties, lose wars. Perhaps Hezbollah's greatest tactical advantage, however, was simply the commitment of its troops. Hezbollah didn't seek to waste its cadres, but it didn't fear losses.

Although only the most fanatical sought death, the average Hezbollah soldier was less afraid of dying than his Israeli counterpart. And more Hezbollah fighters did die—although the number was probably closer to 500 than to the 800 some Israelis claimed. Military loss ratios were thus about five Hezbollah fighters to one IDF soldier. It was a ratio Hezbollah was perfectly willing to accept—and hardly a surprising result, given the IDF's overwhelming strength in technology and troops. At some points of decision, the IDF's advantage was as much as ten to one, yet the Israelis remained hesitant to close with the enemy in urban combat.

Effective Intelligence. This was the truly unexpected asymmetry. With a long-standing reputation for effective work, Israel's intelligence services failed terribly this time (with echoes of 1973). Although capable of identifying key fixed or substantial mobile targets—such as large-signature rocket launchers—Israeli intelligence proved poor at finding operational command sites; underestimated the amount of weaponry available to Hezbollah; missed some late-generation weapons entirely; had no idea how deep, complex, and well-constructed Hezbollah's front-line bunker system had become; and failed to predict Hezbollah's tactical tenacity. Despite decades of contact, Israel did not know its enemy—nor did it accurately read the psychology of the Lebanese people.

Hezbollah, on the other hand, understood Israel's strengths and weaknesses acutely. Although the Hezbollah leader, Hassan Nasrallah, admitted that he did not expect so extensive a military response to the kidnapping of two Israeli soldiers, his organization had sized up the IDF's military capabilities, tactics, personalities, and decision cycle with impressive skill. On paper, the IDF was clearly superior. In practice, its intelligence preparation of the battlefield made Hezbollah surprisingly effective. The terrorist organization also appeared to grasp the political dynamics within Israel far better than Israel read the political complexities of Lebanon.

Israel fought as a limping stepchild of Clausewitz. Hezbollah fought as Sun Tzu's fanatical son.

THE WAR'S PECULIAR PROPHETS

Perhaps the oddest thing about the cellular antitank defense Hezbollah employed is that it had been proposed three decades earlier—for NATO, by off-the-reservation European generals. The prophetic books for Hezbollah-style warfare were impractical, military-utopian tomes written at a time of decreasing European defense budgets and the ascendancy of quantitative analysis—and, ironically, in the shadow of the antitank missile's success in the Yom Kippur War.

Senior officers such as Emil Spannochi of Austria (*Verteidigung ohne Selbstzerstoerung* "Defense Without Self-Destruction"), Franz Uhle-Wettler of Germany (*Gefechtsfeld Mitteleuropa* "Battlefield Central Europe") and Guy Brossolet of France (*Essai sur la non-bataille,* loosely, "The Non-Battle War") suggested that an effective and economical method of defeating massed Warsaw Pact armor would be to field large numbers of small cells equipped with antitank weapons to wage a territorial defense in depth.

The prophets called the European battlefield's dynamics utterly wrong. Relying on faulty math that assumed X number of kills for each team, they failed to take into account the psychological effects of masses of armor on small, isolated groups of European reservists—or even active-duty troops. Although the techniques they recommended varied somewhat in their details, all assumed that soldiers would wait patiently for Soviet tanks to come into range, coolly and accurately discharge their weapons in the required number of volleys, and then safely escape to fight again. The theories also assumed that the right number of antitank teams could be concentrated at precisely the right points along exactly the right avenues of approach to pick off passive Warsaw Pact armored vehicles that would present themselves as cardboard ducks in a shooting gallery. It was utter nonsense in the European context.

But it was exactly right for Hezbollah, an organization that had the two crucial ingredients that were missing in Central Europe and NATO: a relatively small piece of restrictive terrain to defend—and fighters willing to die on the spot to kill their enemies. And the IDF, for all its strength, had nothing approaching the number of Warsaw Pact tanks. Furthermore, the Israelis had a distinctly non-Soviet attitude toward friendly casualties.

It's a bizarre quirk of history that European military thinkers in quest of defense on the cheap unwittingly predicted the tactics of a twenty-first-century terrorist army. And the predictions don't end with the examples above: In a collection of articles edited by Carl Friedrich von Weizsaecker in 1984 (*Die Praxis der defensiven Verteidigung—The Practice of Defensive Defense*), the entry by Alexander Acker is titled "*Einsatz von Raketenartillerie im Verteigigungsnetz*," or "The Employment of Rocket-Artillery in a Defensive Network," although the author didn't quite foresee the use of tactical rockets as strategic terror weapons. Another pertinent essay from the same book dealt with the social and political consequences of alternative concepts of defense—an issue Hezbollah managed to turn into a weapon in and of itself as it lured the IDF to strike civilian targets.

While it wouldn't do to assume that Hezbollah's doctrine designers had read the European texts, it's not beyond the realm of plausibility, given the terrorist organization's extensive ties to northern Europe. But that's a question for historians with time on their hands. What matters is that, however it managed to conceive its battlefield doctrine, Hezbollah developed effective forms of defense and elastic organizational structures superbly suited to its strategic goals. If we can overcome our vanity and set aside, for one moment, our disgust with terrorist organizations, we might recognize that no formal military establishment in our time has done a better job than Hezbollah of preparing for the war it would fight—against a superior enemy. If David didn't kill Goliath this time, he certainly gave the big guy a headache.

Future developments will determine whether Hezbollah won an enduring strategic victory or achieved only the brief illusion of one. Today's champions can turn out to be tomorrow's losers—and the political complexity in Lebanon and the greater Middle East is such that no one can predict with confidence whether Hezbollah will become ever stronger and more influential, or if its moment of triumph was just that—a moment, soon to be eclipsed by greater forces. We do not know what the future holds for Hezbollah, but for now, we would do well to study the prototype it created of an effective twenty-first-century terrorist army.

PART V

The World Beyond

Waters of Wealth and War: The Crucial Indian Ocean

Armed Forces Journal

March 2006

Five hundred years ago, the Portuguese conquered the Indian Ocean with a dozen ships. In the twenty-first century, the U.S. Navy may find itself hard-pressed to maintain control of the same sea-lanes with every vessel it can spare for that distant, difficult theater. If there is one region of the globe in which naval actions and broader U.S. involvement in crises approach a certainty, it's the greater Indian Ocean, including contiguous waters from the Persian Gulf to the Java Sea and the deep littoral areas that harbor over a third of humanity, a fateful concentration of energy and mineral supplies, and a stupendous capacity for violence, local and international.

Riveted by the past century's European wars—hot and cold—the United States, a maritime power, shifted its strategic thinking away from the seas and onto dry land. During a period of unprecedented expansion in global trade, with ever more wealth moving over the face of the waters, our military forgot the strategic importance of commerce—except for a few oil-related brushes near the Strait of Hormuz. Incidentally, the Portuguese held Hormuz for 100 years.

As you read these lines, nearly 20 million shipping containers are underway around the globe—carried by fewer than 4,000 hulls. The explosion of transoceanic trade simultaneously has made that commerce more vulnerable, not only in the obvious sense that economies have grown more interdependent, but also because, even as the volume of shipped goods increased, the number of significant cargo carriers plummeted—because of the increasing size of commercial vessels, from supertankers to container ships. Far fewer transports ply the seas today than a century ago; the sinking, seizure, or blockading of a small portion of the international merchant fleet could bring high-end economies to a standstill. While our Navy—the most powerful and skilled in history—focuses on grand fleet actions (or their postmodern, dispersed equivalent), the strategic weak link across the globe is trade.

This is nowhere more evident than in the greater Indian Ocean (GIO), on whose shores lie great potential wealth and incomparable poverty, along with multiple immediate and potential clashes of civilizations, cultures, and minorities. Here, the world's great religions confront each other; systems of government challenge one another; social systems conflict; and the world's two most powerful states, the United States and China, find themselves in a competition for resources and allies that Beijing, at least, views as a zero-sum game.

And no waters are so vulnerable.

PIRATES AND NUKES

Recently, a U.S. Navy ship entered the twenty-first century by stopping a hijacked vessel off the Somali coast and arresting the pirates aboard. From the Straits of Malacca to the Horn of Africa, piracy is back. Although hijackings and robberies at sea have become increasingly ambitious, most of their victims are still tramp steamers or coastal vessels. Proximity to a Somali dhow in Mombassa last summer convinced me that any pirates strong enough to withstand the smell of its cargo of dried shark probably deserved success. But we live in an age of new confluences: In Iraq, terrorists and insurgents collaborate with criminals. What happens if the growing Islamist-terrorist presence in the Horn of Africa discovers innovative ways to exploit pirates?

The direct damage terrorist-pirates could do would be limited. But their crimes would probably elicit an overreaction that would impede regional trade, while the second-order effects could be greater still: domino economic consequences, from lost business and customs revenue to insurance hikes that damaged fragile

economies and multinational corporations alike. The worse scenario would be terrorist-sponsored pirates who engaged in sheer
destruction. The worst would be terrorists-cum-pirates armed with
weapons of mass destruction.

It may be a blessedly long time before a dhow carrying a nuke
approaches a supertanker or an aircraft carrier, but at the high end
of the threat spectrum, the potential for Iran to field nuclear
weapons could alter the regional equation so profoundly that we
would be hard-pressed to respond effectively within parameters
acceptable to world opinion. Although recent nuclear saber rattling
by French President Jacque Chirac suggests that Europe may not
have come so far from its old bad habits, after all. Will a future generation look back wistfully at the moderation of the George W.
Bush presidency?

The prospect of nuclear weapons controlled by Tehran sum-
mons visions of a new, nuclear holocaust against Israel. But a Shi'a
bomb is at least as likely to be employed against Sunni Muslims,
while a nuclear threat to the Strait of Hormuz could play havoc with
the global economy. Dubai may be the most vulnerable—and over-
priced—patch of real estate on earth.

In his last State of the Union message, President Bush belatedly
called for a dramatic reduction of U.S. dependence on Middle Eastern oil by 2025. Yet, even if this worthy goal is achieved—precipitat-
ing the well-deserved collapse of Arab oil economies—two turbulent
decades loom ahead as the Muslim world argues with itself over the
nature of its faith and the cause of its catastrophic failure. Iranian
nuclear weapons, once married to effective delivery systems, would
not only make it difficult for the U.S. military to operate in the Persian Gulf—could we sustain our efforts in Iraq if our ships feared to
enter the Gulf?—but also would extend Tehran's de facto control
beyond its own oil reserves to those of the Gulf sheikhdoms and
Saudi Arabia. And the position of the Islamofascist Tehran regime
increasingly seems to be *Après nous, le déluge.*

Yet, even this much attention paid to the Arabo-Persian world
reflects only our past misjudgments, not the broader future. The
Arab world, especially, is headed back to history's ward for the ter-
minally ill, with its decades of mismanaged oil wealth an anomaly
whose long-term consequences were political, social, cultural, and

spiritual cancer. Especially if the Iraqi experiment fails, our challenge in the Middle East will no longer be to transform the region but to contain the consequences of its pervasive failure.

SHANGHAI'D

U.S. military and intelligence officers worry, with some justification, about Chinese involvement from Iran through southern Africa. But the Chinese—correctly—are far more worried about us.

Beijing has to play for time. For all the impressive growth statistics coming out of China, that state's internal disparities, excited expectations, financial-system fragility, and dependence on foreign trade to sustain its economy make Beijing nervous and geostrategically (not militarily) aggressive. Paradoxically, the Chinese government could endure a long war but lives on a knife's edge in peace, surviving on bad domestic loans, an undervalued currency, low-end industries, the abuse of human capital, ecological ruthlessness, and the crossed-fingers hope that the economy can transition to the production of more sophisticated goods (in a glutted market) and the development of a service sector for which it is politically, linguistically, and culturally ill-suited. While China is a power to be reckoned with, its greatest reckoning may be internal; meanwhile, if the robustness of any economy is exaggerated, it's China's.

To keep that economy running, China needs more of just about everything except people or corruption: More foreign markets, more domestic infrastructure, more raw materials, more minerals, and, above all, ever more oil and gas. Beijing is well aware of its vulnerability to an interruption of trade and the interdiction of global sea-lanes, and it also understands that its military—especially its navy—is far from becoming competitive with that of the United States. Thus, China's alternative strategy is to build networks of interdependence to conquer markets and build alliances wherever they have the potential to impede the diplomatic and military actions of the United States.

China's initiatives abroad may be divided into those aimed at actively countering American power and those intended to frustrate American actions temporarily in a crisis. In addition to the practical benefits of pursuing natural gas supplies in Bolivia or leveraging a controlling interest in the Panama Canal, China hopes to distract

U.S. attention and divert American energies and resources during a prelude to war or in its initial phase. Beijing realizes its presence in Latin America is no more than an outpost line that would have to be sacrificed. China's fleet will never be able to contest the Pacific sea-lanes. But Beijing will ensure that any wartime retreat from the Western Hemisphere leaves behind a maximum of regional ill-will toward Washington.

The GIO, on the other hand, is integral to Beijing's strategy.

One of China's advantages, at least in the near term, is its willingness to embrace the world's worst rogue regimes; in the longer term, such as strategy can backfire as those regimes implode. The Chinese are active in Sudan and courting Iran, both because of the energy resources possessed by those states and their strategic locations. Elsewhere, Beijing has long since bought a degree of control over Myanmar. Even a decade ago, I found the old Burma Road crowded with goods—trucks making the trip between Rangoon/Yangon port and southern China. Beijing has a major intelligence operation and a quiet military presence in Myanmar, which it views as an emergency lifeline to the Bay of Bengal and the GIO beyond.

Not all of China's engagement initiatives offer so direct a payoff. In distant Zimbabwe, at the inland edge of the GIO, Beijing supports the vile regime of Robert Mugabe. In return, the Chinese have received concessionary terms for their investments, but that only goes so far in a bankrupt, ruined country. It isn't so much a matter of profits, as of presence—and a reliable allied vote in world forums. To an unnoticed extent, the Chinese have begun to belie their reputation for cautiousness. By embracing one rogue regime after another, they're gambling on a continued lack of unity among Western governments as well as on the stability of the world's most repressive states—note their recent approaches to Saudi Arabia. Beijing is building its foreign policy on blasting caps in a world full of dynamite.

As formidable as some of this sounds, first-hand observation of the Chinese abroad suggests that we haven't that much to worry about as far as direct competition goes. Much is made of deepening Chinese involvement in eastern Africa, the far and neglected shore of the GIO. And yes, the Chinese are visible: When I stayed in Dar es Salaam last year, my hotel—long deserted by Westerners—

survived by providing bunks to Chinese delegations whose members displayed a manly disregard for the cockroaches in the dining room. Yet, not only is Chinese trade with Africa still miniscule compared to that with the U.S. or Europe, the geopolitical opportunities for China on that continent peaked in the 1960s, in the wake of the continent's decolonization, in the age of Che in the Congo and Chinese engineers on Zanzibar, when revolutionary rhetoric still seemed a viable substitute for achievement. Beijing's legacy in Tanzania, for example, is of ill-built factories that now stand derelict or function at a fraction of their theoretical capacity. Far from conquering twenty-first century Africa, Beijing blew its best shot decades ago. Now, China's struggling to catch up with Western economies that not only have greater resources, skills, and commercial ties, but whose representatives also are better liked.

We consistently fail to include the human factor in our intelligence analysis. While African states remain hungry for aid and investment, the Chinese are far less welcome than their money or goods. Although you can hardly move around the cities of the old Swahili Coast without tripping over groups of Chinese (never Chinese alone), those batches and bunches of ill-at-ease foreigners smack of the Soviet delegations of the high Cold War—although the Soviets drank harder. The Chinese hold a powerfully racist view of Africans, which Africans do not fail to grasp. The aloofness of the Chinese is one of their greatest weaknesses—even Chinese tourism in a country such as Kenya doesn't help. The Chinese don't tip, either.

On the other hand, Americans are far better liked than the herd-think global media would have one believe. In theory, Africans may not like the United States, but in practice they not only like but also admire America. There are no long lines of Africans waiting for visas to emigrate to China. Conversely, African governments may welcome the Chinese in theory, but no one much cares for them in the flesh.

This matters. At a time when we endure endless rhetoric about how we're losing the culture wars because of Muslim-world trucelence, the evidence I've seen firsthand, from Indonesia to South Africa, is that the American dream is alive and kicking far beyond our shores—if only we look beyond the Middle East. Chinese culture is exclusive and profoundly foreign (kung-fu movies notwithstanding), while American culture is so seductive it addicts even those who attack it. Apart from the failed civilization of Middle Eastern Islam, the future is ours to lose.

In eastern and southern Africa, as well as in the Middle East, the Chinese seek to create webs of obligation sufficiently strong to stymie U.S. diplomatic initiatives in a crisis and to deny the use of GIO port facilities to the U.S. Navy. The Chinese know they can't win in the Pacific but believe they could put up a fight—if an asymmetrical one—in the Indian Ocean, with its indispensable sea-lanes.

And the key to the Indian Ocean is India.

OUR VITAL FUTURE ALLY?

Watch Beijing's attempts to build a relationship with New Delhi. If China's leaders could prevent the United States from developing a closer relationship with any state on earth, they would unhesitatingly pick India.

It doesn't take Mahan or Corbett to understand why. Just look at a map. There's a very good reason why that body of water is called the "Indian" Ocean. China understands that, unless India can be persuaded to maintain a form of neutrality that tilts Beijing's way during a Sino-American confrontation, China's last hope of maintaining even the slightest economic lifeline would collapse; Beijing's semisatellite Myanmar would become worthless; and the region's other states would be far less likely to align diplomatically with a China they perceived as bound to lose.

It often has been remarked that the U.S. and India are natural allies, given that they're the world's two largest democracies and have converging geostrategic and economic interests. Ties between our governments have been growing, if slowly. But for now, three obstacles remain on the Indian side that impede the expansion of cooperative efforts that would benefit both states profoundly: The psychological insecurity of the Indian elite, which manifests itself in roll-your-eyes arrogance; the populist demagogy of politicians still playing the outdated anti-American card; and, most challenging of all, Indian cartel and union resistance to the further opening of the Indian market, which would be of tremendous benefit to the overwhelming majority of the population and India's still-disappointing economy.

Yet, our mutual interests are so strong that a closer alliance appears inevitable. There will be awkward intervals—over Pakistan, for example—but the smart money would bet on Beijing failing to make serious inroads with New Delhi. Beyond old antagonisms, India is deeply worried about the rapid expansion of Chinese wealth and power—and jealousy is a decisive strategic factor.

On a practical level, Indian alignment with the United States not only shifts a billion people to our side, but also effectively blocks China's last trade routes; negates Chinese inroads in the Middle East and Africa; and eases the burden on the U.S. Navy by engaging India's navy, a force with significant regional capabilities.

How India defines its geostrategic interests may decide the fate of the entire region.

THREATS AND OPPORTUNITIES

A magazine column can barely scratch the surface of the incomparably complex GIO theater. Our difficulties in comprehending the strategic interdependence of Australia and South Africa, Kenya and Thailand, Sudan and Myanmar, India and Indonesia are manifested by our division of responsibility for this crucial region between three commands, EUCOM, CENTCOM, and PACOM. While inter-command coordination is better than ever, our outdated division of the world hinders us from understanding the changed strategic environment. For example, the boundary between EUCOM and CENTCOM is drawn as well as it could be (in the absence of a GIO-specific command), yet it fails to acknowledge ties of trade, religion, culture, war, and colonization that date back more than a thousand years. Globalization isn't new, and millennium-old Chinese pottery shards routinely appear in excavations in East Africa.

The Cold War is over, and the twentieth century is over. Our willingness to extend the presence of substantial U.S. forces in northern Europe while slighting the GIO (apart from the Middle East) makes no strategic sense. The future lies below the Tropic of Cancer, in the emerging postmodern empire built overnight by postapartheid South Africa, in the enormous potential of Indonesia to pioneer a more successful, modern path for Islam, in the awakening capacities of India—and even in the enduring importance of Singapore, perhaps the most vital city-state since Athens.

The GIO harbors terrible threats, as well (and not merely that possible, but unlikely, military confrontation between the U.S. and China): Nuclear-armed Pakistan is a Hamlet among nations, unsure of its identity and unable to decide on a decisive course of action. As in the play, the last act could litter the stage with bodies. Bangladesh, a human disaster, is prey to Islamist militancy. Beyond the familiar struggles in the Horn of Africa, the growing tension between jihadi Islam and the African Church Militant has already resulted in regional bloodlettings, from Sudan west to Nigeria. Saudi Arabia is doomed—its violent collapse only a matter of time, be it years or decades. And Iran remains a powerful short-term threat, but is also a potential U.S. ally in the longer term (Persians are a friendless, proud, hated people in a very nasty neighborhood). For now, the world continues to gulp Middle-Eastern oil, creating an immediate set of problems. Tomorrow, a diminished appetite for oil and the implosion of bankrupt regional states may generate other challenges entirely.

No other region of the world offers such potential—and presents so many intractable problems.

How might the future of the GIO look, if the United States thinks clearly and acts deftly (admittedly a tall order)? We should strive to build a new regional alliance aligning the United States with, in the first rank, Australia, Indonesia, Singapore, India, Iran (in the out-years) and South Africa. Desirable secondary allies would include New Zealand, Thailand, Sri Lanka, Kenya (if its government can be reformed), the islands with flags, and, perhaps, Tanzania, Mozambique, and Malaysia. The challenge, of course, is for all of these governments, including our own, to move beyond the past century's prejudices and petty bickering to grasp our commonality of interests.

A greater Indian Ocean strategic alliance could be to the twenty-first century what the North Atlantic Treaty Organization was to the twentieth: A military alliance that prevents a catastrophic war and fosters regional cooperation. But we need to have the vision to see beyond yesteryear's divisions of the world—and to grasp that command of the Indian Ocean will be decisive to the global future.

The "Cartoon Riots": Bigots on Both Sides

New York Post

February 7, 2006

Riots scorch the Islamic world as maddened believers protest Danish cartoons depicting the Prophet Mohammed. Embassies burn, demonstrators die, crazed threats resound. Far more Muslims fill the streets than protested the invasion of Iraq.

Astonished Europeans insist on their right to press freedom. Muslims are outraged at the willful violation of a widespread Islamic belief: The Prophet's image must not be depicted.

Now the confrontation's gone too far for either side to back down. And both sides are wrong.

First, consider the Europeans. The Danish newspaper that first published the cartoons last September was not standing up courageously for freedom of expression. The editors and cartoonists were so oblivious to any reality beyond their Copenhagen coffee bars that they just thought they were pulling an attention-getting prank. They got attention, all right. As did the papers elsewhere in Europe that reprinted the offending cartoons last week. In the name of press freedom, of course.

The problem is that with freedom comes responsibility, a quality to which Europe's become allergic (nothing is ever a European's fault). Breaking a well-known taboo of Islam was irresponsible. No other word for it.

There's plenty to criticize in the failed civilization of Middle Eastern Islam. But the European press avoids the serious issues. They could've run cartoons about al Zarqawi's savagery, al Jazeera's hypocrisy, or the oppression of women. Instead, they attacked a religion's heart. Gratuitously.

Those cartoons said more about Europe's own arrogance toward religious believers and intolerance of faith than they do about Islam. Today's Europeans consider religious belief as beneath their sophistication. They've come so far that they no longer grasp how intense faith can be—and how furiously the faithful can react.

Through their clumsiness and vanity, the Europeans have made this an all-or-nothing issue. What began as a nasty little Danish problem has been globalized. If the Europeans appear to capitulate now, it will only encourage Muslim extremists around the world.

Wasn't it those oh-so-clever Europeans who complained about a heavy U.S. hand in the Middle East? Who made excuses for 9/11, the Madrid bombings, street murders, terrorist kidnappings and beheadings, the London bombings, French suburbs aflame, and no end of hate speech? Then treated Islam the way a dog treats a fire hydrant?

That's Europe for you: A continent of cowards who start fights they can't finish themselves. Thanks, Hans. Merci, Pierre.

Of course, the blame doesn't fall solely on the Eurotrash. The overreaction within the Muslim world is psychotic—yet another indication of the spiritual and practical collapse of the Middle East and realms beyond. Will the Europeans figure it out this time? How many corpses, cracked heads, arrests, boycotts, and smoldering embassies will it take before Europe realizes that militant Islam isn't benign?

The Arab world, especially, is a pile of tinder waiting for random sparks. And the alacrity with which regional governments and Islamist groups have moved to blow up the cartoon issue into a conflagration is as tactically astute as it is despicable.

What we're seeing in the Middle East is strategic theater, benefit performances for the Syrian government (now playing the Islam card), Hezbollah, Hamas, and every tough customer in the neighborhood.

No accident that the largest number of demonstrators busted in Beirut were Syrian nationals. And does anyone really believe that Syria's police and security services couldn't control those crowds in Damascus?

Meanwhile, the nuts-for-Allah boys in Tehran are using the issue to whip up support for Shi'a nukes. Kashmiri separatists are milking the controversy, as are the remnants of the Taliban in Afghanistan. The protests stretch from Indonesia to England.

Expect more blood.

It's hard not to feel a certain amount of *Schadenfreude* after enduring endless lectures from Europeans about how the Middle East's problems were all made in America. It will be fascinating to watch the Europeans attempt to come to grips with fanaticism. Even a French philosopher can't forever glorify a civilization that puts more energy into calling for death to cartoonists than it does into human rights, education, or good government.

For once, we Americans can sit back and watch the fight (pass the popcorn, please). The Europeans are going to get a few more teeth knocked out. As for the Islamist bigots intent on destroying what's left of their own decayed societies, they'll lose at least a few of their European apologists—the sort who make excuses for terrorists, as long as they only kill Americans (or Muslims).

Looking at the pigheaded intolerance driving the Europeans and Islamist fanatics alike, the healthy response is, "A plague on both your houses."

The Worst Plague

New York Post

February 17, 2006

What does a standoff between a Texas sheriff's department and Mexican soldiers over a drug bust have in common with the electoral victory of Hamas and the current government crisis in Kenya? Here's a hint: They all tie in with the fate of Iraq's new government, the Enron trials, and environmental degradation in China.

The winning—and losing—answer is: corruption. No single factor has been as destructive of good government and the hopes of billions of struggling human beings. AIDS? Malaria? Avian flu? Corruption undercuts efforts to provide decent health care—just as it wrecks education systems and corrodes social bonds. Corruption is the great plague that makes all others worse.

Corruption kills. Sometimes directly, as when Mexican narco-insurgents shielded by regional politicians assassinate journalists fighting to clean up their country. Or when a crusading African politician dies in an "accident."

Usually, though, corruption kills indirectly. By robbing honest chances for better lives. By siphoning off funds meant for sewage systems or piped water. By delivering medicines long past their expiration dates—or no medicines at all.

From Latin America to China, university spaces and grades are for sale, while government jobs and contracts require kickbacks. Meritocracy—that great human hope—doesn't have a chance. Markets are distorted, and capitalism, which relies on the rule of law, gets a bad name where it never had a chance. The poor suffer. And they vote their desperation, putting fanatic religious parties in power in Palestine or electing a demagogue to the presidency in Venezuela.

Corruption makes a mockery of every religion, every system of government, every public institution. From Argentina through Nigeria to Pakistan, countries that should've punched their way to the economic middleweight bouts failed miserably instead—while privileged citizens bought luxury homes in Europe.

Corruption makes wars worse, too. Illicit arms deals, the lure of profits from "blood diamonds" or narcotics, or simple land grabs increase human misery geometrically. The Vietnam-era slogan "War is Good Business" applies far more viciously to the crippled "developing" world than it ever did to our own country.

Yes, we have corruption in the United States. You bet. After sex and violence, corruption's easily the third-oldest human pastime. But we don't look away. When we encounter corruption, we get angry. And we prosecute. Whether the case involves executives so rich they think they're untouchable, arrogant D.C. lobbyists—or members of Congress. It may take time, but here the corrupt go to jail.

Elsewhere, they go to Paris. Or Geneva. Or Parliament. Elsewhere, billions of human beings are born without hope if they don't belong to the right family, the right clan or tribe, or the right religion. Elsewhere, the rich and powerful not only steal from the poor and helpless, they rub their superiority in the faces of those they've dispossessed.

If you want to see cruelty more pernicious than physical torture, study corrupt societies. Much of the immigration, legal and illegal, to the USA isn't just a flight toward hope but a flight away from corruption and its consequences.

Corruption undercuts our strategic ambitions, too. In the course of a how-to-fix-Iraq discussion on Capitol Hill last fall, I remarked that, as long as we don't quit, the greatest threat to Iraq's future isn't terrorism, but the deeply embedded tradition of corruption. I don't think the senator hosting the meeting believed me, but I was deadly serious.

Without a sense of social responsibility that transcends blood and sect, it's hard to build a rule-of-law democracy. Corrupt politicians don't just steal money—they steal their country's future.

While we don't tolerate corruption here at home, we're still too willing to overlook it abroad. Yes, we have sound anti-corruption laws for our multinational corporations. But the scrutiny still isn't what it should be. And laws are worthless unless enforced.

As you'd expect, the hypocritical Europeans are much worse— despite holier-than-thou European Union antibribery rules (honored about as often as the old Soviet constitution). As for the Chinese and other up-and-coming economic players, they don't even pretend to obey international anticorruption codes. And we don't call them on it. Back in the overrated 1960s, a now-forgotten novel had a great title, *Everybody Knows and Nobody Cares.* When it comes to global corruption, that's a perfect slogan.

Yes, fighting corruption abroad is tough. We lose contracts. "Friendly" governments turn against us. Demagogues blame us for their own sins. Nationalists are outraged.

But doesn't the fate of billions of human beings matter more?

Washington has to take an uncompromising stand against corruption—and not just a rhetorical one. If we're remotely sincere about democracy, human rights, or religious tolerance, the battle starts with the fight against corruption.

It's about self-interest, too. 9/11 had its roots not only in religious fanaticism but also in the suffocating corruption of the Middle East. Nothing will deter hardcore fanatics, but give the average man or woman a chance and they're far less likely to strap on a suicide bomb.

Meanwhile, those Enron trials aren't about what's wrong with our system. They're about what's right with it.

Emerging Hot Spots

Armchair General

May 2006

Love the Brits, but they blew it. Watch southern Iraq, where the British military's "light touch" peacekeeping ops allowed Shi'a extremists to build parallel power structures that have made Coalition forces all but irrelevant.

No question about it: Man for man, Brits in uniform are the equal of any soldiers in the world. But they fell prey to one of the oldest mistakes in the military book: In Basra and the surrounding region, they applied peacekeeping lessons learned in Northern Ireland. But what works in one peacemaking or peacekeeping effort doesn't necessarily transfer to a radically different cultural environment. With the best intentions in the world, the Brits "fought the last war."

Now their forces are struggling to control pervasive death squads, an Iraqi security apparatus controlled by Shi'a radicals (many of them pro-Iran), and local governments either onboard with the extremist program or terrified to resist it.

With whopping bad judgment, a senior British officer recently chastised the U.S. military for too heavy-handed an approach in Iraq—even as the Brits were effectively turning over the south to anti-Western firebrands.

If Iraq still exists as a unified state a decade from now, the most backward and troublesome provinces won't be in the notorious Sunni Triangle, but in the Shi'a south where the Brits' light touch opened the door to Islamist heavies.

The New Burma Road: Watch China's engagement in Burma/Myanmar. *Armchair General* readers know the Burma theater was one of the cruelest in World War II, but who thinks about Burma today? There may be a passing headline about the continuing detention of Aung San Su Kyi, the courageous democracy advocate, but without oil reserves to attract the world's attention, the Burmese military junta pretty much gets a pass—despite massive human-rights violations.

What's happening under our noses is crucial to China's plans for regional hegemony—and its preparations for that hope-it-doesn't-happen future war with the USA. Even ten years ago, I witnessed stunning Chinese penetration while on a government mission to combat the heroin trade. In Mandalay, Chinese buyers had priced the Burmese out of the city's center; the (crumbling) Burma Road was choked with Chinese trucks ferrying goods between southern China and the Rangoon port; and Beijing's military had already established a listening post on the Bay of Bengal.

Why does it matter? Because the Indian Ocean is even more important to China's security than the Pacific: It's the route for the oil and gas that fuels China's economy. And Beijing grasps that the distant theater is operationally the toughest for our military (logistics rule). In a crisis, Burma/Myanmar would provide a lifeline for southern China and a military base to confront U.S. regional deployments.

Meanwhile, the Chinese have convinced Burma's ruling generals that the Yankees are coming to overthrow their regime. As a result, the already-paranoid junta recently uprooted the entire government, forcing it hundreds of miles inland from Rangoon—transplanting tens of thousands of functionaries to an undeveloped jungle site where the government will further lose touch with global reality.

China is effectively colonizing the country—and gaining its first port that feeds into the crucial Indian Ocean theater. Future key player? India. If India aligns with the USA, Burma/Myanmar won't help China much.

Watch for Chinese efforts to derail the accelerating relationship between Washington and New Delhi.

Could the day come when U.S. forces once again fight in Burmese jungles?

Democracy's Global Crisis

RealClearPolitics.com

April 19, 2006

Not so long ago we were told that democracy would sweep the world. A new age of governmental decency would dawn for hundreds of millions. Peace, constructive trade and general goodwill would follow.

Now, as the number of real and nominal democracies continues to grow, we see little improvement in the human condition, no diminution of corruption, burgeoning discontents—and turmoil where we meant to implant peace. Even in the West, where democracy is deep-rooted, there's a crisis of mediocrity and will. Elsewhere, democracy has been taken as a license to loot, as a launching pad for demagogues, or as a means of settling old scores.

Have we been wrong? Is democracy a tailored suit that fits only the most developed forms? Is it culturally determined, after all? Does it fail to guarantee freedom and a population's general welfare?

Have we overestimated democracy's utility?

The problem isn't with democracy. It's with us. We expected too much of a tool, forgetting that specific skills are required to use it well. We imagined that others could master in a day what we spent a millennium practicing. And we failed to allow for basic human emotions and bigotries: Hatreds, jealousies, ethnic and religious rivalries, and the fierce competition for resources in the lands of never-enough.

Democracy remains by far the most promising form of government—but it's much more difficult to master than we pretended. A series of elections does not constitute democracy. Democracy also requires a spirit of compromise, of shared values and ultimate goals, of social and personal integrity, and a still-rare-in-this-world measure of identification with the state—not just with ties of blood or belief.

To function as we demand, democracy also may require general wealth sufficient to prevent violent struggles over resources or the legitimization of theft from one group for the benefit of another.

Today, there are two crises of democracy, neither of which need prove fatal, but both of which must be faced honestly.

The worst crisis is in the developing world, where democracy too often has been used to implement the dictatorship of the largest tribe; to legitimize the postcolonial kingship of "presidents for life"; to divide minorities, rather than unite them; and to erect reactionary regimes that masquerade as populist governments.

In too much of the world, election to public office remains a license to steal, to suppress, and to oppress. In states with dysfunctional economies, frequent government upheavals stymie progress. And in those ill-drawn states that have no deep sense of collective identity, democracy succumbs to a constant redivision of spoils.

In Venezuela, Argentina, and Bolivia, the recent votes for leftist regimes were not triumphs of democracy, but expressions of dissatisfaction with democracy's inability to meet popular expectations (and, of course, the balloting also reflected destructive populism in the tragic Latin-American tradition).

In Africa, from Nigeria to Kenya, elections prove frustratingly unable to deliver good government. A vote may change the party in office, but fails to alter the culture of the candidates. On that tragic continent, the recent progress has been largely rhetorical, with a new generation of leaders saying the right things but continuing to practice theft-by-incumbency.

In the Middle East, elections are either nonexistent, wildly rigged, or won by Islamist parties (the lure of primitive identities may trump the desire for Western-model freedoms). Iran's "democracy" is poisoned with fraud, and Turkey has been raped and left bleeding by decades of corrupt party politics (paving the way for fundamentalist victories). Iraq, with its bitter history and truculent factions, is the great laboratory for the region. While there is reason for sober optimism, the experiment in Baghdad is far from a guaranteed success.

India is a national success story, but, at the local level, its democracy is that of the gun, the boss, and the bribe. Pakistan has proven itself incompetent to master democracy and probably will remain so. Afghanistan may surprise the world with its success—but only if the Kabul government can assert a monopoly of coercive power. And Russia, that other troubled Asian state, is less a democracy today than Chavez's Venezuela.

Still, none of this means that democracy must fail—only that it is not "a machine that will go of itself." Democracy takes time, labor, commitment, and, sometimes, the willingness to fight against the forces of the past. It also requires that rarest of human commodities, honesty. Contrary to our illusions, the one thing democracy isn't is easy.

Which brings us to the other, unremarked crisis of democracy— the descent into governmental mediocrity in the West. In Europe, the end of the Cold War brought democracy, but rarely inspiring leadership. Eastern Europe celebrated, then woke up with a hangover. Old Europe slipped backward.

At a time when Europe's moribund socioeconomic systems urgently need reform, the continent is strikingly devoid of promising leaders. Germany hasn't had first-rate leadership since the 1970s, and France has been poorly led since the late 1960s. Italy never had great leadership in the postwar era. Britain was blessed with the glorious Mrs. Thatcher and the early Mr. Blair, but the current political landscape looks bleak.

On the continent, a new tyranny of the haves threatens the soul, if not the outward forms, of democracy. The recent strikes in France were an attempt to stop the clock, and Euro-apartheid separates not only white skins from brown or black, but the securely employed from the never-to-be-employed. Soft socialism has created a general malaise among populations, forging a continent of critics, not creators. And the European Union has deadened, rather than enhanced, the continent's prospects with its dictatorship of the Eurocrats.

Even here in the United States, the past few decades have seen the triumph of the mediocre. Was Ronald Reagan our last visionary? Other than John McCain, is there a single galvanizing presidential possibility in either political party?

Has our gotcha culture driven greatness from the political stage, leaving it to the burrowing little souls? Is it to be an enduring American paradox that a country that facilitates internet porn and celebrates Oprah-style public confessions demands a private and public blandness in political leaders that eliminates the aptitude for greatness?

Have we entered the age of "little presidents"? Can America lead the world, if America is not led well? Make no mistake: This is not a Democratic or Republican problem. The self-interested corporatist leadership in Washington is a bipartisan problem.

Democracy isn't "over." It's only beginning. No other system of government approaches its potential for decency, opportunity and equity. But democracy is also hard. Those who prescribed it as a cure-all now must face the possibility that the medicine may make the patient sicker for years before recovery can begin.

Russian Roulette

Armchair General

July 2006

The Russians are coming (back)! With attempts to bully Ukraine and Georgia earlier this year by turning off their supplies of natural gas in midwinter, crackdowns on free speech and pro-democracy groups at home, diplomatic cozying up to rogue regimes—not least through the sale of nuclear technology to Iran—support for the worst dictatorships in the former Soviet Union, security-services backing for Russian-sponsored secessionist regimes on Georgian territory in South Ossetia and Abkhazia, and the endless, astonishingly clumsy violence in Chechnya, Moscow has proved, yet again, that it "never misses an opportunity to miss an opportunity."

Is there something just plain wrong with the Russians? Apologists cite insecurities born of the "Tartar yoke" and Muscovy's centuries of serving as Christianity's frontier state against Islam. Yet, Ukrainians suffered far worse from the long struggles with the Ottoman Empire and its clients, such as the Crimean Tartars. History as an excuse for viciousness goes only so far.

In the early 1990s, those of us who had studied the Russians and traveled throughout the Soviet Union tried to tell Washington that Moscow's shrunken empire was *not* going to become a model Jeffersonian democracy. We were mocked as unreconstructed Cold Warriors. Well, welcome to the future. Russian president Vladimir Putin, raised in the KGB, has proved incapable of seeing beyond a paranoid, security-service view of the world. No country enjoyed so much international goodwill after the Soviet collapse as the new Russia. And the Russians squandered their moral credit.

Can Russia reform itself and get back on track to popular democracy? The signs aren't good. While Ukrainians, Balts, Georgians, Armenians, and even Azeris and Kyrgyz stand up for freedom and democracy, the silence from the Russian population has been deafening. Putin knows his people: He's given them social and some economic freedoms, while restricting their political freedoms again. And the Russian population has accepted the deal. They want security and fear liberty.

Does this mean we're headed back toward a military rivalry with Russia? Absolutely not. The Russian military is pathetically broken, its systems in disrepair and its morale lower than it must have been in the summer of 1941. The brutal tradition of *Dyedovshchina,* the savage hazing of recruits, still results in the torture deaths and suicides of junior enlisted men (how's that for a morale builder?). The generals are still drunks. The troops still do maintenance with sledgehammers. And the fleet—or what's left of it—can't be trusted to get out of its home harbors without a disaster.

But Moscow can still make infernal mischief diplomatically and by trading with rogue regimes. The Putin regime's blindness to the country's real interests is stunning. Moscow's bullying has further hardened the fears—and Western orientation—of Eastern Europe and key former-Soviet states. The rise in oil prices has allowed the Russian economy to survive—but at the price of a failure to diversify and long-term vulnerability. Increasingly, Russia looks like a shabby discount version of Saudi Arabia (with hookers).

Watch Moscow's relationship with Tehran. If Putin puts profits from the nuclear trade above global security, we'll need to reassess our relationship with Russia and stop pretending we're pals. While Putin thinks he has the Europeans over the barrel with the Euro-reliance on Russian natural gas, he may be in for a surprise there, too (Europe's turning mean again). Meanwhile, the Russian military is so far diminished since its Cold War days of glory that it can't control an internal state the size of Rhode Island.

The new Russia "could've been a contender." Instead, Moscow's chosen to make enemies of the powerful and allies of the doomed. While it poses no direct threat to the United States (and won't), Putin's Russia has the capacity to make plenty of regional mischief.

French Twisted

New York Post

June 19, 2006

This spring, I visited French-speaking West Africa. Wherever I went, two things remained consistent: The French government was hated, and Africans looked to Washington for a square deal.

President Jacques Chirac and his racist minions know it, and they don't like it, and they're trying to do something about it:

Sucker America into showing "solidarity with an ally in the War on Terror." The French want our military and diplomatic cooperation—but not our economic presence, of course. Let me translate what the parasites of Paris really mean: "Support our brutality and exploitation of West Africa, stiff-arm tens of millions of Africans yearning to be free of French neo-imperialism—and just maybe we clever Frenchmen will toss you stupid Americans a little bone now and then." And we're in danger of falling for it.

In the half-century since France thrust a phony independence on colonies such as Ivory Coast, Senegal, and Mali, the French government and French business interests have looted everything they possibly could. To Paris, African "independence" meant business as usual, except that Paris would no longer accept any responsibility for the welfare of the local populations.

It was a free ride, guaranteed by a French military that had failed everywhere else but remained sufficiently competent to bully unarmed Africans. One French government after another supported pro-Paris strongmen, from the relatively benign Houphouet-Boigny of Ivory Coast, who merely bankrupted his country with

nutty construction projects, to Jean Bedell-Bokassa, a literal canni-
bal who frequently played host to then-President Valery Giscard-
D'Estaing.

But the winds of freedom have been blowing, often in unexpected places. The era of African "Big Men" is over, even if a few
linger on. And Africans want real freedom this time, not French
colonization in disguise.

In Ivory Coast, the French utterly mismanaged a 2002 rebellion
they thought they could manipulate. Their efforts at playing the factions off against each other exploded, shattering a country that had
been a source of pride and great profit to Paris. Muslim or Christian, northerner or southerner, the one commonality I found
among the people of Ivory Coast was that they all now hate the
French.

Even in Senegal, the country that has had the most benign relationship with France, the people are tired of French bullying and
condescension.

Throughout the region, animosity toward Paris—especially the
ham-handed government of Jacques Chirac—has reached a tipping
point past which legitimate anger threatens to turn into irrational
fury.

In Abidjan, in Ivory Coast, I even found myself in the unusual
position of defending the French, arguing that nobody could be as
omnipresent and cagey as my local friend believed French agents to
be.

We hear a great deal about global anti-Americanism, but, as this
column has noted, much of it is superficial or concentrated among
the usual suspects, while a tremendous reservoir of goodwill toward
us is still overflowing in much of the world. Even those who reflexively complain about American power long for a green card.

In West Africa, everyone has a friend or relative, or the friend
of a relative, in one of New York's boroughs or in Chicago. Their
vision of America is of hardworking immigrants building prosperous lives impossible elsewhere. The American dream is alive and
well—in Dakar or Abidjan.

In contrast, West Africans know that their relatives imprisoned
in the suburban slums of Paris or Lyon have no hope of getting
ahead, but suffer relentless discrimination.

As a result, street-level Africans consistently express tremendous goodwill toward Americans (although they're mystified by African-American heritage tourists who complain about their lot—Africans would gladly swap places). Either George Bush or Bill Clinton could win an election by a landslide in any West African country I visited.

Meanwhile, the French know they're in trouble. They know that their African victims are sick and tired of being robbed and treated as inferiors. They want the French out of their economies, out of their elections, and out of their countries.

The French response is to offer "cooperation" with the United States. Implying none too subtly that "white powers should stick together, after all," they misread the times, and they wildly misread America. For our part, we can only lose prestige, influence, and goodwill by being associated with the French in West Africa.

But that's the point, as far as Paris is concerned: The Chirac government wants to present a united Western front to Africans yearning for real freedom, to show them that Washington isn't an alternative because America's on France's side.

This duplicity is especially dangerous, given that many French-speaking African countries have majority-Muslim populations—Muslims who are not anti-American. On the contrary, they practice tolerant, local forms of Islam and resent Wahhabi extremist efforts to "purify" their religion.

Islam is deathly sick in its Middle Eastern heartland, but it's vibrant and healthy on its frontiers, from Jakarta through Dakar to Detroit. The struggle for the future of Islam is cruel and discouraging in the Middle East, but elsewhere the good guys are winning.

By accepting the proffered French embrace in Africa, we risk needlessly alienating tens of millions of Muslims who are our natural allies in the war against Arab fanaticism.

Certainly, we should cooperate with France when it's genuinely in our interests. But, in West Africa, the cooperation Paris wants is a sham that would benefit only French neocolonialists, while doing America's image and cause great harm.

If we really believe in freedom and democracy, we should stand up for the striving people of Africa, not for the crumpled imperialists on the Seine.

Nigerian Nightmare

Armchair General

September 2006

There's trouble in the oil fields, and this time it's not in the Middle East. Nigeria, the dominant state in West Africa and a consistent disappointment, has been troubled since it gained independence over four decades ago. The horrific civil war in the 1960s between the government and secessionist Biafra led to almost three decades of military rule with brief, failed interludes of civilian government. Nigeria became one of the world's most corrupt states as crime exploded, government officials hid stolen funds offshore, and life expectancy for the average citizen fell to below forty-seven years.

Now, the country faces its worst series of crises since Biafra. There's no hope of a perfect solution. The alternatives facing this vast country of 130 million deeply divided people are either to muddle through with intermittent bloodletting or crack apart in genocidal violence.

Nigeria matters. The world's eighth-largest oil and natural gas producer, it's a vital supplier for the United States. China and India increasingly look to Nigeria for petroleum, as well. Rebel operations in the oil-rich southern delta—where local populations suffer ecological catastrophe as profits disappear into government pockets—include guerrilla attacks, assassinations, kidnappings of foreign oil workers, pipeline bombings, and oil platform seizures. The government responds with a heavy, incompetent hand.

And that's only one set of violent problems facing this Franken-stein's monster of a country that imperial Britain patched together from ill-fitting parts.

The sharpest divide is between the Hausa-Fulani north—Mus-lim and politically dominant—and the Yoruba, Igbo, and other tribes of the Christian-animist south (Nigeria has over 250 tribes in all). The Brits favored the Muslims, allowing them to dominate the military's upper echelons—as they still do. The situation was bad enough in the past, before the recent upsurge of Islamist funda-mentalism. Now it's explosive.

Attempts to impose Islamic Sharia law in the north spark Chris-tian outrage. Terror campaigns against transplanted Christians result in deadly backlashes against Muslims living in the south. Last winter's global disturbances over Danish cartoons of the Prophet Mohammed turned ugliest in Nigeria. Southern Christians responded to northern Muslim repression with a rampage in provincial cities. Dozens of Christians and hundreds of Muslims died.

The Muslim-shaded government lashes out violently but inef-fectively. Nigeria's internal problems make a mockery of its regional leadership pretensions. It sends troops abroad as peacekeepers but can't keep the peace at home. Recently lauded as a democratic suc-cess story, Nigeria's corruption-addled government looks increas-ingly fragile. Heralded as a unifier after his free election as president, former general Olusegun Obasanjo now wants to change the law that limits him to two terms. Expect a spike in turmoil by 2007, if not before.

Watch for military repression in the oil-rich south. Almost 100 percent of Nigeria's official export earnings (which doesn't include the country's hefty income from transnational crime) comes from southern oil and gas, but northern powerbrokers refuse to allow southerners a fair share of the revenue. If the central government relies on force alone to keep the oil flowing, the south could erupt. Meanwhile, the Chinese have begun supplying Nigeria with weapons as human-rights violations slow U.S. support.

If Nigeria implodes, the consequences will go far beyond tight oil supplies. The web of potential conflicts could spread across West Africa, reversing the fragile progress in ravaged Liberia and Sierra

Leone, plunging the troubled Ivory Coast into chaos, overwhelming smaller states, and flooding the region with refugees, insurgents, and criminal cartels.

The best hope is government compromise that localizes the violence. But the worst Christian-Muslim bloodshed in sub-Saharan Africa may be coming to Nigeria.

The Undecided Continent:
The New Struggle for Africa

Armed Forces Journal

August 2006

Africa has suffered many curses, from massive corruption to AIDS to dysfunctional borders drawn by cynical Europeans. Oppression, illiteracy, deadly ethnic and religious rivalries—Africa's litany of disadvantages resembles that of Europe in the fourteenth century (when the Black Death struck far harder and more swiftly than AIDS has done south of the Sahara). But there is one inexcusable curse: the casual assumption on the part of Americans that Africa is all of one hopeless piece.

In fact, there are many Africas, some as nearly irredeemable as any territories on earth, others remarkably promising. Writing off black Africa is as wrong strategically as it is morally, and lumping together countries as diverse as South Africa, Congo, and Senegal is as foolish as assuming that, because they're both North American states, Mexico and the U.S. must be identical.

Four research trips to Africa over the past four years have made me a cautious optimist. If they make only a few more correct decisions, states such as South Africa, Mozambique, Ghana, and Senegal may escape, at last, most of the curses that have made sub-Saharan Africa the mockery and pity of the world.

Increasingly, African states have realized that the ultimate price of corruption is far higher than the mere tally of money changing hands, that socialist economies cannot deliver progress, and that markets work. In numerous states, there's a new sense of self-reliance and disgust with the begging bowl. While Africa will need development aid for many years to come, the regulation and application of that aid—while still imperfect—is more effective than it was during the decades when Western donors and lenders did little more than drop money on the ground.

Men and women are making a positive difference in Africa. And this time around, they're Africans.

ADMITTING THE FAILURES

No sane observer would claim that all's well with Africa. It is utterly impossible for the vast region known as Democratic Republic of the Congo (aka Zaire) ever to function effectively as a unitary state. The series of wars that have engaged Congo and its neighbors for the past dozen years, with combat from Kigali to Kinshasa, adds up to the worst man-made death toll since Mao's Cultural Revolution. And intermittent cease-fires do not promise a final end. Few of the volatile issues plaguing Congo and its neighbors have been admitted, let alone solved. Local power brokers and international diplomats alike deny that a state such as Congo can fail irredeemably. So the misery continues.

Nor is there much to be hopeful about in another vast country, Nigeria. Diseased by oil revenues, one irresponsible government after another—military and civilian—has only worsened the plight of Nigeria's poorest citizens while polarizing religious and tribal rivals. With routine Muslim-on-Christian and Christian-on-Muslim violence, growing insurgencies in the oil-haunted Niger Delta, and the most corrupt major military on earth, the best that can be hoped is that Nigeria will continue to muddle through, avoiding all-out civil war and a bloodbath that could not be contained within its borders.

Zimbabwe, recently an agricultural export power with a promising civil society, has been torn apart by the egomania of its president-for-too-long-a-life, the octogenarian Robert Mugabe. With populist rhetoric and cynical policies, Mugabe guaranteed his personal power by destroying a farming culture that profited Zimbabwe's white and black citizens alike. Famine claws yesterday's breadbasket of southern Africa, with the minority Matabele tribe purposely starved and even Mugabe's majority Shona tribe suffering miserably (while regime supporters, black and white, party on caviar and fresh lobster flown in on pirate aircraft by crews from the former East Bloc—frequently funded by Chinese "investment" money).

The indifference of Zimbabwe's neighbors to the suffering of millions thrown out of work, made homeless, and left hungry revealed a significant African weakness: the reluctance of African leaders to criticize one another or challenge another state's internal abuses. Once a hero of the liberation struggle, Mugabe has been permitted to savage his people to a degree that the bigoted, but not genocidal, Rhodesian government never did.

Ivory Coast, once France's model colony (and thereafter a neo-colonial model of successful exploitation), is struggling to move beyond a ruinous civil war condoned initially by Paris—which sought to play the sides against each other. But the demons of factional strife are hard to put down once unleashed, and Ivory Coast may continue to play out its delayed postcolonial dramas in blood. If they take place as planned, the elections scheduled for October could begin to patch up the country—or lead to yet another round of fighting.

The recent Islamist takeover in Mogadishu forced Somalia back into the international spotlight, exposing yet again the Clinton-era fallacy that neglected problems simply go away. The world community also failed by refusing to recognize Somaliland, Somalia's successful, peaceful northern territory, as the independent state it claims to be. By their reluctance to accept changes in international boundaries, no matter how sensible and just, the world community and Somalia's fellow African states may have condemned the promising and comparatively tolerant society of Somaliland to civil war with Islamic extremists supported by al Qa'eda.

Yet, listing present and looming crises such as these—the usual approach to Africa—tells only the dark half of the story. Long ignored, Africa is becoming a global center of attention for the first time since the 1960s and the depths of the Cold War. And it isn't only the U.S. European Command and U.S. Central Command that are interested: The Chinese are back.

China's contact with the East African coast dates back at least a thousand years. A matter of trade goods, the first, long period of wealth transfers peaked with the visit of a mighty Chinese fleet 600 years ago. Thereafter, China curled up like a porcupine—as China has done intermittently though its history.

The second, more aggressive wave of Chinese involvement in Africa splashed over the continent in the 1960s, when liberation (and communism) was supposed to arrive at the barrel of a gun. China invested far more heavily then, in proportion to its available resources, than it is doing now, sending military trainers, doctors, engineers, and money it could ill-afford to build ill-constructed factories that stand today as derelict monuments to the failures of socialism. In recent discussions with American analysts, I've felt as though sentinels were running through the halls, screaming, "The Chinese are coming! The Chinese are coming!" Yet, the truth is that the Chinese have already been in Africa in force—and they failed miserably.

Beijing is on a path that will lead to ultimate failure again. While it is only sensible to monitor Chinese involvement in Africa, the correct response is "Chinese," in the sense that we should be patient, watch, and wait. Many of China's seeming successes are hollow—the results of desperation rather than clever strategy. While there are ever more Chinese in the streets of African cities, there are no Chinese in African hearts. There are no long lines outside Chinese embassies with Africa's best and brightest begging for the equivalent of a green card.

Our fears regarding Chinese engagement in Africa blind us to China's weak hand (and low investment levels). Our fears also incorporate tacit racism—an assumption that Africans aren't wise enough to see dangers that seem obvious to us. But Africans aren't fools, nor are their powers of observation in any way inferior to ours. Indeed, if anyone has a distorted view of African reality, it's the foreign players—American, European, or Chinese. Africans, delighted to play the Chinese against the French, wouldn't mind playing Americans against the Chinese, either.

Instead of panicking over the "Return of Fu Manchu," consider China's difficulties in attempting to exploit Africa over the long term:

- China's support for rogue regimes, such as those in Sudan or Zimbabwe, alarm us—but they damage China's image terribly in African eyes. Africans have no more taste for Chinese imperialism than they do for French neocolonialism. Beijing's choice of prime clients makes Africans wary, not welcoming. And the Chinese are making the classic error Americans made in the past: believing that repugnant regimes (remember the shah of Iran?) are stronger and more durable than they really are.

- China isn't in Africa because Beijing is brilliant but because Beijing's desperate. With popular expectations and the consumption of raw materials soaring at home, the Chinese are searching the world frantically for any possible sources of oil, minerals—and markets. Yet, every significant tie China has with Africa depends on sea-lanes that Beijing cannot begin to control. No matter how successful its diplomacy might be on the African continent, the U.S. Navy's control of the Indian Ocean negates any strategic advantage Beijing might hope for in a crisis.

- The Chinese aren't liked in Africa. Wherever I've gone, I've found packs of Chinese. And they stay in packs. They do not mix with the locals, and Africans have no difficulty identifying the nineteenth-century intensity of Chinese racism. Nor are Chinese goods considered desirable—Africans buy them only when they cannot afford European or American goods.

And despite exaggerated claims of global anti-Americanism, a visitor to Africa who breaks free of the politician-academic-journalist web of reflexive prejudice finds that no country on earth so fascinates and attracts Africans as does the U.S.

In dealing with Chinese meddling in Africa, we need to have the wisdom to let China fail. Let a desperate China overextend itself. And keep the U.S. Navy strong.

THE GREAT MULTICOLORED HOPE

At least one-fifth of the population is HIV positive; it has the highest rape rate in the world, along with massive unemployment, forbidding slums, and simmering tribal rivalries: Those are the usual things said of South Africa from a distance. But South Africa also offers a stunningly different aspect to those who look more closely.

It's becoming a postmodern empire, a power whose reach exceeds that of any historical empire on the African continent in terms of scale and wealth.

What deceives observers about South Africa is that the contours and concerns of its growing empire do not fit traditional templates. South Africa isn't in the business of conquering its neighbors militarily. It's in the business of business. And its sprawling business empire stretches as far north as Kenya and as far northwest as Ivory Coast. From supermarkets to cell phone networks, South Africa is an African power catering to African markets. Its penetration dwarfs China's. In Nairobi and Accra, I found that locals fear the fierce competitive skills of South African companies—owned and run by aggressive teams of blacks, browns, and whites who cracked the code the moment the old apartheid regime fell: By cooperating, all could grow rich.

Admittedly, there are dark sides to South Africa's success. First, it has been built on a willingness—resembling that of India's upwardly mobile class—to ignore the poverty of millions of citizens, tossing them a few placating programs and a wealth of empty promises. AIDS, crime, inadequate medical care and housing, poor schools— such issues have been slighted to free up capital for investment.

Capitalism works. But it doesn't work evenhandedly.

Second, South African businesses are ruthless abroad. The utter destruction of Mozambique in three decades of liberation struggle and civil war taught South Africans a lucrative lesson: Anything destroyed in southern-African countries will have to be rebuilt. And South Africans are best positioned to profit from the needs of shattered neighbors. Directly or indirectly, South Africans control Mozambique, where they bought in at rock-bottom prices in war's wake. They are now applying the lesson to Zimbabwe, where the Mugabe regime has been allowed to run up debts it cannot begin to repay while ruining the country. When Mugabe finally disappears, South Africans will own the country's treasures. Nor does South Africa worry about the present engagement of Chinese or Libyan players in Zimbabwe, because South Africa has the power to close the direct-access routes through Mozambique, leaving a long and tortuous route through Tanzania as the only—and fragile—lifeline for players who do not follow South Africa's rules.

That ruthlessness may be inhumane, but it is proving to be the best formula for success and constructive wealth accumulation the continent has seen. But South Africa is approaching a crucial point internally. Its next presidential election will be the most important vote the continent has seen—it will decide not only the fate of South Africa, but also potentially that of much of sub-Saharan Africa. If South Africans elect a skilled technocrat as their next president, there will be no stopping the country. If, however, South Africans fall into the old regional trap of voting for a populist demagogue, all of the progress to date could fall apart, leading to internal strife, capital flight, and an economic breakdown. One man, Jacob Zuma, a populist firebrand recently acquitted on the charge of raping an HIV positive family friend, stands an ugly chance of becoming South Africa's next leader. If he does, one man may destroy not only a country's hopes, but also a continent's.

BRIGHTENING LIGHTS ELSEWHERE

If Mozambique has been conquered by South African investors, it nonetheless may turn out to provide the most successful development model yet seen in Africa. A darling of the aid community for more than a decade, Mozambique has defied the pattern of failure that has afflicted so many postindependence African states. One of the world's poorest countries, ravaged by war, Mozambique has struggled to avoid becoming an aid addict, seeking instead projects that allow it to help itself, to get the training wheels off the development bicycle as quickly as possible. Lacking everything, Mozambique avoided the trap of trying to do everything at once, only to fail on all fronts. Instead, there has been a steady concentration of infrastructure development—and the government has battled corruption more aggressively than any other regional state except South Africa.

That said, corruption remains the biggest hurdle to long-term success. Mozambique's poverty has exposed it to Nigerian and Pakistani criminal organizations, and it has become an important transit point for heroin and laundered money. Whether or not this battle can be won is undecided for now, but a visitor to Mozambique cannot help feeling optimistic. This is a country trying hard to get better—and without making unreasonable demands or indulging in paralyzing blame. It is also the only country in Africa in which I was never asked for a handout.

To the north, Tanzania, which avoided the internecine savagery that ravaged so many of its neighbors, is rebounding from its long romance with socialism. Despite spotty election-cycle violence, the country's minority Muslims (on the coast) and majority Christians and animists (in the interior) have achieved a functional identity as Tanzanians—a triumph in a region of my-tribe-first loyalties. Fostered by Julius Nyerere and abetted by the absence of a single dominant tribe, Tanzanian identity may still be fragile, but it exists—something that simply is not the case elsewhere, where tribal identity consistently trumps national identity. Poor and underdeveloped, Tanzania nonetheless has a chance to become a healthy state—and a helpful U.S. ally.

Across the continent, where the regional psyche is trapped between the brutality of the recent civil wars in Liberia and Sierra Leone and the potential for a violent collapse of the Nigerian state, two very different countries offer hope.

Comparatively rich at independence only to be bankrupted by its first president, Kwame Nkrumah, and his impulsive socialism, Ghana has been on a long road to recovery. Ten years of damage under Nkrumah, followed by another decade of rule by weak, grasping governments, has taken multiple decades to repair. But today's Ghana has begun to show the potential to build a viable economy and make meaningful improvements in the lives of its citizens.

Confounding liberal Western prejudices, it was the coup-maker (and later elected president) Jerry Rawlins who set the country on the strenuous path back to health. Now, with a succession of free—and generally fair—elections behind it, the population has acquired a taste for democracy, as well as for education and hard work. Ghana is never going to be a regional powerhouse. But it may serve as a regional example and a stabilizing force—although it, too, could be swamped by a flood of violence emanating from Nigeria. Barring Nigerian self-destruction, though, Ghana has the potential to be a key building block in the reconstruction of West Africa.

Another building block and encouraging example is Senegal, a stable, overwhelmingly Muslim state that has refused, adamantly, to be radicalized by Wahhabi or Salafist extremists. For those who insist that all Muslims are uniform in their desire to subvert and dominate Western civilization, Senegal offers abundant evidence to the contrary.

One point that Western Muslim-baiters refuse to recognize is that Islam comes in many varieties, some of which are tolerant and humane, and many of which are tied to cherished local practices and beliefs. From Indonesia to West Africa, I've seen how Muslims, confident in their faith, reject the proselytizing of Saudi-funded zealots—who insist that Senegalese Muslims, for example, have gotten Islam all wrong.

Nobody much likes to be told that traditions they've cherished for a thousand years are false and devilish. And the Senegalese, with their Sufi influences, marabout holy men, and religious brotherhoods, much prefer their own form of Islam, thanks, to the joyless faith inflicted by the Saudis.

A poor country, Senegal nonetheless has refused to be bought by the Saudis and Gulf Arabs. Leopold Senghor, a minority Catholic and the only "big man" leader of post-independence Africa to leave an unblemished legacy, created a state of institutions, rational ambitions, and ethnic equity. A long tradition of peace, foreign and domestic, has enabled Senegalese society to develop without succumbing to the internal stresses that ravaged so many other African states. Even the French presence has been relatively benign— although it's increasingly resented.

It's easy for rich states to be tolerant. But the tolerance practiced by a poor state such as Senegal is a triumph of the human spirit. Senegal is never going to be a great power, but it's already a stabilizing force and an encouraging example in West Africa—and proof that Islam does not equal anti-Western hatred. To the contrary, the Senegalese love to regale visitors with tales of friends and relatives who've "made it" in America, while decrying the prejudice they've encountered in the Middle East, either as workers or pilgrims.

The key point this article seeks to make is simply that Africa isn't monolithic or doomed to failure. While it's difficult to have much confidence in a gleaming tomorrow for Congo, Sudan, or Somalia—and many other African countries will have to be content to muddle through—there are also states that should offer us encouragement, such as Senegal, Ghana, South Africa, Mozambique, Tanzania, Namibia, and even savagely poor Mali.

We cannot afford to write off an entire continent. On both strategic and humanitarian grounds, our engagement in Africa is essential. Instead of obsessing on the growing Chinese presence, we should concentrate on continuing to outperform Beijing—not very hard to do, especially given the latent goodwill toward the U.S. felt by the average African (if you want to find pro-American extremists, visit any state colonized by the French). We see Africa in terms of resources and threats to stability, but we need to teach ourselves to understand its greater potential and to encourage those trends that hint at a spreading recovery from the traumas of the colonial and postcolonial eras. This doesn't mean huge giveaway aid programs, but intelligent cooperation and a respect for Africa's own capabilities.

For all the sufferings of Eastern Europe, the Cold War may have been hardest on Africa. Not all of the continent's failures were homemade. But Africa's recent successes, from Capetown to Accra, are stamped "Made in Africa." It's only the failures, from Harare to Khartoum, that wear an increasingly visible stamp "Assembled in Beijing."

Africa won't belong to us. But it won't become Beijing's property, either. After centuries of tribulation, Africa has begun to belong to Africans again.

The "Eurabia" Myth

New York Post

November 26, 2006

A Rash of pop prophets tell us that Muslims in Europe are reproducing so fast and European societies are so weak and listless that, before you know it, the continent will become "Eurabia," with all those topless gals on the Riviera wearing veils.

Well, maybe not.

The notion that continental Europeans, who are world-champion haters, will let the impoverished Muslim immigrants they confine to ghettos take over their societies and extend the caliphate from the Amalfi Coast to Amsterdam has it exactly wrong.

The endangered species isn't the "peace loving" European lolling in his or her welfare state, but the continent's Muslim immigrants—and their multigeneration descendents—who were foolish enough to imagine that Europeans would share their toys.

In fact, Muslims are hardly welcome to pick up the trash on Europe's playgrounds.

Don't let Europe's current round of playing pacifist dress up fool you: This is the continent that perfected genocide and ethnic cleansing, the happy-go-lucky slice of humanity that brought us such recent hits as the Holocaust and Srebrenica.

The historical patterns are clear: When Europeans feel sufficiently threatened—even when the threat's concocted nonsense—they don't just react, they overreact with stunning ferocity. One of their more humane (and frequently employed) techniques has been ethnic cleansing.

And Europeans won't even need to rewrite "The Protocols of the Elders of Zion" with an Islamist theme—real Muslims zealots provide Europe's bigots with all the propaganda they need. Al Qa'eda and its wannabe fans are the worst thing that could have happened to Europe's Muslims. Europe hasn't broken free of its historical addictions—we're going to see Europe's history reprised on meth.

The year 1492 wasn't just big for Columbus. It's also when Spain expelled its culturally magnificent Jewish community en masse—to be followed shortly by the Moors, Muslims who had been on the Iberian Peninsula for more than 800 years.

Jews got the boot elsewhere in Europe, too—if they weren't just killed on the spot. When Shakespeare wrote *The Merchant of Venice*, it's a safe bet he'd never met a Jew. The Chosen People were long gone from Jolly Olde England.

From the French expulsion of the Huguenots right down to the last century's massive ethnic cleansings, Europeans have never been shy about showing "foreigners and subversives" the door.

And Europe's Muslims don't even have roots, by historical standards. For the Europeans, they're just the detritus of colonial history. When Europeans feel sufficiently provoked and threatened—a few serious terrorist attacks could do it—Europe's Muslims will be lucky just to be deported.

Sound impossible? Have the Europeans become too soft for that sort of thing? Has narcotic socialism destroyed their ability to hate? Is their atheism a prelude to total surrender to faith-intoxicated Muslim jihadis?

The answer to all of the above questions is a booming, "No!" The Europeans have enjoyed a comfy ride for the last sixty years—but the very fact that they don't want it to stop increases their rage and sense of being besieged by Muslim minorities they've long refused to assimilate (and which no longer want to assimilate).

We don't need to gloss over the many Muslim acts of barbarism down the centuries to recognize that the Europeans are just better at the extermination process. From the massacre of all Muslims and Jews (and quite a few Eastern Christians) when the Crusaders reached Jerusalem in 1099 to the massacre of all the Jews in Buda (not yet attached to Pest across the Danube) when the "liberating"

Habsburg armies retook the citadel at the end of the seventeenth century, Europeans have just been better organized for genocide.

It's the difference between the messy Turkish execution of the Armenian genocide and the industrial efficiency of the Holocaust. Hey, when you love your work, you get good at it.

Far from enjoying the prospect of taking over Europe by having babies, Europe's Muslims are living on borrowed time. When a third of French voters have demonstrated their willingness to vote for Jean-Marie Le Pen's National Front—a party that makes the Ku Klux Klan seem like Human Rights Watch—all predictions of Europe going gently into that good night are surreal.

I have no difficulty imagining a scenario in which U.S. Navy ships are at anchor and U.S. Marines have gone ashore at Brest, Bremerhaven, or Bari to guarantee the safe evacuation of Europe's Muslims. After all, we were the only ones to do anything about the slaughter of Muslims in the Balkans. And even though we botched it, our effort in Iraq was meant to give the Middle East's Muslims a last chance to escape their self-inflicted misery.

And we're lucky. The United States attracts the quality. American Muslims have a higher income level than our national average. We hear about the handful of rabble-rousers, but more of our fellow Americans who happen to be Muslims are doctors, professors, and entrepreneurs.

And the American dream is still alive and well, thanks: Even the newest taxi driver stumbling over his English grammar knows he can truly become an American.

But European Muslims can't become French or Dutch or Italian or German. Even if they qualify for a passport, they remain second-class citizens. On a good day. And they're supposed to take over the continent that's exported more death than any other?

All the copy-cat predictions of a Muslim takeover of Europe not only ignore history and Europe's ineradicable viciousness, but do a serious disservice by exacerbating fear and hatred. And when it comes to hatred, trust me: The Europeans don't need our help.

The jobless and hopeless kids in the suburbs may burn a couple of cars, but we'll always have Paris.

The Damned of Darfur

The New York Post

December 11, 2006

A half-million dead in Darfur; 2.5 million refugees—not counting the corpses lost in the sands or terrified survivors in hiding. Surely, the world will act?

No. The world talks. While the militias kill—and years pass. The United Nations looks away—its signature gesture when human rights are violated.

Welcome to the triumph of global hypocrisy.

Europe wrings its hands—as Europe always does—but declines an invitation to the dance. After all, "responsible" governments can't play fast and loose with another state's sovereignty. No dictator or president for life would be able to get a decent night's sleep.

So Sudan's Islamo-fascists continue to kill with impunity.

Our own left mourns theatrically for Darfur's dead—but no one has formed a new Lincoln Brigade to take on Sudan's Muslim fanatics. And the uncomfortable fact that Arab Muslims are slaughtering black Muslims goes ignored. It doesn't fit the left's comfortable worldview.

Oh, yes: Those on the left demanding that we "bring the troops home" from Iraq would be delighted to send American troops to rescue Khartoum's victims. But our military is occupied with other cases of fanaticism and genocide in the Muslim world this holiday season.

Isn't it curious that, when it comes to liberation, Iraq didn't count? For the endlessly hypocritical left, there's one magic difference between the half-million dead of Darfur and the 1.5 million people killed by Saddam in his internal massacres and neighborhood wars: Bush.

Now the global intelligentsia is getting yet another lesson in what happens when the United States and its fellow English-speaking democracies are otherwise engaged: When the "Great Satan" doesn't act, the killing continues.

It doesn't matter that those oh-so-much-wiser Europeans have plenty of troops available. Latin America, that beacon of liberation, has plenty of soldiers, too. Asia has a number of excellent militaries—and China certainly has troops to spare.

But the world outside of Africa won't fight to save black lives. And China backs the Khartoum government at the United Nations—for the sake of Sudan's oil. Europe does what it loves to do: Weep piteously over the dead, but do nothing to save the living.

It tells you all you need to know about Europe's "conscience" that Guantanamo matters more to its citizens than the genocide in Darfur.

The problem is that changing the world for the better costs blood. Only Anglo-American civilization has ever provided the leadership necessary to stop this kind of killing. For which we receive only abuse from the world's hypocrites and cowards.

As the massacres and mass rapes continue in Darfur, rich countries watch the destruction of an entire culture while arguing sanctimoniously that "We must let Africans solve Africa's problems"—knowing full well that Africa's militaries are too weak and poor, too ill-trained and ill-led to cope with so grave a crisis.

The oil-rich states of the Middle East could have funded the now-failed African military mission—after all, the victims in Darfur are fellow Muslims. But to the bloated princes and sheiks of Arabia, there are Muslims and then there are Muslims. Khartoum's Arabs count as "real" Muslims—unlike the black-skinned Africans who foolishly believed the Prophet's teachings that all believers are equal before Allah.

And the sanctimonious mourners realize that a mission to Darfur wouldn't be for peacekeeping. There's no peace to keep. It would be for peacemaking. And none of these folks thinks black lives are worth a fight.

Whether our domestic laments for Darfur come from *The New York Times* or a website, there's no indication that the left is really serious. Even those who want to send in our troops refuse to acknowledge that, in order to rescue Darfur from its "sovereign" government, an intervention force would need no-nonsense rules of engagement, resolute leaders behind it—and the intention of staying for years.

Indeed, the only way to build a lasting peace would be to break up the artificial state seated at the United Nations as "Sudan"—but the U.N. would never countenance such an act of justice. So the Khartoum junta will just go on killing its "own" people—as it has done not only in Darfur in the country's west, but in its impoverished south and east, as well.

One begins to suspect that all too many on the left enjoy pitying Darfur as they wait in line for their lattes. Others, of course, just refuse to accept the troubling fact that this broken world's problems demand more profound solutions than a chant of "Stop the killing."

The killing will never stop until we stop pretending that every dictator or junta seizing power is entitled to claim sovereignty over the millions who never had a voice in choosing their government. After the oppression of women, the sovereignty con is the world's greatest human-rights abuse. And for all of its damnable incompetence, the Bush administration understood that one great truth.

Darfur deserves more than self-satisfied words. As does Iraq. And Afghanistan. And Zimbabwe. And Burma/Myanmar, Cuba, Iran, North Korea, and so many other "sovereign states."

But if we're ever going to stop the killing, we first have to stop the lying. Especially the lie we tell ourselves about the universal desire for peace: Try telling that one to the Janjaweed militaman raping your wife, burning your house, taking your children into slavery—and cutting your throat.

Meanwhile, the Sudanese government laughs at all of us. Khartoum is so confident that the world doesn't give a damn about black Africans that it's recently moved to destabilize neighboring Chad.

The hypocrisy of the intelligentsia, here and in Europe, stinks to the throne of God. No campus seminar ever provoked a ceasefire, and no demonstration ever halted a massacre. Those who are unwilling to fight injustice will ultimately face injustice and a fight.

Terror's Surprise Loss— Islamists Fold in Somalia

New York Post

January 2, 2007

The new year is off to a bad start for Muslim extremists and their admirers in the media: After only a few months in power, the Islamist regime in Mogadishu collapsed overnight as Ethiopian troops drove out the fanatics.

The global media line held that the Islamic Courts Council, which seized power last year and immediately imposed Sharia law, was in firm control of the country, with the legal government in Baidoa destined to fall. And Somalia did become the new Terror Central, a safe haven for al Qa'eda and a strategic base for Islamist subversion in Africa.

Then Ethiopia stepped in and spoiled the goat roast. Unconvinced by Western myths that military force is useless against terrorists, Addis Ababa's troops intervened to support Somalia's internationally recognized government against the jihadis. The nononsense use of force worked.

An Islamist regime that supposedly had broad support collapsed so quickly the international media couldn't keep up: On New Year's morning, newspapers warned that the Islamists, who'd fled Mogadishu, were digging in to defend their "stronghold," the vital port city of Kismayo. By the time those sanctimonious papers hit the streets, the hardcore extremists had high-tailed it, their mass of recruits had deserted, and the Ethiopian military had gained control of Kismayo without a battle.

Now the media line is that it was all a plan, that the Islamists intended all along to fight a guerrilla war. Sure, right. We've heard this one before, folks: The same pundits argued that Saddam never intended to fight a conventional war, but had always planned to hide in a hole in the ground while his sons were killed so he could eventually be dragged out by our troops and hanged by his own people.

Will the Islamic Courts Movement resort to terror and guerrilla operations? You bet. But trust me: They would've preferred to stay in power. The truth is that they were shocked by the speed and resolve of the Ethiopian attack—their al Qa'eda advisers had grown used to dithering Western powers crippled by our superstitious faith in the power of negotiations.

The Ethiopians fought. And won. Could there be a lesson here? Of course, Somalia won't become the new vacation spot of choice for the mega-rich—Somalis will show up with Kalashnikovs on the Day of Judgment. Yes, the Islamists will default to terror. But just as it's better to have the Taliban raiding in the boonies rather than ruling Afghanistan, it's vastly preferable to have Somalia's Islamists and their foreign-terrorist allies conniving to regain power than to have them in charge of a strategically located state.

To Americans, Somalia is "Black Hawk Down" country, where our forces won a lopsided military victory only to have President Bill Clinton surrender to our enemies—the greatest single act of encouragement our government ever gave to the Islamist movement. We picture Somalia as a poor, dusty, war-ravaged place (all true) and as small, remote, and unimportant (all wrong).

Somalia is the size of Texas with the Panhandle trimmed back; it has the longest coast on the African continent—over 2,000 miles of shoreline vitally positioned on the Indian Ocean and Red Sea. An artificial country slapped together by retreating colonial powers (who pretended that endlessly warring tribes would all just get along), its population by current guesses is just under nine million.

The province of Somaliland, in the country's north, is peaceful, relatively prosperous—and anxious to secede. But the international community insists that all borders are sacrosanct. The United Nations would have preferred to hand over Somaliland to the

Islamists rather than accept the will of Somaliland's people—who don't want a damned thing to do with Sharia law.

The United Nations did formally recognize the national coalition government—then, when faced with the Islamic Courts Council's aggression, did what the U.N. always does when confronted with fanaticism and terror: Nothing.

Fortunately, Christian-majority Ethiopia had had enough of Somali-backed Islamist subversion among its Muslim minority. Despite its serious internal flaws, the government of Prime Minister Meles Zenawi did civilization a great favor by ignoring diplomatic table manners and confronting the Islamists in Mogadishu.

There's some history there—in the last half-century, Ethiopia fought (and defeated) Somalia twice. Less-formal conflicts go back centuries. The only sub-Saharan territory never colonized (the Italians tried and failed miserably), Ethiopia is justly proud of its martial heritage.

Of course, the Somalis are proud, too. Somali patience with an Ethiopian military presence won't last indefinitely. There's turbulence ahead. But that's still better than terrorists in power.

For now, it's worth popping that leftover bottle of champagne. Somalia's homegrown fanatics and their al Qa'eda allies are on the run; the Ethiopian military is hunting down wanted terrorists (including several implicated in the bombing of our embassies in Kenya and Tanzania), and our enemies have lost a safe haven, a money-laundering capital, a smuggler's paradise, and a launching pad for subversion.

The ideal of a perfect, eternal victory—to which the media hold those who battle terrorism—is an unfair standard. A win that overthrows a terrorist regime, whether in Afghanistan or Somalia, is worth the fight, even if the enemy can't be completely eradicated. Desperate terrorists struggling for survival are always preferable to a terrorist regime in the capital city.

There's plenty more trouble to come in the Horn of Africa. But the good guys won this round, and nay-saying pundits can't put the terrorists back in power in Mogadishu.

Terrorizing Terrorists

New York Post

January 10, 2007

We'll get you. No matter how long it takes, we'll get you. That's the message our specialoperations forces just sent to al Qa'eda fugitives in Somalia—and everywhere else.

With AC-130 gunships pounding terrorist hideouts and training sites in the badlands near the Kenyan border, we may have nailed senior al Qa'eda figures involved in bombing our embassies in Nairobi and Dar Es Salaam. At the very least, we killed some really bad hombres.

As always, terrorist propagandists will claim that only innocent civilians suffered, and media sympathizers will echo their nonsense.

Fortunately, though, most proterrorist journalists and "human-rights advocates" are preoccupied just now with the awful mistreatment of poor, misunderstood Saddam Hussein.

And the devastation left behind by our gunships is only part of a very big U.S. win:

- Thanks to resolute military action by Ethiopia's government (quietly backed by Washington), the terror regime in Mogadishu crumbled overnight—collapsing the lie that extremist Islam is on the march to an inevitable victory.
- The speed of the Ethiopian advance cornered hundreds of hardcore Islamist fighters in a forlorn backwater, where they can be killed out of sight of their media defenders. And be killed they will.

- Islamist outrages and subversion inspired unprecedented cooperation between moderate Somalis, Ethiopians, Kenyans, and Americans. For its part, the Kenyan government grew sick of Somalia exporting hatred, weapons, and terror. Now Kenyan troops have sealed their border so al Qa'eda's agents can't escape.
- Far from being a growing threat—as Americahaters insist— al Qa'eda's on the run. Confident that they had a new refuge in Somalia, international terrorists instead find themselves scrambling to escape justice.
- Our special-ops forces are getting their revenge: After Army Rangers and Delta Force troops won a hands-down victory in the streets of Mogadishu back in 1993, President Bill Clinton sold them out (as the Pelosi-Reid Democrats threaten to do to our soldiers in Iraq on a greater scale). Now they're killing al Qa'eda fanatics and their local allies with the full support of a new Somali government.

Much remains unresolved in Somalia—it won't turn into a quiet garden spot any year soon. But no amount of rationalizations by anti-American voices can disguise the fact that this has been a huge defeat for radical Islam and its terrorist vanguard: They're homeless again.

Fanatical dreams of reestablishing—and extending—the Muslim caliphate on the African continent are suddenly in shambles (although our enemies, from al Qa'eda to the Saudi royal family, won't give up just yet). Far from impressing the world with its strength, extremist Islam just revealed its inherent weakness again: Average Muslims don't like it and won't defend it.

Yes, there's plenty of anti-Ethiopian emotion in the streets of Mogadishu today—but that's not the same as pro-Islamist sentiment.

As for al Qa'eda's media pals, they'll try to play down the scope of this defeat, lying that only a few foreign terrorists were in Somalia. But even apart from the number of fanatics now lying dead in mango swamps, snake-ridden forests, and scrubland, the psychological blow to al Qa'eda has been huge:

Mired in Iraq and hunkered down in remote rat-holes in Pakistan, Terror International, Inc., has been robbed of its biggest success story since 9/11.

The Islamists lost their vital beachhead in the Horn of Africa. Even Sudan, for all its villainy, is wary of associating with al Qa'eda today (Khartoum has enough problems).

Of course, not all in the region is exactly as it seems on the surface. The do-it-in-the-dark boys—our military special-operations forces and CIA personnel—have been deeply involved in getting this one right. Joint Task Force Horn of Africa, the American regional headquarters in Djibouti, has been a consistently effective player, too, punching well above its weight. JTF-HOA is an economy-of-force operation that returns a huge strategic dividend on the taxpayer's investment.

We owe all of our engaged military and intelligence personnel—overt, covert, and clandestine—a debt of thanks. But the thanks won't be public. As always, our special operators will fade back into the strategic mist. Some may have been on the ground in Somalia throughout this operation, helping out with intelligence and targeting, nudging key actions along, and hunting specific terrorists. The use of AC-130 gunships—incredibly effective weapons—against massed terrorists may have been cued by cell phone intercepts, but I wouldn't discount brave Americans on the ground directing those airstrikes.

That's speculation, of course. But I can guarantee two things to *Post* readers: First, Somalia and the world are better off with the Islamists on the run and living in terror themselves, and second, our special operations forces—from all of the services—are greater heroes than the history books or Hollywood films will ever be able to capture.

Whack 'em again, guys.

Strategic Invisibility

Armed Forces Journal

March 2007

No strategic arena is so readily ignored or, arguably, as little understood by the U.S. government as Latin America. Yet no state is more vital to our security, economy, and contemporary society than Mexico, while the combined populations of only two Latin American countries, Brazil and Mexico, exceed by ten million the number of U.S. citizens and residents. Geographically, Brazil is nearly the size of the United States, Mexico is three times larger than Texas, and Argentina, with its forty million citizens, is one-third the size of the lower forty-eight. With growing markets, rising per capita incomes, and ever-sturdier democracies, such states are natural partners for Washington. Yet, even Africa (certainly deserving of attention) enjoys richer coverage in our media and more enthusiastic government engagement.

Of course, much of Latin America—a vast and various region stretching from the Rio Grande south to Tierra del Fuego—suffers from grotesque social and economic distortions, cultural impediments to development, and a fickle taste in guiding philosophies. Rising per capita income figures mask the enormous gulf between rich and poor, while corruption blights all. From the Andean Ridge northward through Mexico, crime competes with government, whether one speaks of narcotics cartels or gangs—entities that run their own foreign policies vis-à-vis the United States, frequently doing so with greater acuity than the states that produced them.

Latin America's problems can easily be ridiculed, yet they fade in comparison with abysmal conditions elsewhere—not least, in the Middle East, a region the U.S. embraces with passionate blindness. Latin America stumbles now and then but continues to move forward. That claim could not be made for any Muslim state on the Eurasian land mass or for a single country in the great triangle of misery bounded by Egypt, Nigeria, and Congo. If any stretch of the globe offers still-untapped potential for a mutually beneficial relationship with the U.S., it's Latin America.

All parties would have to want such a relationship, and plenty of tired myths would need to be discarded. The old stew of resentment, neglect, animosity, condescension, and jealousy simmering at the back of the geopolitical stove may provide convenient helpings for demagogic politicians but poorly serves the people of Latin America—or the U.S.

Strategically speaking, it's time for us all to grow up.

MEXICO CONTRADICTORIO

After the U.S. itself, the saddest victim of September 11 was Mexico. Prior to the attacks on the World Trade Center Towers and the Pentagon, forging a closer, healthier relationship with Mexico (and, by extension, the rest of Latin America) was a top priority for the new administration of President Bush. A "my ranch or yours?" friend of Mexico's then-President Vicente Fox, Bush spoke passable Spanish and, as governor of Texas, had faced the issues impeding bilateral relations. A long-overdue confluence of interests seemed to be near. Then the hijackers struck, border animosities soared, and Fox became just another distraction to be shoved aside as Washington stripped for action and went to war. Relations with Mexico fell back into the hands of hysterics north of the border. To the south, collapsed expectations destroyed the Fox presidency.

But if Washington's attention wandered, Mexico and the issues it posed didn't go away. By 2006, our neighbor appeared to be in its deepest crisis—a series of crises—in eight decades. The interminable comic-opera rebellion in Chiapas spread to Oaxaca next door, as a mob occupied the state capital. Elsewhere, drug-cartel violence soared, with turf wars between syndicates claiming more than 2,000 lives in less than a year. A bitter presidential election gave Felipe Calderon, the conservative candidate, a microscopic lead over a charismatic leftist, Manuel Lopez Obrador—but Lopez Obrador refused to accept the vote count, summoning his followers to Mexico City. Hundreds of thousands camped out in the Zocalo—the city's ancient heart—crippling the municipality for months. Meanwhile, cities along the U.S. border had turned into killing fields.

Then events kicked over the projections of linear thinkers who saw Mexico bound for chaos. It was as if the Virgin of Guadalupe—Mexico's patroness—had decided a miracle was in order. The protests withered. Despite an entertaining display of bad manners by opposition legislators, Calderon took his oath of office. And he immediately took actions his predecessors had deemed impossible.

Instead of blaming Mexico's ills entirely on the United States (the traditional stance of Mexican politicians from all parties), Calderon broke with tradition and began extraditing drug kingpins—a controversial move in a country obsessively sensitive to perceived infringements of its sovereignty. Even more boldly, Calderon sent the army and federal police reinforcements into the cartel-plagued state of Michoacan, as well as to cities such as Acapulco and Tijuana, which had been haunted by drug-related violence. At present, 27,000 soldiers and special police officers have been deployed. While the Mexican military is far from corruption free (as our border agents can attest), it remains the most dependable major institution in the country and its no-nonsense employment by the new president signals a level of determination in confronting Mexico's home-grown problems that raises hopes for a rejuvenation of Mexican politics and society—and makes Calderon the likeliest candidate for assassination of any Mexican president in living memory.

Corruption has become so endemic in Mexico (and throughout Latin America) that Calderon faces daunting odds. The encouraging aspect is that someone has finally begun to accept the gravity of Mexico's internal problems. Meanwhile, opposition politicians continue to do all they can to undermine the president, orchestrating new demonstrations in the capital in January to protest rising tortilla prices—an issue that, once again, demonstrates the inseparability of all three North American economies: The soaring demand for corn-based ethanol in the U.S. drove up the price of the Mexican dietary staple, since Mexico purchases nearly a third of its corn from U.S. farmers.

It cannot be stressed sufficiently that Mexico is strategically positioned on our southern border (and no one's going to tow it away), with a population of 110 million that remains our No. 1 source of legal and illegal immigration—providing indispensable additions to the lower echelons of our work force, if we would only be honest about the matter. Our neighbor is a huge land of internal contradictions, with booming export industries and infuriating poverty, plush vacation spots, and urban killing fields. A major source of oil for the U.S., its impoverished south belongs to Central America, while Mexico's comparatively well-to-do north is ever more closely integrated with the rest of North America. Famous for its anti-American traditions, Mexico is the top retirement destination for U.S. expatriates— who live safely and happily as valued residents.

With a trillion-dollar economy, troubled borders (north and south), and ever-expanding ties of blood and culture to the U.S., it should be obvious to Washington that Mexico deserves first-rank priority in our diplomatic strategy. Instead, this vital country is treated as a banana republic. If Mexico's behavior has not always been satisfying to us, our own comportment has been callous, dishonest, and generally counterproductive.

While serving in our Army, I routinely attempted to persuade officers to study the Mexican Revolution, that complex and bloody prototype of so many rebellions that followed around the globe. I might as well have asked my peers to study tribal spats in New Guinea. Its richness, flamboyance, and above all, pertinence make Mexico's history a subject as inexhaustible as it is instructive—yet we ignore the striking human pageant next door, preferring to watch yet another miniseries about long-dead English royalty. (Try dissecting the Civil War-era French installation of a puppet regime and the furious Mexican response as a case study for our mishandling of Iraq.)

The bad blood and mutual ignorance on both sides must be overcome. The U.S. and Mexico are bound together inextricably. Our present attitude, that Mexico is nothing more than a source of problems, neglects the country's enormous strategic and economic potential, as well as inextinguishable cultural affinities. Certainly, we need to control our southern border and have every right to do so—but we also need to be honest about our labor-market needs and reasonably humane in our approach. For all the name-calling over the decades, when it comes to Mexico, we're our own worst enemies.

With a new and promising president in Mexico City, we have a fresh chance to move our relationship forward. President Calderon has made the first, difficult steps. Can the flagging Bush administration recall the bright hopes with which it assumed office?

THE COUNTRY OF THE FUTURE

An old joke (also told about Argentina) runs that "Brazil is the country of the future—and always will be." Well, the future's here. A state with even greater internal contradictions than Mexico, Brazil may host the most complex society in Latin America. White at the top, brown in the middle, and black at the bottom, the economic racism in play can obscure more nuanced gradations. With contrasts between primitive tribes at the back of beyond and the *Blade Runner* city of Sao Paulo, fantastic wealth, and one-third of its 190 million citizens struggling below the poverty line and barracked in slums the police enter only in well-armed force, Brazil presents "conclusive" evidence to optimists and pessimists alike.

Essentially a nuclear power, Brazil exports advanced aircraft to the U.S. but has yet to fully map its Amazonian interior. While recent growth rates have disappointed, its economy continues to dwarf all others in South America. A continent-sized country, it includes pristine rain forests and jungles from prehistory, as well as vast tracts of ecological devastation. And, beyond the inertia leaving both sides on their lumpy strategic couches, there is no reason why Brazil should not be one of the closest and best allies of the U.S. in the twenty-first century.

Singling out Mexico and Brazil for scrutiny in this article is not meant to slight the other states of this sprawling region—they simply offer the most striking examples of enormous potential largely ignored by Washington. Their political courses also provide a useful counterpoint to the "common knowledge" that "Latin America is turning left." In fact, Latin America is becoming ever more democratic, leading to leftist electoral victories that garner headlines and obscure the fact that most recent ballots have returned centrists or conservatives to power from the Sonoran Desert to the Andean glaciers.

Brazil's recently reelected president, Luiz Inacio "Lula" da Silva, serves as the region's best advertisement for the importance of not overreacting when Latin American populations vote in ways that disappoint us. With a working-class, trade-union background, Lula alarmed the Washington establishment: He was classed as a socialist and radical who was bound to drag Brazil on a fatal leftward course, erasing economic gains and polarizing society. Instead, Lula turned out to be a reformer (corruption scandals notwithstanding) with a balanced foreign policy and a wariness of leftist extremism. Anxious to reassure the domestic business community and international investors, he also kept Venezuela's histrionic president, Hugo Chavez, at arm's length, refusing to subscribe to Chavez's neo-Fidelista agenda or oppose Washington on principle.

The obvious lesson is that, if we truly believe in democracy, we need to allow people to make their own choices at the ballot box—even if we sometimes deplore those choices. In love and politics, human beings have to make their own mistakes and learn from them (with the learning process more streamlined in politics than in love). It takes time and frustrates the impatient North American temperament, but attempts to steer election results (or a rush to support ill-judged coups) only radicalize voters and turn us into hypocrites. Just as our clumsiness "made" Fidel Castro, we fumbled our Venezuela policy so awfully that we ended up amplifying Chavez's appeal and making a hero out of an erratic clown.

Time is on our side. Socialism, to say nothing of outright Marxism or Maoism, doesn't work, can't work, and won't work. The recent elections that returned hardcore leftists—notably in Bolivia and Ecuador, with Nicaragua a mere sideshow featuring an aging accused child-molester—will only provide a direct lesson to the people of those countries that rhetoric is no substitute for sound economic policy. Fortunately, Washington's handling of the new heads of state in Ecuador and Bolivia has been intelligently low-key, letting them fail on their own. It's consistently the wisest policy: Democracy works, if not always with full and immediate efficiency. The only trigger for confrontation should be when elected leaders use democracy to destroy democracy—as Chavez appears to be doing. Yet, even in such instances, confrontation has to be executed artfully so that the U.S. can't be portrayed in yesteryear's imperialist-bully terms.

Two further examples that should encourage us are Chile and Argentina. In the former, a market economy and increasingly robust democracy allowed the recent election of a socialist-lite candidate, Michelle Bachelet, to the nation's highest office—without leading to a radical change of course. The election results resembled a party transition in Washington, not the "mood swing" pattern that so long prevailed in Latin America.

Argentina, a state whose frontier history bears a remarkable resemblance to our own, presented a more difficult case. Officially espousing market economics in the 1990s, then-President Carlos Menem, in fact, presided over an orgy of corruption stunning even by regional standards. The result, paradoxically, was to give the marketplace—which never had a fair chance to develop—a bad name, while corruption met with a business-as-usual shrug. The inevitable economic collapse led to a series of brief, weak governments prior to the election of the current president, Nestor Kirchner. Kirchner came to office with an anti-American chip on his shoulder and a socialist agenda. Yet his priority was paying off foreign debt and nursing the economy back to a semblance of health. Confronted with the realities of his office, Kirchner evolved from a noisy pal of leftist demagogues to a responsible leader who recently has played down his relationship—briefly warm—with Venezuela's Chavez. Shunning leftwing jamborees, such as the recent opportunity to meet for a photo op with Chavez and Iran's President Ahmedinejad, Kirchner's priorities today are creating jobs and a favorable investment climate—while toning down his blame-the-Americans rhetoric.

Yet a fundamental question remains. All of the major (and most minor) Latin American states gained their independence two centuries ago, having fought under banners proclaiming the goals of freedom and democracy. With so many countries only beginning to reach political maturity and others still lagging, why on earth has it taken so long?

CULTURE IS FATE—BUT FATE EVOLVES

A story told to me years ago in Bolivia runs as follows: A well-born and well-educated South American matriarch, glancing northward with irony and envy, shrugged delicately and remarked, "If the English had settled South America and the Spaniards had settled North America, South America would be the superpower today."

At a time when it's politically incorrect to explore cultural differences, anyone possessing even a superficial acquaintance with both regions recognizes that different values, social models, and priorities prevail. While the old caricatures of the lazy Latin or the unscrupulous gringo are as misleading as they are convenient to bigots in both cultures, there nonetheless are profoundly different historical inheritances at work—and the differences continue to restrict progress in Latin America today, although change for the better has been accelerating at last.

First, it must be noted that there is no single Latin American culture; on the contrary, the region offers more variety than Europe does. Cultures vary wildly even within states: The German-seasoned tone of lowland Santa Cruz de la Sierra seems a world away from the indigenous culture of the Bolivian Altiplano, and highlanders from Bogota bear as little resemblance to Colombia's coastal population as Lombards do to Sicilians. Italianate Argentina's neurotic artistic brilliance hardly resembles the raucous popular culture of Brazil, where Portugal and Africa collided. Second, cultural analysis demands book-length investigations, not the simplifications of magazine articles. Yet, allowing for those caveats, there are some commonalities that retarded development in Latin America as the hemisphere's two northernmost states marched relentlessly forward.

Choosing founding archetypes for Latin America and Anglo-America is so easy—the conquistador in his armor and the pilgrim armed with his Bible—that it's tempting to dismiss them from serious consideration. Yet those two figures embody the deepest values that shaped the Western Hemisphere's often-discordant cultures. The religious refugee who plodded ashore in New England expected to build a new world; the Spanish knight set sail to conquer someone else's world. While both dealt harshly with indigenous populations, the former expected to work himself, while the latter intended that conquered men should work for him. The English-speaking colonist in Massachusetts expected hard and life-long labor as part of God's design, while the Spaniard (and the Por-tuguese) expected to fight hard then rule luxuriously with God's blessing. In Protestant civilization—especially in the Calvinist strains that shaped Britain's northern colonies—work was pleasing to God, a form of worship. In Latin culture, God was bribed with gifts and the requirement to sweat for a living marked a man as socially infe-rior. The results were the contrasting ideals of the workaholic and the gentleman of leisure, the yeoman farmer versus the haciendado.

It's striking how persistent those inherited behavioral patterns and values remain. Jokes about playing golf every day aside, most of us cannot imagine lives without work and insist on volunteering for community service even after age forces us from our professions. In Latin cultures, there's certainly a willingness to work hard to get ahead—as anyone who has firsthand familiarity with Hispanic immi-grants knows—but the desired end state is different. Machismo isn't simply about strutting around and seducing women; even more profoundly, it reflects an attitude to labor. In Latin America, the purpose of work is, first, to survive, but at the next stage of achieve-ment, to accumulate sufficient wealth never to need to break a sweat again. Of course, there are countless exceptions to this pat-tern, and attitudes toward business have changed mightily in Latin America in recent decades—yet the model of the caudillo, the man of power who, capable of inflicting violence when necessary, dis-penses largesse to his inferiors and "never saddles his own horse," remains a seductive ideal, from Paraguayan generals to the Latino gangbangers of Los Angeles.

That model traces back to conquerors such as Cortez and Pizarro. But the conquistadors' values reflected, in turn, those of the Moorish lords Spaniards fought for 800 years—and, inevitably, emulated. The disdain for weakness, studied indolence, and erup-tive violence of the Hispanic gang leader in El Salvador or San Diego is an inheritance from the Islamic warriors who swept out of the Middle East to conquer an empire in Europe hardly a century after Mohammed's death. Even Spanish Catholicism was influenced by the behavioral strictures of Islam, from the sequestration of women and the obsession with their purity, to the association of learning with a religious vocation. The Latin American strongman always bore a closer resemblance to an Arab emir than to a feudal nobleman in Europe beyond the Pyrenees.

Globalization isn't new.

Different attitudes toward work, women, violence, learning, pride, financial integrity, and faith (in New England, religious freedom won through; in Latin America, the Inquisition followed closely behind the conquistadors) unquestionably shaped the contrasting developmental patterns of Anglo-America and Latin America. Unpopular though such views may be today, the evidence is so pervasive that only an academic could reject it.

BOOM AND BUST

Another pattern—this time, macroeconomic—that hindered Latin American development and continues to hamper economic diversification has been the boom-bust cycle, which has haunted Latin America since the earliest days of the Conquest. Initially, colonists in North America were disappointed by the apparent paucity of mineral deposits that might lead to instant wealth and had to rely— for the first few hundred years—on the wealth of the soil. In contrast, Latin America was cursed with "found" wealth (much as the oil-rich states of the Middle East are today). The Spanish knights went in search of fortunes to be looted, and they found them. Since then, successive booms, some long and others brief, have distorted Latin America's economic development: The colonial-era silver boom, the Andean tin boom, the Argentine and Uruguayan beef boom, the Brazilian rubber boom, successive oil booms, and more recently, the cocaine boom.

The decisive characteristic of booms is that they end. Consistently, Latin Americans have squandered their profits on displays of wealth (the Montevideo mansion or the drug gang leader's "bling"). As a result, colonial cities gained magnificent civic architecture, but never developed healthy economies. Spanish trade policies also crippled development, but even after independence, the loot-and-display pattern remained in force: Beef-boom-era Buenos Aires erected some of the world's finest art nouveau architecture, while the cocaine boom built the "offshore" high-rises of Panama City in the 1990s. The thread that sews the centuries together is that no one believed his boom would end and wealth was spent on inert monuments to vanity, instead of being invested in economic diversification.

North of the Rio Grande, the discovery of tremendous mineral wealth occurred only after the industrial revolution had created a complex economy—the exception being the cotton monoculture of the American South, which, resembling parts of Latin America, relied on slave labor and failed to pursue balanced development. Yankee ingenuity wasn't a matter of luck, but a necessity for survival. The paradox is that one of the reasons Latin America has lagged developmentally is that riches came too easily and too soon.

Of the immediate inhibitors of development, the worst is corruption—but this is a near-global phenomenon. The worst affliction diseasing the developing world, corruption is the cancer that aggravates all other social ills. As attitudes toward work, education, gender issues, and even religion accelerate their evolution in Latin America, the best indicator of which states and societies are apt to move ahead most swiftly is the willingness of their governments to fight corruption and the consistency with which the struggle is waged.

Cultures and civilizations, like individuals, make their own fates.

THE COWBOY AND THE GAUCHO

Despite the cultural divergences highlighted above, more factors bind English-speaking North America and Latin America together than keep us apart. Even our histories have as much in common as they do in conflict. From the Argentine and Chilean Indian wars on their nineteenth-century frontiers back to the obvious fact that we all spring from colonial cultures erected on a pre-Columbian past, we share a sense that the future need not repeat yesteryear's failures (even if it persistently does so) and that new forms of greatness remain possible. If the pragmatic Yankee does continue to contrast with the fatalistic Latin (the tango is a soundtrack for suicides), the differences are not nearly so pronounced as they were a generation ago. Increasingly, the elites throughout the Americas attend the same schools, share corporate identities—and political values. At the lower social levels, cultural cross-fertilization continues to intensify, and the influence of North American social and political values more than counterbalances our new preference for salsa over ketchup.

In that vein, perhaps the most ludicrous claim made by any U.S. citizen in recent history is the insistence that "Latino immigrants want to take back the Southwest for Mexico." The silly posturing of a goofball minority aside, the message immigrants, legal and illegal, take back home is that they'd rather turn Mexico into the U.S. Southwest. We chronically underestimate our country's seductive and exemplary powers: No one who has been able to send his children to decent schools, cope with officials without paying bribes, and get ahead through hard work decides that bad schools (or none), corrupt government, and chronic unemployment constitute a preferable way of life. Even as governments posture, mobile immigrants are transforming their native cultures far more profoundly than they alter ours.

What can Washington do to accelerate progress, a hemispheric rapprochement, and strategic cooperation? There are countless specific initiatives that might be recommended, but the fundamental answer is straightforward: Treat others with respect and live up to our rhetoric. Latin America isn't our backyard; it's a complex collection of neighbors with various personalities and interests. And those neighbors ask one thing above all: respect. The worst thing we do to Latin America isn't economic imperialism (a myth) or bumbling CIA antics (as ineffective as ever). The worst thing is treating a vast region of enormous potential as not worth serious attention.

Latin American states have plenty of internal problems they must confront, but we have to confront our own failings, as well— not least our outdated regard for Europe and our ignore-all-else obsession with the Middle East. Latin America is far more important to the U.S., both in our day-to-day lives and in our strategic future, than France or Saudi Arabia. Yet we continue to pull along in the old harness designed by yesteryear's Europhiles and craven oil companies.

After all of the revolutions through which Latin America has suffered, let's try a revolution of our own: treating our hemispheric neighbors as equals.

Return of the Tribes

The Weekly Standard

September 4, 2006

Globalization is real, but its power to improve the lot of humankind has been madly oversold. Globalization enthralls and binds together a new aristocracy—the golden crust on the human loaf—but the remaining billions, who lack the culture and confidence to benefit from "one world," have begun to erect barricades against the internationalization of their affairs. And, from Peshawar to Paris, those manning the barricades increasingly turn violent over perceived threats to their accustomed patterns of life. If globalization represents a liberal worldview, renewed localism is a manifestation of reactionary fears, resurgent faiths, and the iron grip of tradition.

Except in the commercial sphere, bet on the localists to prevail. When the topic of resistance to globalization arises, an educated American is apt to think of a French farmer-activist trashing a McDonald's, anarchist mummers shattering windows during World Bank powwows, or just the organic farmer with a stall at the local market. But the swelling resistance to globalization is far more powerful and considerably more complex than a few squads of dropouts aiming rocks at the police in Seattle or Berlin. We are witnessing the return of the tribes—a global phenomenon, but the antithesis of globalization as described in pop bestsellers. The twin tribal identities, ethnic and religious brotherhood, are once again armed and dangerous.

A generation ago, it was unacceptable to use the word tribes. Yet, the tribes themselves won through, insisting on their own identity—whether Xhosa or Zulu, Tikriti or Barzani, or, *writ large,* French or German. In political terms, globalization peaked between the earnest efforts of the United Nations in the early 1960s and the electoral defeat of the European constitution in 2005 (the French and Dutch votes weren't a rebuff, but an assassination). In Europe, which was to have led the way in transcending nationalism, the European Union will stumble on indefinitely, even making progress in limited spheres, but its philosophical basis is gone. East European laborers and West European farmers alike will continue to exploit the E.U.'s easing of borders and transfers of wealth, but no one believes any longer in a European super-identity destined to supplant one's self-identification as a Dane or Basque. Far from softening, national and other local identities are hardening again, reverting to ever-narrower–blood-and-language relationships that Europe's dreamers assumed would fade away.

Who now sees himself as fundamentally Belgian, rather than as a Fleming or Walloon? Catalans deny that they are Spaniards, and the Welsh imagine a national grandeur for themselves. In the last decade, the ineradicable local identities within the former Yugoslavia split apart in a bloodbath, while a mortified Europe looked away for as long as it could. The Yugoslav disaster was written off as an echo from the past—anyway, Serbs, Croats, Bosnians, and Kosovars were "not our kind"—but the Balkan wars instead signaled a much broader popular discontent with pseudo-identities concocted by political elites. The collapse of Yugoslavia hinted at the future of Europe: not necessarily the bloodshed, but the tenacity of historical identity.

Even as they grabbed from one another in Brussels, European elites insisted that continental unification was desirable and inevitable. Until the people said no.

Now, in 2006, we see one European state after another enacting protectionist measures to prevent foreign ownership of vital industries (such as yogurt making). France paused, as hundreds of thousands of its best and brightest protested the creation of new jobs for the less privileged in a spectacular defense of the *ancien régime*. And a new German chancellor has called for saving the European project by destroying it—or at least by hewing down the massive bureaucracy in Brussels that alienated the continent. The future of

Europe lies not in a cosmopolitan version of the empire of Charlemagne, but in a postmodern version of the feudal fragmentation that succeeded the Frankish empire. Brussels may be the new medieval Rome, its bureaucratic papacy able to pronounce in limited spheres, but there is ever less fear of excommunication.

Elsewhere, the devolution of identity from the state to the clan or cult is more radical, more anxious, and more volatile. In Iraq, religious, ethnic, and tribal identities dictate the composition of the struggling national government—as they do in Lebanon, Canada, Nigeria, and dozens of other countries (we shall not soon see a Baptist prime minister of Israel—or a Muslim Bundeskanzler, despite those who warn of Eurabia). Even in the United States, with our integrative genius, racial, religious, and ethnic identity politics continue to prosper; we are fortunate that we have no single dominant tribe (minorities might disagree). Still, the success of the United States in breaking down ancient loyalties is remarkable—and anomalous.

While the current American bugbear is Hispanic immigration, most Latinos establish worthy lives in the American grain, just as the Irish and Italians, Slavs and Jews, did before them. American Indians may still think in tribal terms (especially when casino profits are involved), and there is no apparent end to the splinter identities Americans pursue in their social and religious lives, but not even imperial Rome came remotely so close to forging a genuinely new, inclusive identity.

Our peculiar success blinds us to failures abroad. Not only have other states and cultures failed to integrate *Einwanderer* or to agree upon composite identities, they do not desire to do so. The issue of who and what a Frenchman or German is appeared to idealists to have been resolved a century ago. It wasn't. Now, newly forged (in both senses of the word) identities in the developing world are dissolving in fits of rage.

European-drawn borders have failed; European models of statehood and statecraft have failed; and, in global terms, European civilization has failed. Unable to see beyond those models, the United States fails to exert influence commensurate with its power, except in the field of popular culture (even Islamist terrorists like a good action flick). With the end of the colonial vision and the swift crack-up of postcolonial dreams—not least, of a socialist paradise—there is a worldwide vacuum of purpose that the glittering trinkets of globalization cannot fill. From the fear mongering of our own media to the sermons of Muqtada al Sadr, the real global commonality is the dread of change. Whether in Tehran or Texas, the established orders have gone into a defensive crouch. Men dream of change, but cling to what they know.

Far from teaching the workers of the world to love one another (or at least to enjoy a Starbucks together), the economic and informational effects of globalization have been to remind people how satisfying it is to hate. Whether threatened in their jobs, their moral code, or their religion, human beings dislocated by change don't want explanations. They want someone to blame.

THE NEW GLOBAL ARISTOCRACY

There is, indeed, a globalizing class, and hundreds of millions of human beings share the consumer tastes that announce their membership: Prada handbags for the striving women of Tokyo and Manhattan; the poverty-born music of Cesaria Evora for well-off fans from Frankfurt to San Francisco; the Mercedes sedan and the credit card; voyeuristic leftism for professors in Ann Arbor, Buenos Aires, and Vienna; computers for the literate and solvent from Budapest to Bangalore; wine from the region-of-the-week for London suburbanites or Shanghai's *nouveaux riches;* media conglomerates that eschew patriotism; and, for the platinum specks on that golden crust of humanity, private jets and $30,000-per-week vacation rentals when they weary of their own three or four homes.

Such people may well be more at home with foreigners of their own cultural stratum than with their less fortunate countrymen. For the upper tier of these new aristocrats of globalization, place of residence and citizenship are matters of convenience, tastes, and tax codes. This is a nobility with no sense of responsibility to the serfs, and its members are shielded as never before from life's inconveniences. For the billions remaining, globalization and its consort, the information revolution, merely open a window into an exclusive shop they are not allowed to enter. A secondhand Pittsburgh Steelers shirt on a Congolese beggar isn't globalization, but only the hind end of global trade.

The new awareness of the wealth of others is hardly pacifying. On the contrary, it excites the conviction (which local demagogues are delighted to exacerbate) that *they* can only be so rich because they stole what was *ours*. The uneven ability to digest the feast of information suddenly available even in the globe's backwaters doesn't bring humanity together (even if Saudi clerics and American bureaucrats visit the same online porn sites). Rather, it disorients those whose lives previously had been ordered, and creates a sense simultaneously of being cheated of previously unimagined possibilities while having one's essential verities challenged. Feeling helpless and besieged, the victim of globalization turns to the comfort of explanatory, fundamentalist religion or a xenophobia that assures him that, for all his material wants, he is nonetheless superior to others.

The confident may welcome freedom, but the rest want rules. The conviction that a new man freed of archaic identities and primitive loyalties can be created by human contrivance is an old illusion. Rome believed that the new identity it offered not only to its citizens, but also to its remote subjects, must be irresistible. Yet imperial Rome faced no end of revolts from subject tribes, from Britain to Gaul to Palestine. In the end human collectives with stronger, undiluted identities conquered the empire. From the brief, bloody egalitarianism of the French revolution, through socialist visions that promised us the brotherhood of man and an end to war (a conviction especially strong in 1913), to the grisly attempt to create Homo Sovieticus and export him to the world, there has been no shortage of visions of globalization. Even the most powerful attempts to unite humanity failed: the monotheist campaigns to impose one god.

ONE GOD, ONE WAY, ONE WORLD

Monotheism replaced Rome's law codes with the law of God. The first near-success of globalization was the bewildering survival and spread of Christianity, the transitional faith between the exclusive tribal monotheism of Judaism and the universal aspirations of Islam. Beginning as a cult uncertain of the legitimacy of proselytizing among those of different inheritances, Christianity quickly developed a taste for salesmanship, adapting its message from one of local destiny to one of universal possibility. Furthermore, its message to the poor (a constituency contemporary globalization ignores) had as exemplary an appeal among the less fortunate of the bygone Mediterranean world as it does today in sub-Saharan Africa. Christianity was an outsider's religion co-opted by rulers, while Islam meant to rule—and include—all social classes from the years of its foundation.

Globalization really got moving with the advent of Islam. Open to converts from its earliest days, Islam moved rapidly, in just a few centuries, from voluntary through coerced to forced conversions. While the latter were never universally demanded, they were frequent (as were forced conversions to Christianity elsewhere). The immediate and enduring conflict between Christianity and Islam involved different visions of globalization, a competition of quality, design, and power (think of it as Toyota vs. Ford in a battle for souls). Those Christian and Muslim visions continue to experience drastic mutations in the battle for new and local loyalties, having now reached every habitable continent. Their success has blinded us to their weakness: Neither religion has been able to subdue their old antiglobalist nemesis: magic.

When we speak of religion—that greatest of all strategic factors—our vocabulary is so limited that we conflate radically different impulses, needs, and practices. When breaking down African populations for statistical purposes, for example, demographers are apt to present us with a portrait of country X as 45 percent Christian, 30 percent Muslim, and 25 percent animist/native religion. Such figures are wildly deceptive (as honest missionaries will admit).

African Christians or Muslims rarely abandon tribal practices altogether, shopping daily between belief systems for the best results. Sometimes, the pastor's counsel helps; other times it's the shaman who delivers. The Anglican priest in South Africa decries witchcraft but fails to see that his otherworldly belief system offers no adequate substitute for solving certain types of daily problems. Quite simply, Big Religion and local cults are inherently different commodities. From Brazil to Borneo, local Christians don't see imported and traditional belief systems as mutually exclusive any more than a kitchen fortunate enough to have a refrigerator should therefore be denied a stove.

There's an enormous difference between Big Religions—Islam, Christianity, Hinduism, and the others—and the local cults that endure long beyond their predicted disappearance. This distinction is critical, not only in itself, but also because it is emblematic of the obstacles that local identities present to globalization as we imagine it.

Big Religion interests itself in a world beyond this world, while the emphasis of local faiths has always been on magic (bending aspects of the natural world to the will of the practitioner of hermetic knowledge). Magic affects daily life in the here and now, and its force and appeal can be far more potent than our rationalist worldview accepts: What we cannot explain, we mock. (An advantage Christianity enjoys among the poor of the developing world is the image of Jesus, the Conjure Man, turning water into wine and walking on water—he's a more-promising shaman than Muhammad.)

Another aspect of identity that we, the inheritors of proselytizing world religions, fail to grasp is that local cults are exclusive. They not only do not seek new members, but can't imagine integrating outsiders (the politicized tribal beliefs of the Asante in Ghana are a limited exception, since they were devised to confirm the subjugation of neighboring tribes). Cult beliefs are bound to the local soil, the trees, the waters. Tribal religions are about place and person, an identity bound to a specific environment. While slaves did take voodoo practices with them to the new world, the rituals immediately began to mutate under the stress of transplantation. Tribal religions form an invisible defensive wall, as local practices do today, from the Andes to the Caucasus. Even ancestor worship, one of the commonest localist practices, supposes the intervention of the dead in the affairs of living men and women. Built on bones, local religions are cumulative, rather than anticipatory. While both Big Religions and local belief systems proffer creation myths, universal faiths are far more concerned with an end-of-times apocalypse (in the Hindu faith, with recurring apocalypses), while local cults rarely see beyond the next harvest. The great faiths lift the native's heart on one day of the week, while local beliefs guide him through the other six.

What we lump together under the term "religion" is better divided into the distinct categories of religion and magic. The reason that so many local cults, from Arizona to Ghana, persist under Christianity or Islam, and why they remain a source of endless frustration to Wahhabi and evangelical missionaries alike, is that they answer different needs. Big Religion is about immortal life. Magic is about acquiring a mate, avoiding snakebite or traffic accidents, gaining wealth. African tribes, as well as the indigenous populations of the Western Hemisphere, can accept a global faith with full sincerity, while seeing no reason to abandon old practices that work.

Even as they change their names, the old gods live, and our attempts to export Western ideas and behaviors are destined to end in similar mutations. Our personal bias may be in favor of the frustrated missionaries who try to dissuade the Christians of up-country Sulawesi from holding elaborate, bankrupting funerals with mass animal sacrifices (death remains far more important than birth or baptism), but the reassuring counter is that in the Indonesian city of Solo, where Abu Bakr Bashir established his famed "terrorist school," the devoutly Muslim population drives Saudi missionaries mad by holding a massive annual ceremony honoring the old Javanese Goddess of the Southern Seas. Likewise, Javanese and Sumatran Muslims go on the hajj with great enthusiasm (on government-organized tours) but continue to revere the spirits of local trees, Sufi saints, and the occasional rock. In Senegal, I found local Muslims irate at the condescending attitudes of Saudi emissaries who condemned their practices as contrary to Islam. With their long-established Muslim brotherhoods and their beloved *marabouts*, the Senegalese responded, "We were Islamic scholars when the Saudis were living in tents."

From West Africa to Indonesia, an unnoted defense against Islamist extremism is the loyalty Muslims have to the local versions of their faith. No one much likes to be told that he and his ancestors have gotten it all wrong for the last five centuries. Foolish Westerners who insist that Islam is a unified religion of believers plotting as one to subjugate the West refuse to see that the fiercest enemy of Salafist fundamentalism is the affection Muslims have for their local ways.

Islamist terrorists are all about globalization, while the hope for peace lies in the grip of local custom.

Uninterested in political correctness, a Muslim from Côte d'Ivoire remarked to me, "You can change the African's dress, you can educate him and change his table manners, but you cannot change the African inside him." He might have said the same of the Russian, the German, or the Chinese. By refusing to acknowledge, much less attempting to understand, the indestructible differences between human collectives, the twentieth-century intelligentsia smoothed the path to genocide in Rwanda, Bosnia, and Sudan, as well as to the age of globalized terror. Denied differences only fester; ignored long enough, the infection kills.

Our insistence that human beings will grow ever more alike defies the historical evidence, as well as practical and spiritual needs. Paradoxically, we make a great fuss of celebrating diversity, yet claim that human values are converging. We, too, have our superstitions and taboos.

MAGIC VS. JIHAD

The spread of Islam into Europe and Africa struck very different, but equally potent, barriers in the north and south. In Europe, it could not overcome a rival monotheist faith with its own universalist vision. In West Africa, Islam stopped roughly five centuries ago when it left the deserts and grasslands to enter the African forest, that potent domain of magic.

It should excite far more interest than it has that a warrior faith with an unparalleled record of conquest and conversion dead-ended when it reached the realms of illiterate tribes that had not mastered the wheel: In the forests of sub-Saharan Africa, Islam could not conquer, could not convert, and could not convince. On their own turf, local beliefs proved more powerful than a faith that had swept over "civilized" continents.

Forests are the abodes of magic. Look to forested areas for resistance to innovation. Even European fairy tales insist on the forest's mystery. Islam, with its abhorrence of magic, had nothing to offer African forest tribes to replace the beliefs that enveloped them. In northern Europe, too, monotheism faced its greatest difficulty in penetrating forested expanses, and the persistence of essentially pagan folk beliefs in the forested mountains of eastern Europe can startle a visitor today.

The forest, with its magic, is the opponent of globalization. Unlike the monotheist faiths with their propulsive desert origins, it only menaces those who insist on entering it. Now the worrisome question is whether the vast urban slums of the developing world are the world's new forests—impenetrable, exclusive, and deadly. From Sadr City to Brazil's *favelas*, slum dwellers are converting the great monotheist religions back into local cults, complete with various forms of human sacrifice. Far from monolithic, both the Muslim and Christian faiths are splintering, with radical strains emerging that reject the globalization of God and insist that His love is narrow, specific, and highly conditional. The great faiths are becoming tribal religions again.

THE LIMITS OF GLOBALIZATION

After approximately a century of Christian expansion inward from its coasts, Africa remains a jumble of faiths: Muslim in the north of states such as Nigeria, Ghana, Côte d'Ivoire, Sudan, or Kenya, while Christian in the south—and persistently fond of local beliefs throughout. Christian televangelists (the real advance guard of globalization) rail against traditional practices in Ghana, while, at the continent's other extreme, on remote islands off the coast of Mozambique, the population remains strictly Muslim by day but brings out the drums and incantations at night.

The attitude of missionaries, Christian or Muslim, is that such beliefs and practices are a combination of bad habits, naive superstitions, and general ignorance. But the conviction has grown in me as I travel that the missionaries themselves are—willfully—ignorant of systems they cannot respect and so refuse to understand. Religions are like businesses in the sense that they must provide products that work with sufficient regularity to keep customers coming back. Results matter. The psychological comfort and beyond-the-grave promises of Christianity and Islam function transcendently but leave immediate needs unanswered.

In developed societies, civil, commercial, and social institutions fill the gap; elsewhere, magic must. Magic endures because local populations experience sufficient evidence of its power. This is hard for Westerners to accept, but, whether training African militaries or running an aid program in Peru, those who ignore the role of magic in the lives of others will always fall short in their results: When Global Man goes home, the shaman returns.

We laugh at this "mumbo jumbo" from the safety of our own parochial worlds, but the hold of magic remains so tenacious that it continues to inspire human sacrifice in up-country Ghana and self-mutilation from New Mexico to Sulawesi. One way to read the grave discontents of the Middle East is that Sunni Islam, especially, anni-hilated magic, but, unlike Western civilization, failed to substitute other means to satisfy human needs. There is a huge void in the contemporary human experience in the Islamic heartlands: no reassuring magic, no triumphant progress. Islam in the Sunni-Arab world—the incubator of global terror—is all ritual and no results, while even modern, Western Christianity imbues its rituals with sat-isfying mysticism, from the experience of being "born again" to the transubstantiation of bread and wine into body and blood.

What if magic—ritual transactions that address spiritual, psy-chological, and practical needs—is a strategic factor that we've missed entirely? We would not wish to send our troops anywhere without good maps of the local terrain, but we make no serious effort to map the spiritual world of our enemies or potential allies. Even if magic and local beliefs are merely a worthless travesty of faith, our convictions are irrelevant: What matters is what the other man believes.

The power of local beliefs and traditions will continue to frus-trate dreams of a globalized, homogenized society beyond our life-times. If we can recognize and exploit the power of local customs, we may find them the most potent tools we have for containing the religious counterrevolution of our Islamist enemies. If, on the other hand, we continue to deny that local traditions, beliefs, and habits constitute a power to be reckoned with, we will lose potential allies and many a well-meant assistance project will falter as soon as we remove our hand.

As for the potential for violence from insulted local beliefs, con-sider this statement: "They can preach holy war, and that is ever the most deadly kind, for it recks nothing of consequences." This doesn't refer to mad mullahs and postmodern suicide bombers. It's a quotation from a historical novel by Rosemary Sutcliff, *The Eagle of the Ninth*. Published half a century ago for adolescents, it describes a Druid revolt against the Romans in Britain.

Globalization isn't new, but the power of local beliefs, rooted in native earth, is far older. And those local beliefs may prove to be the more powerful, just as they have so often done in the past. From Islamist terrorists fighting to perpetuate the enslavement of women to the Armenian obsession with the soil of Karabakh—from the French rejection of "Anglo-Saxon" economic models to the resistance of African Muslims to Islamist imperialism—the most complex forces at work in the world today, with the greatest potential for both violence and resistance to violence, may be the antiglobal impulses of local societies.

From Liège to Lagos, the tribes are back.